Globalization and Literature

Themes in Twentieth- and Twenty-First-Century Literature and Culture

Series Adviser: Rod Mengham

Modernism, Tim Armstrong
Globalization and Literature, Suman Gupta
The Postcolonial Novel, Richard Lane

Globalization
and Literature

Suman Gupta

polity

First published in 2009 by Polity Press

Polity Press
65 Bridge Street
Cambridge CB2 1UR, UK

Polity Press
350 Main Street
Malden, MA 02148, USA

ISBN-13: 978-0-7456-4023-5
ISBN-13: 978-0-7456-4024-2 (pb)

A catalogue record for this book is available from the British Library.

Typeset in 10.5 on 12 pt Bembo
by SNP Best-set Typesetter Ltd, Hong Kong
Printed and bound in Great Britain by MPG Books Ltd, Bodmin, Cornwall

The publisher has used its best endeavours to ensure that the URLs for external websites referred to in this book are correct and active at the time of going to press. However, the publisher has no responsibility for the websites and can make no guarantee that a site will remain live or that the content is or will remain appropriate.

For further information on Polity, visit our website: www.polity.co.uk

To Ayan-Yue

Don't kid yourself,
The Child is not father of the Man,
But he may already be *il miglior fabbro*,
And that's worrying enough for this dad.

Contents

Acknowledgements		ix
1	**The Nuances of Globalization**	1
	Narrative Performance	1
	Travels of a Term	3
	Plan of this Study	10
2	**Movements and Protests**	13
	Plucking a Theme	13
	Anti-Globalization Protests	14
	Peace Movements	23
	V-Day	31
3	**Global Cities and Cosmopolis**	37
	Global Teens	37
	Global Cities	38
	Global City Transactions	43
	Cosmopolitan Order and Cosmopolis	48
	Virtual Cosmopolis	53
4	**Literary Studies and Globalization**	62
	Literary Entanglements	62
	Turning to Literary Studies	65
	Globalization Thematized	66
	Literary Text	71
	Culture and Identity	85
5	**Postmodernism and Postcolonialism**	97
	Postmodernism	97
	Postcolonialism	107
6	**Academic Institutional Spaces**	123
	English Studies	123
	Comparative Literature/World Literature	136
	A Note on Translation	146

7   **The Globalization of Literature**   151
    Dying Authors   151
    Literary Industries   159

    References   171
    Index   185

Acknowledgements

I have run various arguments and ideas that figure in this study past friends, and have benefited immensely from their responses. I am particularly grateful to the following for clearing up some of my confusions: Tapan Basu, Taieb Belghazi, Milena Katsarska, Tope Omoniyi, Bob Owens, Zhao Baisheng and, as ever, Xiao Cheng. Andrea Drugan had suggested the theme of this book to me and encouraged me to pursue it; I am grateful for this and will remain so even if she regrets it all later. Thanks are due to my colleagues in the English Department of the Open University for bearing with me while this was being written; and to Roehampton University for continuing to give me access to space and resources. No one but I am responsible for the shortcomings and errors in the following pages.

Suman Gupta
July 2008

1 The Nuances of Globalization

NARRATIVE PERFORMANCE

American novelist Richard Powers's *Plowing the Dark* (2000) revolves around an early (1980s) prototype of a virtual reality chamber, the 'Cavern'. Our familiarity with global electronic networks and virtual environments, which characterizes the new millennium at the portal of which this novel appeared, is prefigured in the 'Cavern'. Protagonists from different disciplines are invited to use this nascent space to realize their visions and advance their understanding of the world. The main protagonist, artist Adie Klarpol, struggles to find an effective aesthetic output from the 'Cavern' and doesn't achieve much beyond creating a 3-D version of Henri Rousseau's Jungle paintings. Others (mathematicians, meteorologists, etc.) are more successful in advancing their fields. Economist Ronan O'Reilly, like Klarpol, also reaches towards failure in his engagement with the 'Cavern', but, unlike Klarpol's, it is a grand world-encompassing failure. O'Reilly's ambition is to use the 'Cavern' to create a model of the whole globe, and thereby to compute economic futures by taking into account not just a mass of existing economic data but also all kinds of social and political histories and scenarios. His model works – or ultimately doesn't – as a visualizable virtual environment: in the 'Cavern' a virtual globe containing all the information within easy access is thrown up. O'Reilly can simply step into the globe and see the whole physical-social-economic world from the inside, as it were, and call up and compute with all the data he needs from anywhere in the world. O'Reilly's achievement is first described in Powers's economical yet vivid style as follows:

O'Reilly assigned the wand's thumbwheel to a zoom function. A little scrolling and the Earth swelled to a medicine ball or imploded into an atom. With the rub of a thumb, Afghanistan, as it had lately in the world's imagination, ballooned from an invisible speck to a billboard that filled the field of view.

When the globe grew large enough, O'Reilly simply stepped inside. The Cavern knew where his head was at all times, and rehung its coordinates accordingly. The crust of countries that the projectors served up looked even better from the underside than from the out. Inside, from the vantage of the earth's core, O'Reilly could inspect the whole theatre at one glance, with no hidden hemisphere on the far side of a projection. The unbroken surface spread out above him in all directions, like the constellations of the night sky.

He set the wand's buttons to throw various layers over his planetarium display. The slices of tonal register tracked the range of a variable as it wrestled its way through the proving grounds. Armed with canned data, O'Reilly took the globe out for a test spin. Per capita GDP, in single-year frames. As a function of energy consumption. As a function of consumer spending. All the classical formulae, for which he had only clinical patience, ran as ten-second, color-stabbing short subjects before Our Feature Attraction.

To this clean, coherent display, Ronan fused his ten-dimensional recursive cellular automata. All the furious systems, the flex and tensions of abductors and carpals clasped together in an invisible hand to rock a cradle now eminently observable. On the surface, sunsets and dawns illuminated the familiar jigsaw of the world's nations. Underneath, a seething snake's nest of cooperation and competition rippled through the global markets, deciding them. (Powers 2000, 119)

O'Reilly's extraordinarily ambitious programme fails, it later emerges, because it doesn't do what it's designed to do: predict economic futures with a reasonable degree of accuracy.

What is successfully conveyed in this passage is not a foreboding of failure but an apprehension of the enormity, the wholeness, of this splendid construct. There are several interesting ideas that run across that passage. First, there's the apprehension of the world itself, as a whole, as a complex function of parts and levels, caught between its natural patterns of 'sunsets and dawns' and its artificial unfolding through patterns of 'cooperation and competition'. Second, there's the notion that the world itself has been grasped through the artifice of O'Reilly's simulation, brought within his reach by the curious perspectival manoeuvre of being inside the globe and looking at its under-surface, and amenable to his control (subject to a 'test spin', open to expansion or contraction, a 'theatre' or 'planetarium'). Third, there's the somewhat distinct understanding that this simulation is for an instrumental purpose and is at the service of an agent. This agent is an economist cum programmer, O'Reilly, at the controls. Not only does this simulation clarify our understanding of the world, it also thereby bends the world to O'Reilly's will – the 'invisible hand to rock a cradle now eminently observable'. Fourth, there's the tacit understanding that all the above ideas are being conveyed through means, by devices, from a point of view outside the quoted passage. This has to do with the manner in which the language of the quoted passage works. Mediations take place through a descriptive language which is not transparent but curiously opaque, drawing attention to itself. Within the carefully crafted description, clearly visualizable metaphors ('from an invisible speck to a billboard', the 'theatre' and the 'planetarium', 'the constellations of the night sky', 'a seething snake's nest') and barely visualizable technical abstractions ('rehung its coordinates accordingly', 'slices of tonal register tracked the range of a variable', 'ten-dimensional recursive cellular automata') are negotiated. An implied narrative consciousness obviously mediates between seeing the simulation both from within (like the 'constellations of the night sky'), as O'Reilly does, and from without ('the crust of countries', 'on the surface'). This narrative consciousness also tells the reader both what O'Reilly intends (do a 'test spin', 'inspect the whole theatre', with 'clinical patience') and what it's like for someone watching him (the metaphors of 'the constellations of the night sky' and the 'seething snake's nest' are evidently not descriptions of O'Reilly's feelings). The invisible narrator tacitly tracks progression in the passage too, so that the function and scope of the simulation becomes gradually clearer for the reader. The language of the passage, in brief, *performs* these mediations to convey the enormity of an economist's global vision and ambition.

O'Reilly's economic ambition and vision cohere broadly with ideas and processes that are now understood as related to globalization. These ideas and processes occupy scholarship in fields as widely dispersed as economics, sociology, culture and media studies, technology, politics, geography and history. I return to the connotations of the term 'globalization' shortly. More immediately, I would like to pause on the narrative performance that conveys O'Reilly's globe-embracing ambition, where language is used to perform and convey something of the intellectual scope and aesthetic stimulation of ideas of globalization. This language is not as precise and systematic as the scholarly language in which globalization is usually discussed. And what is conveyed of globalization is not quite as well ordered as in academic texts about globalization – it is impressionistic. Yet, what is conveyed is suggestive. The quotation from Powers's novel could be thought of as a snap-shot literary apprehension of globalization. As such, this is a particular sort of literary expression which is of interest to a particular kind of student or researcher: those engaged in literary studies. To pay attention to such literary expressions of globalization is one (there are others) of the objectives of this study, addressed as it is to the relationship between literature and globalization, and written as it is for the purposes of literary studies.

TRAVELS OF A TERM

Impressionistic though such literary expressions of globalization might seem, they are obviously cognisant of the more precise scholarly discussions of globalization. These discussions are as prolific as they are diverse, but the general drift can be quickly grasped by contemplating a few influential definition-like statements. Such succinct statements are invariably given on the understanding that they need systematic elaboration, which is thereafter provided. But even when contemplated in themselves they make immediate and relevant sense. Anthony Giddens's definition of globalization as 'the intensification of worldwide social relations which link distant localities in such a way that local happenings are shaped by events occurring many miles away and vice versa' (Giddens 1990, 64) is useful in this fashion. So is Martin Albrow's observation that 'globalisation effectively means that societies now cannot be seen as systems in an environment of other systems, but as sub-systems of the larger inclusive world society' (Albrow 1990, 11); as is Roland Robertson's understanding that 'Globalization as a concept refers both to the compression of the world and the intensification of consciousness of the world as a whole' (Robertson 1992, 8); and as is David Held's attempt to present the manifold aspects of globalization as 'a process (or set of processes) which embodies a transformation in their spatial organisation of social relations and transactions – assessed in terms of their extensity, intensity, velocity and impact – generating transcontinental or interregional flows and networks of activity, interaction, and the exercise of power' (Held et al. 1999, 16). These definition-like attempts to characterize the *nature* of the processes ('intensification', 'compression', 'transformation', at levels of 'extensity', 'intensity', etc.) denoted by 'globalization' are supplemented by numerous succinct attempts at emphasizing the connotative *content* of 'globalization'. Martin Albrow's example can serve here as representative:

GLOBALIZATION

1. Making or being made global:
    (a) in individual instances
         (i)   by the active dissemination of practices, values, technology and other human products throughout the globe
         (ii) when global practices and so on exercise an increasing influence over people's lives
         (iii) when the globe serves as a focus for, or a premise in shaping, human activities
         (iv) in the incremental change occasioned by the interaction of any such instances;
    (b) seen as the generality of such instances;
    (c) such instances being viewed abstractly.
2. A process of making or being made global in any or all of the senses in (1).
3. The historical transformation constituted by the sum of particular forms and instances in (1). (Albrow 1996, 88)

The emphasis in the latter is obviously more on the range of meanings embraced by the term 'globalization' than on the description of processes alluded to by it.

Such definition-like statements give the term 'globalization' a tractable and definite quality, without thereby restricting its superlative reach. They convey the enormity of globalization's geographical and disciplinary border crossings and the transgression of different linguistic registers and areas of application and usage. The elaborations that surround these (and such) definitions both recognize the enormity of thinking about globalization and build upon that foundation of tractability and definitiveness that such a succinct definition-like moment makes available. And yet, even in offering such clear definitions and elaborating on them coherently, a kind of anxiety about the term 'globalization' – as a term – is often found. It is as if the scholars offering these definitions and elaborations by way of taming the concept and manifestations of globalization nevertheless feel that it has not been correspondingly tamed. The term seems to possess an autonomous momentum, an uncontrollable currency, which no amount of careful systematization and analysis of its connotations can cover. Put otherwise, it appears to have its own passages and history which are not quite unpacked by charting and theorizing the social, political, economic, cultural processes of globalization. There is therefore an oft noted mismatch between the history and discernment of globalization as process and the history and usage of the term 'globalization'. This tension is noted by almost all the above-mentioned scholars. Roland Robertson thus observes that:

In academic circles [globalization] was not recognized as a significant concept in spite of diffuse and intermittent usage prior to that, until the early, or even middle, 1980s. During the second half of the 1980s its use increased enormously, so much so that it is virtually impossible to trace the patterns of its contemporary diffusion across a large number of areas of contemporary life in different parts of the world. By now, even though the term is often used very loosely and, indeed, in contradictory ways, it has *itself* become part of 'global consciousness', an aspect of the remarkable proliferation of terms centred as 'global'. (Robertson 1992, 8)

A similar anxiety about the term occupies Martin Albrow momentarily too:

The term 'globalization' binds the syntax of the global and its derivations into a ramifying set of meanings. They are thus effectively entwined in an unfolding story over time. It conveys a widespread sense of transformation of the world. But this tendency to blanket coverage should in itself indicate how unlikely it is to have a precise analytical set of reference points. (Albrow 1996, 86)

And this anxiety appears with almost an air of impatience by the time Zygmunt Bauman begins his study of some of the less observed human consequences of globalization:

'Globalization' is on everybody's lips; a fad word fast turning into a shibboleth, a magic incantation, a pass-key meant to unlock the gates to all present and future mysteries. [. . .] All vague words share a similar fate: the more experiences they pretend to make transparent, the more they themselves become opaque. (Bauman 1998, 1)

Perhaps attention to such linguistic tensions and anxieties is most aptly given by students of literature, and this study is therefore structured more emphatically around the passages, rather than any given definition or conceptualization, of the term 'globalization'. To come to grips with the relationship between globalization and literature and literary studies it is, this study assumes, more useful to follow the manifold accruals and dynamics of the term 'globalization' than to fit in with any one way or a few ways of conceptualizing and demonstrating globalization. This is all the more expedient here since the term 'globalization' has crept into literary studies only very recently. It has shouldered its way, in an as yet uncertain manner, alongside other far more familiar terms that are as embracing and transgressive of boundaries for literary students, such as 'postmodernism' and 'postcolonialism'. The currency of 'globalization' has developed largely outside literature and literary studies, mainly at the behest of sociologists and social theorists such as those quoted above – even though the term seems to spin out of their control and impinge everywhere, even upon literature and inside literary studies. Literature and literary studies do not pick up globalization as a concept that emerges, so to speak, from *within*, but somewhat resistantly as a term that batters on them from *outside* and will not be denied, and is larger and more dynamic than its past and present masters.

What follows, therefore, to set the ground for this study of globalization and literature are some cursory observations on the travels and shifting nuances of the term 'globalization' – undertaking in a very superficial fashion what Robertson regards as the virtually impossible task of tracing 'the patterns of its contemporary diffusion'. In effect this also enables a delimitation of the scope of this study, which is largely contained to the relatively short period within which the term 'globalization' has had currency. It is assumed that the circulation of the term 'globalization' and its manifold meanings demarcates a space–time within which the relationship between globalization and literature can be meaningfully examined.

Richard Kilminster traces the first appearance of the term 'globalization' in the Webster dictionary in 1961 and in the Oxford English Dictionary Supplement in 1972 (Kilminster 1997, 257). It was somewhat later that it entered academic parlance in a decisive manner, in the late 1970s and early 1980s, mainly by thrusting aside 'international' or 'world' or 'universal' processes and systems. Most of these initial academic evocations came clearly from a specific North American location and with concordant interests. Though the term itself wasn't used, Marshall McLuhan's observations on technological developments in communication and media, implicitly informed by his North American perspective, seemed to set the tone – especially in statements such as: 'The new electronic interdependence recreates the world in the image of a global village' (McLuhan 1962, 31); and: 'Today, after more than a century of electric technology, we have extended our central nervous system itself in a global embrace, abolishing both space and time as far as our planet is concerned' (McLuhan 1964, 3). By the late 1970s the term 'globalization' itself started appearing in various academic and specialist forums. It connoted variously the desire to develop the study of sociology in the USA as a world-embracing enterprise or to track such study as it expanded into domains outside the USA (Lamy 1976; Goreau 1983; Parker 1984). More importantly it expressed the desire of

US business leaders and management gurus to extend US business interests, and exploitation of resources and labour, to a global domain (Hopkins 1978; Levitt 1983). Since then the term has gradually been distanced from the specific contexts and interests with which it was initially associated and understood as gesturing towards an increasingly acontextual world condition. In this some of its other early associations helped. The impetus for this direction was given, to some extent, by left-wing intellectuals in the 1970s who associated a growing consolidation of global economic processes and markets with advanced capitalism – e.g. in Eric Hobsbawm's 'drawing together of all parts of the globe into a single world' (1975, 65) – a notion that was more rigorously theorized with the late twentieth century in view in Immanuel Wallerstein's 'world capitalist system' (1974) and Ernest Mandel's 'late capitalism' ([1972] 1978).

The tendency towards decontextualizing the term was underlined in the Brandt Commission report, published in 1980 as *North–South*. This was the result of deliberations in an independent think-tank under the chairmanship of former German Chancellor Willy Brandt to resolve the impasse between poor and rich nations on terms of loans and assistance through the World Bank. Eighteen countries (none from the communist bloc) were represented in this. The report that followed called for a 'globalization of policies' to counter the 'globalization of dangers and challenges' (Independent Commission on International Development Issues 1980, 19). Rather contrary to the recommendations of this commission, the ironic result was the devising of a lending system through the World Bank and IMF (structural adjustment loans or structural adjustment facilities) whereby loans to poor countries were made conditional on extensive infrastructural changes, often with unpopular and counterproductive effects (Stiglitz 2003; Chua 2003; Peet 2003). Localized resistance to the consequences of accepting such conditions were evidenced widely, in Algeria, Benin, Bolivia, Ecuador, Jamaica, Jordan, Mexico, Niger, Nigeria, Russia, Sudan, Trinidad, Uganda, Venezuela, Zaire (Congo) and Zambia, among other countries. These coincided with expressions of disaffection with single-party politics and centralized economic arrangements in a number of communist countries. In the course of the 1980s, these resistances were gradually given some coherence as 'new social movements' (in a timely fashion in Touraine 1981 and Habermas 1981).

Roughly until the end of the 1980s the term 'globalization' usually appeared unambiguously with the ideological weight of its North American–Western European capitalist associations and affirmations, and was located (despite the spread of 'new social movements') in the polarized ideological discourse of the Cold War. With the symbolic end of the Cold War (marked by the fall in 1989 of the Berlin Wall) the term 'globalization' really came into its own. There were, it seems, two noteworthy sides to manoeuvres around the term 'globalization' at this point: 1) it was adjusted to cohere with the vocabulary of activists and NGOs, which in turn impinged upon establishment, mass-media and academic usage; and 2) the term's public, mass-media and particularly academic uses proliferated exponentially, essentially with the effect of firmly decontextualizing it and neutralizing its ideologically partisan affirmativeness. The two sides of these shifting nuances of 'globalization' unfolded simultaneously and with extraordinary speed.

The advent of 'globalization' in the vocabulary of activists and NGOs has a great deal to do with the antonymous coinage 'anti-globalization', which was primarily a media invention and rarely used before 1995 elsewhere. The alignments to which the term 'anti-globalization' was and continues to be applied – those involved in activism in 'new social movements', against global economic regulation and hegemony, and often in favour of local sustainable development – seldom accepted it happily (e.g. Klein 2001). Its thrust in the mass media was (and still is) a largely pejorative one (presenting 'anti-globalization' as a disabling, anarchic, anti-technological/anti-modernization stance), evoked while descrying such large-scale and multi-front protests as the Seattle anti-WTO demonstrations of 30 November 1999, the Genoa G8 summit protests of July 2001, etc. However, the negative thrust of much mass-media use of 'anti-globalization' was turned on its head by deliberately and positively engaging 'globalization' to oppose the neoliberal capitalist associations of 'globalization'. Some of those who were (and continue to be) placed in the so-called anti-globalization alignment coined the phrases 'globalization-from-above' and 'globalization-from-below' and aligned themselves with the latter. A sort of contest of 'globalizations' thus seemed to be set up, a hegemonic and an oppositional anti-hegemonic taking possession of 'globalization', perhaps best exemplified in the early 1990s in Brecher, Childs and Cutler 1993. The overall effect of these shifts in 'globalization's' career in the course of the 1990s was of (a) giving the term a greater sense of normative complexity than heretofore – which has thereafter been played upon in a variety of ways by Richard Falk, Naomi Klein, Joseph Stiglitz, Antonio Negri, Michael Hardt, Tim Jordan, David Graeber and numerous others – while, at the same time, (b) stripping it of its earlier one-sided liberal capitalist associations and rendering it more or less normatively neutral, acontextual, applicable to claims from contrary ideological positions.

Such negotiations of the term 'globalization' merged into the other kind of proliferating engagements with the term mentioned above, especially in academic and other establishment discourses (political, corporate, media). This entailed simply defining 'globalization' as ideologically neutral and as connoting sociologically, economically, politically, culturally and historically relevant transnational processes. Contributions in this direction have been too numerous to be discussed at any length here. I have cited some definitions in this mould at the beginning of this section, and further definitions and elaborations of the term by Jürgen Habermas, Ulrich Beck, Saskia Sassen, Arjun Appadurai, Mike Featherstone and Scott Lash, among numerous others, come to mind. Most of these gave content to the term by noting processes: in terms of disciplinary emphasis, geopolitical spread, measurable effect and so on. Various strategies for embracing the term 'globalization' without immediately entering an arena of ideological battles and contests have worked within these negotiations. These include both defenders of 'globalization' as a spontaneous process against 'anti-globalization' (e.g. Bhagwati 2004), and those who hold that globalization from above and below should be regarded as a single conjoined process of 'globalization' (e.g. Held and McGraw 2002; Held 2004). Further, through these moves the term also became gradually abstracted from specific histories and cultures. 'Globalization' seemed to become applicable with retrospective effect, spilling out of its contextual specificities and circulations as a term. Every kind of historical transaction across boundaries, every encounter and imperial venture across history, everything that passed as 'international' or 'world'-based or 'universal' in history, could now be invested in the term 'globalization'. Unsurprisingly, historians accordingly recruited it with this retrospective throw-back effect to stretch far before its existence as a term – markedly in, for instance, O'Rourke and Williamson 1999; Nederveen Pieterse 2003; and Gills and Thompson 2006.

Through these shifts and negotiations 'globalization' is now available as one of the most markedly protean and thickly connotative words in our vocabulary. The passages of the term charted briefly above have subsisted to a remarkable degree on the play of terminology, on the deployment of rhetorical strategies. Thus, the above manoeuvres have constantly involved the suggestive deployment of 'globalization' in relation to other equally abstract terms, neologisms, variations – such as 'local', 'regional', 'nation-state', 'transnational', 'glocal', 'globalist', etc. Through continuous shifts between decontextualization and repossession, accruals of meanings and abstractions, rhetorical play and redefinitions, 'globalization' can now be thrown in apparently meaningfully with regard to almost any kind of issue: so not just in the 'globalization of media', the 'globalization of culture', the 'globalization of labour', but also, by the same token, in the 'globalization of crime', the 'globalization of surveillance', the 'globalization of entertainment', and so on – including naturally, and of particular moment now, the 'globalization of terrorism'. The situation that obtains at present with regard to the term 'globalization' is usefully summarized by Norman Fairclough:

We cannot get away from the fact that although 'globalization' is a set of changes which are actually happening in the world (though what the set includes is highly controversial), it is also a *word* which has quite recently become prominent in the ways in which such changes are represented. But this is a simplification because the word 'globalization' is used in various senses within more complex discourses, which are partly characterized by distinctive vocabularies in which 'globalization' is related in particular (and differing) ways from other 'keywords' such as 'modernization', 'democracy', 'markets', 'free trade', 'flexibility', 'liberalization', 'security', 'terrorism', 'culture', 'cosmopolitanism' and so forth. And these discourses are more than vocabularies – they also differ in grammatical features (e.g. in some discourses but not others, 'globalization' is represented as an agent which itself causes change in the world, as in 'globalization opens up new markets'), as well as forms of narrative, forms of argumentation and so forth. (Fairclough 2006, 4)

PLAN OF THIS STUDY

That excursus into the travels of the term 'globalization' should not be regarded as setting us adrift from literature and literary studies. As I have noted in passing, it actually enables several methodological decisions to structure this study, and focus it where it should be focused.

First, it provides a loose chronological frame to work with. As I have observed already, 'globalization' has become increasingly decontextualized and has been rendered ideologically neutral and tends now to spill outside any chronological frame. If we assume that the relationship of globalization to literature and literary studies is not unconnected to its passages and resonances as a term (a respectable literary assumption) we have a roughly delimited chronological field. This study is consequently focused largely on the last two decades of the twentieth century and thereafter, wherein the circulation of the term 'globalization' goes through the convoluted shifts briefly charted above. In this the present study differs from some other attempts at coming to grips with the relationship between globalization and literature/literary studies, such as, for instance, the January 2001 *PMLA* special issue *Globalizing Literary Studies*, coordinated by Giles Gunn. Gunn sets the tone in his introduction to the latter by suggesting that globalization should allude to the 'historical process, by which the world has for several thousand years, rather than for several hundred, been woven and rewoven into an increasingly interconnected organism' (Gunn 2001, 21), and most of the other contributors concur. Paul Jay feels that a project of globalizing literary studies would benefit from taking a long 'historical view of globalization' (Jay 2001, 37); Stephen Greenblatt observes that the 'globalization of literary studies is not principally a phenomenon of the Internet or Apex fares or the spread of English on the wings of international capitalism' but should be coeval with the recognition that 'a vital global cultural discourse is ancient' (Greenblatt 2001, 50); Rey Chow avers that 'it is important to remember that globalization is not a new phenomenon, that it has been going on for some time under different rubrics' (Chow 2001, 69); and so on. Notably though, in the same collection, it is clear to Edward Said that 'political and economic globalization [has] since the end of the Cold War [. . .] been the enveloping context in which literary studies are undertaken' (Said 2001, 66). It seems to me curiously contradictory that, in emphasizing the need for a historical and contextual awareness in literary studies, the above theorists mostly choose to empty the term 'globalization' of its historical and contextual content, to extend it retrospectively in an ahistorical and acontextual fashion. This study differs in confining itself to the period where the shifting nuances of the term are contextually deployed and received, and suggests that literature and literary studies relate to it, within their historical and contextual specificities, accordingly.

Second, the attempt to extricate the extraordinarily protean and accommodative nuances of 'globalization' as a term offers certain entanglements with other equally protean and accommodative terms which are understood at present to be more squarely *within* literary studies and the ken of literature. 'Modernism'/'postmodernism' and 'postcolonialism' in particular have a similar sort of socio-political edge, and are similarly transgressive and interrogative of given boundaries (of, for instance, language, nation-state, identity), often in ways that coincide with debates about globalization. And yet those terms have evolved in close connection with the discursive space of literature and literary studies. More interestingly, they have ensconced themselves in the institutional arrangements of literature and literary studies over roughly the same post-1970s period in which the term 'globalization' has extended itself to its current eminence. The evolution and institutional inculcations of these terms in academia (research and pedagogy) and what could be called the knowledge industry (media, policy formation, publishing, archiving, etc.) have had a kind of conjoined momentum, and have been impelled by similar political, social, cultural and economic imperatives. Their place in the larger knowledge-production industry, and in the institutional space of literature and literary studies particularly, has already received some attention (see, for instance, Gupta 2007). These are significant considerations for the present study too.

Third, following the terminological turns of 'globalization' also opens up a rationale and structure for this study. At one level, globalization is something that is happening out there, so to speak, characterizing the economic, social, political, cultural contemporary world. This cannot but be represented or reflected or constructed within literature and literary studies, themselves inevitably of the world. At another level, and particularly in view of the more recent acontextual and ideologically-neutral and process-centred nuances acquired by the term, globalization is something that has everything in its grip – including literature. In this sense, we could say 'literature and literary studies are becoming globalized', and it seems to make immediate linguistic sense, though it remains to be seen in what exactly that sense consists insofar as the practice or doing of literature and literary studies – the reading and writing and transmissions of literature and literary studies – goes. This discernment of two levels enables a bipartite structure for this book, addressing each separately and in relation to each other.

Accordingly, this book falls into broadly two uneven parts. The following two chapters, chapters 2 and 3, address the extent to which processes of globalization are registered *within* literature, at the level of being represented in a literary manner or discussed as literary themes. In this instance, I have focused these chapters on two particular areas of globalization which have received substantial attention from globalization scholars: global or transnational or anti-globalization protest, and global or world cities. Four chapters after that, chapters 4 to 7, are devoted to examining the senses in which literature and literary studies may be regarded as themselves becoming globalized. Of these, chapters 4 and 5 contemplate the manner in which globalization has impinged upon literary studies at a conceptual level, in terms of doing literary criticism and engaging with literary theory (chapter 5 picks up the relationship of literary postmodernism and postcolonialism to globalization theory). And chapters 6 and 7 attend to the effects of globalization upon the institutional practices of literary studies and in relation to literary industries. In particular, chapter 6 focuses on the institutional spaces of English studies and comparative literature, and chapter 7 on the influence of corporate arrangements on literary production, circulation and consumption.

That is a rather schematic way of presenting the structure of this study, and is done only to give an initial sense of what's to come. The arguments in the following do not actually break down in this schematic fashion, and are not arranged to make any such schema explicit. Instead, the study is presented as a continuous argument, a kind of flowing engagement with the considerations that surface when the relationship of globalization and literature/literary studies is contemplated.

2 Movements and Protests

PLUCKING A THEME

As it stands now, 'globalization' is one of those extraordinarily protean terms of our time which seems to be relevant, and is increasingly accepted as meaningful, everywhere. In it the absolute embrace of the core word, the 'globe' itself, struggles against the modification of the suffix, the process marked by '-ization'. A wide variety of possibilities slip through that slight disjuncture between the absolute and the potential: the possibility of active globe-making, discernment of a global teleology, mediation between the bits (the local) and the whole of the globe, reference to systems that span the globe, the ambition of constructing global concepts, the desire of tapping into the material (resources, labour, markets) of the globe, etc. These possibilities do not necessarily sit together comfortably, and yet they are contained in the fertile suggestiveness of the term. Arguably, the term's protean nuances are represented and given flesh in literature most self-consciously where it has everyday currency, in contexts which constantly present themselves as centres of globalizing processes. Contemporary North American and British literature therefore often describe various strands of everyday and social life that are symptomatic of globalization. These often deal with protagonists and events caught in the machine of multinational business, located in the confrontation of global political forces from above and below, placed in the cosmopolitan spaces of global cities or moving fluidly across national and cultural boundaries, etc. Such themes are naturally intermeshed with each other to convey something of a process that is ultimately uncontainable in any single narrative or descriptive effort. These literary works also register the enormity and flux of globalization within their forms, and in the deliberateness of their use and recording of language. To come to grips with literary *representation* (expression) of globalization in the first part of this study, a focus on some contemporary North American and British literary works seems apt. The diffuse relationship between literary representation and a globalizing social world argues for a more or less arbitrary foothold to begin contemplation: a focus on any relevant theme could be expected to unravel into others under the purview of globalization, and into the disposition of literary form and language. To set this part off therefore a theme is plucked out: the literary representation of global movements from above and below, pro- and anti-globalization. Others are drawn out from that as we proceed.

ANTI-GLOBALIZATION PROTESTS

Consider the following fictional description of an anti-globalization protest:

Someone flung a trash can at the rear window. Kinski flinched but barely. To the immediate west, just across Broadway, the protesters created barricades of burning tires. All along there'd seemed a scheme, a destination. Police fired rubber bullets through the smoke, which began to drift high above the billboards. Other police stood a few feet away, helping Eric's security detail protect the car. He didn't know how he felt about this.
    'How will we know when the global era officially ends?'
    He waited.
    'When stretch limousines begin to disappear from the streets of Manhattan.' (DeLillo 2003, 91)

The scene is from Don DeLillo's *Cosmopolis* (2003), set in one April day of 2000, when billionaire financial speculator Eric Packer plays havoc with the world markets in his stretch limousine, which is equipped with internet screens for tracking world markets and phones for trading, as he goes around Manhattan and runs into a violent anti-globalization protest. Eric appears to represent free market capitalism. With him is his 'chief of theory' Vija Kinski, whose function seems to be to theorize (conveniently for the reader) the contemporary world without understanding either the technology or the economics of Eric's operation. The question and answer in the quotation are both Kinski's. Her theorizing up until this point had been confined to how digitized and speeded-up information transfers in the interests of free market capitalism have captured the contemporary world. On encountering the protest, Kinski naturally gives it a concordant theoretical turn, arguing that such protests are a necessary part of, and almost in continuity with, free market capitalism:

'They are working with you, these people. They are acting on your terms,' she said. 'And if they kill you, it's only because you permit it, in your sweet sufferance, as a way to re-emphasize the idea we all live under.'
    'What idea?'
    [. . .]
    'Destruction,' she said.
    [. . .]
    'The urge to destroy is a creative urge.'
    'This is also the hallmark of capitalist thought. Enforced destruction. Old industries have to be harshly eliminated. New markets have to be forcibly claimed. Old markets have to be re-exploited. Destroy the past, make the future.' (DeLillo 2003, 92–3)

As she proceeds with this line of thinking, the protesters are described as engaged in a quite extraordinarily reckless and desperate series of actions, which the police fail to contain with their considerably less reckless methods. In the midst of that Eric spies the defining slogan of the protest:

The top tier of the electronic display across the avenue showed this message now:

A SPECTER IS HAUNTING THE WORLD –
THE SPECTER OF CAPITALISM.

He recognized the variation on the famous first sentence of *The Communist Manifesto* in which Europe is haunted by the spectre of communism, circa 1850.

They were confused and wrongheaded. But his respect for the protesters' ingenuity grew more certain. (DeLillo 2003, 96)

As Eric watches the spectacle he feels exhilarated, and continues trading on the phone. The protest ends with a protester attempting self-immolation. The sight of the burning man impresses Eric, and it crosses his mind that: 'Kinski had been wrong. The market was not total. It could not claim this man or assimilate his act' (ibid., 99–100), though Kinski then observes that the protester had copied images of Vietnamese monks self-immolating, it wasn't an original gesture.

An interesting set of juxtapositions are at work here. Eric's mobile office with its global reach, the site where precisely the kind of 'enforced destruction' that Kinski attributes to 'capitalist thought' occurs, is juxtaposed *against* the destructive action of the anti-globalization protest. Kinsky mediates as the theorist of globalization, in command of those generalizing academic discourses where globalization is apprehended and conceptualized. That the theorist of globalization is in the representative capitalist's protection and pay suggests complicity between globalization theory and capitalist practice. This is immediately evidenced by the lines of co-optation and continuity that Kinski draws between the destructiveness of 'capitalist thought' and the destructiveness of anti-capitalist action, and in the suggestion that the protests inspire Eric and are within his control. The polarized opposition between thought and action is, however, set to slip out of that view of co-optation and continuity. Eric thinks, his various subordinates think, Kinski thinks that the paraphernalia of financial trading somehow conquer reality and enable the sway of speculation (in both senses). When the contemplative movement of Eric's world-embracing capsule in Manhattan hits upon the reckless abandoned desperate activity of the protest, the polarized opposition between thought and action is jarringly reinserted. If there is a pattern or strategy in the protests it is for Eric and Kinski to contemplate and for the protesters to spontaneously enact. Insofar as the protesters express a point of view, it always appears to be a derivative one: the deliberate and indicative misquotation of *The Communist Manifesto*, a re-enactment of a famous image of protest as martyrdom. This derivativeness itself conveys a kind of world-embracing quality or global consciousness too, but only insofar as Kinski or Eric can contemptuously ('they were confused and wrongheaded') discern it. The slippage of the polarized opposition between thought and action from a view of capitalist co-optation and continuity is most cogently conveyed in Eric's misgivings that the act of self-immolation has somehow eluded or defeated the totality of markets.

It doesn't take a veteran of anti-globalization protests to recognize that this description is of a strangely and exaggeratedly violent and destructive affair. It is more a protest of the imagination than based on any recognizable reality. This perception fits the contrived character of the situation itself, the neatness of the juxtaposition of Eric's limo with theorist inside against the raging protests without, the formal structures of the plot which seem to collude in the construction of these juxtapositions. In fact, it seems plausible that this imaginary protest is a product of the literary mode, and comes with licence of a fictionalizing arrangement where situations are posed against each other, and downplayed or played up, for maximum effect. Some sense of literary appositeness underlies the description of this protest. The ideological import of this description is not to be discerned simply by focusing on the scene I have picked on, but against the novel as a whole. The protest scene is a highlight in the simmering and occasionally explosive violence that stretches across the novel. The abstract violence of Eric's sheer power (a kind of, often literally, sexual drive) dovetails into the evidence of real violence which surrounds him, which he is aware of, and which he even enjoys as spectacle. He watches pictures of two assassinations on his screens in the limo: of Arthur Rapp, managing director of the International Monetary Fund, and of Nikolai Kaganovich, 'owner of Russia's largest media conglomerate' and Eric's friend. He is also being stalked by a real assassin, Richard Sheets alias Benno Levin, who ultimately kills him. In the course of the day he is attacked by a fake assassin, 'André Petrescu, the pastry assassin, a man who stalked corporate directors, military commanders, soccer stars and politicians' (DeLillo 2003, 142). In the scheme of the novel the visceral violence of the anti-globalization protesters appears in the middle as an intensification and widening (to the masses) of the different strands of violence that knit the plot together.

At different points of the novel this sort of real violence is presented as a concretization of the abstract violence of global capitalism itself. As observed above, this occurs in Kinski's theorizations, and, more importantly, towards the end of the novel when Eric himself disintegrates into real violence. He murders, quite gratuitously, his chief of security Torval, and in his final moments, as he faces his murderer, he shoots himself in the hand:

He pressed the muzzle of his gun, Eric did, against the palm of his left hand. He tried to think clearly. He thought of his chief of security flat on the asphalt, a second yet left in his life. He thought of others down the years, hazy and nameless. He felt an enormous remorseful awareness. It moved through him, called guilt, and strange how soft the trigger felt against his finger. (DeLillo 2003, 196)

But Eric's own descent into physical violence is rather different from the violence of the protest. In shooting his bodyguard he effectively removes his own armour, in shooting himself he finally removes that capacity that made him a success, 'the predatory impulse, the sense of large excitation that drove him through the days, the sheer and reeling need to be' (ibid., 209). Eric's violence is directed against what he stands for. It becomes parcel of the violence that is described through the novel, in assassinations of capitalists, in the shattering violence of the anti-globalization protesters. Eric is the opposite of Bateman in Brett Easton Ellis's novel *American Psycho* (1991), the 1980s Wall Street banker in Manhattan who spends his time in conspicuous consumption and fantasies (perhaps realities) of serial killing. In the millennial moment where DeLillo sets *Cosmopolis*, Eric seems to move against the grain of Ellis's portrayal of capitalist psychopathology; Eric's violence is directed against himself and what he stands for just as the protesters' violence is. DeLillo's novel presents a world in the grip of an abstractly destructive and dehumanizing global capitalism which even incorporates its opponents. But its main agents appear to be peculiarly vulnerable and mortal, and its ostensible opponents – the anti-globalization activists and protesters – seem to have a near monopoly on real violence. The imaginary anti-globalization protests described in the novel are a deliberately exaggerated and manipulative envisioning of this idea. DeLillo's fictional ploys may leave his ideological take on globalization processes and free market capitalism hazy, and may deliberately evade theoretical academic pinning down, but are used to present a relatively clear placement of anti-globalization protests. They are a co-opted product of and in continuity with what they oppose, and have a near monopoly on real violence. Even the state's violence (through the police), traditionally regarded (by Weber's celebrated definition) as exercised through its monopoly on force, wanes in significance before the protesters' sweeping destructiveness. The police shoot their rubber bullets uselessly over the billboards.

That the anti-globalization protest in DeLillo's *Cosmopolis* belongs to the sphere of the imaginary, is constructed according to the exigencies of fictional structure, is sufficiently clear within that novel. Its character as an anti-globalization (or, for that matter, anti-capitalist) protest makes immediate sense only within that artificial structure of the novel; its relationship to real protests and public gestures which are sometimes contentiously dubbed 'anti-globalization' in the mass media is equally immediately distant. In the latter, protesters are typically far from being conceptually derivative or agents of physical action and typically identify, as observed in the previous chapter, with 'social movements' or 'globalization from below'. A fictional account of such real-world protest, carefully constructed to convey a sense of historical and contextualizable reality, could be usefully considered alongside *Cosmopolis*, and the obvious candidate is Robert Newman's *The Fountain at the Centre of the World* (2003), published in the same year.

Newman's *The Fountain* presents, as its climax, a day-by-day description of the celebrated protests organized in Seattle during the WTO meeting in December 1999. In the course of the novel, as the fictional characters traverse internal and international boundaries across Britain, Mexico and the United States, to converge in Seattle in December 1999, numerous factual (or sometimes factual-sounding) details are thrown in. Details of the South American disease *chagas*, the nuances of VNRs or video news records, the dangers of working in a Componentes Mecánicos factory in Mexico, the political and economic situation in Mexico, proceedings in Global Power Forum summits, the legal meaning of a private corporation, how to make a fertilizer bomb (this, though convincingly technical sounding, is actually unworkable), 1989 statements by Secretary of State Madeleine Albright, etc., are woven seamlessly into the plot. These factual details work alongside and within the fiction, which involves the central character Chano Salgado, who is on the run from the Mexican police for bombing a multinational company's toxic waste plant, his brother and powerful international corporate PR guru Evan Hatch, from whom he was parted in childhood, and his long lost son Daniel. Just as DeLillo juxtaposes the protesters, the powerful financial speculator, and the globalization theorist within a single space, so Newman engineers meetings and partings between the brothers as representatives of diametrically opposed ideological positions. But these contrivances coalesce with details which serve to convey a concrete historical context that is documented and verifiable. The 1999 Seattle protests are presented within that frame.

Since a specific historical event is now at issue, some registering of discussions of social movements and protests similar to the 1999 Seattle one (visibly and effectively staged since at meetings of transnational economic and military alignments such as the World Bank, IMF, WTO, NAFTA, and G8 – Montreal 2000, Genoa 2001, Davos 2001, Calgary and Ottawa 2002, Cancun 2003, etc.) is called for. So, a brief digression from *The Fountain*, outlining the key ideas relevant here follows; I return to the novel below.

Discussions of social movements and protests have broadly centred on the following perceptions. First, the increasing frequency and visibility of such protests are merely the tip of the iceberg – symptoms or surface manifestations of a larger and deeper phenomenon. These represent the convergence of a range of identity-based or local issue-based activities and gestures (addressing poverty, localized oppressions, culture-specific disaffections, the operations of corporations/states on specific ecosystems, etc.) within the global South or East; left- and right-oriented marginal political factions with specific agendas (ending Third World debt and mistreatment of migrants, protecting the environment or animal rights, extending Christian charity, etc.) in the global North or West; and locally as well as transnationally active NGOs. The global scale of the phenomenon merits attention. Behind such moments of convergence lie an enormous variety of protest activities dispersed among interest groups in a large number of locations. Second, these moments of convergence present an opportunity to announce some degree of commonality of objective and purpose in them, or perhaps to generate such commonality of purpose among them. These very divergent interests can be presented as aligned in a specific direction through the adoption of an inclusive terminology, as in 'social movement', 'globalization from below' and 'movement of movements'. Third, though the impetus of such protests is provided by the moments of convergence of diverse interests, the fact still remains that these are momentary convergences involving provisional pacts that retain their diverse and fragmentary character at all times. To retain the promise of the convergence, and yet at the same time not disturb the diversity of interest groups entering provisional pacts, is a tricky business. This is to a great extent a matter of presentation, and may involve disposing different kinds of interests into a finite number of structurally related categories (such as identity-based, issue-based and region-based), presenting the different interests as aligned with a finite number of ideological positions (radical, liberal, moderate), or presenting the diverse kinds of protests and activities involved as falling into a limited number of types (direct action against transnational/state/corporate entities, reform of existing state and transnational entities, NGO-based facilitations, enabling communal autonomy). Fourth, the balance between convergence and divergence in social movements is necessarily a kind of mirror-image of that which such social movements seem to oppose, and in fact a great deal of transfer or co-opting of the norms avowed by globalization champions is unproblematically possible. Thus, for instance, social movements often seem to enter into some sort of competition with establishment alignments in claiming democratic legitimacy. In their book *Globalization/Anti-Globalization* (2002), Held and McGrew are therefore understandably able to see little contradiction between the promise of democratization through globalization processes and that through anti-globalization movements. However, social movements and protests do demand change of the establishment in clearly enunciated, and often radical, ways. Callinicos's *An Anti-Capitalist Manifesto* (2003), for example, presents a clear exposition of the kind of radical changes that may be demanded. Fifth, and finally, combining ideas of radical change with existing understandings of social movements does recall transformative agendas rooted in the history of Marxism and the international working-class movement. To a certain extent, social movements are conceptualized both as replacing and correcting the problems in that history and as retaining the spirit of the historical working-class movement against the exploitations of industrial, agrarian and colonial capitalism and with universal human interests at stake. DeLillo's linking of anti-globalization protests with *The Communist Manifesto* gestures towards this.

Newman's *The Fountain* actually represents various levels of local disenchantment and rousing of protest which are brought to converge in the great 1999 Seattle anti-WTO protest. The main protagonist, Chano Salgado, who gradually comes to represent the spirit of the Seattle protest, is introduced as follows:

But what can a protest march achieve? asked Chano Salgado.

We have to do something, right? replied Oscar, his forearm flat on the table like the shadow on a sundial pointing at Chano. The others at El Café Fuente were all looking at Chano too. Yes, they'd known him a long time – but a long time ago. Did they still?

Of course you have to act, Chano replied, but we need to find, well, some other way, a new way. (Newman 2003, 9)

In this instance the proposed march is against a toxic-waste plant constructed by a multinational water corporation that is pumping up to 60,000 gallons of water a day and depleting the local water resources. The alternative way that is later suggested to him by his friend Ayo, and that Chano reluctantly accepts, is bombing the toxic-waste plant. Chano can make bombs – he has a past as a student activist, his wife Marisa was killed while attending a strike meeting at a Ford *maquilla* (border factory), and he had spent time in prison. The end result is that Chano successfully bombs the plant, but his own house unfortunately explodes too, and he has to go on the run. Chano's friend Yolanda, to pick up another thread, worked in the Componentes Mecánicos ('subsidiary of a famous US make of car' – ibid., 61) *maquilla*, where she, like many of her co-workers, was gradually poisoned by the chemicals that she had to deal with without protection. As a result her son was born with a fatal disease, Sturge–Weber Syndrome. Yolanda and fellow sufferer Elena discuss the different options for seeking redress here – Elena is in favour of raising consciousness through the media and taking legal action; Yolanda wants to organize a different sort of more inclusive protest (Elena speaks first in the quotation, contemplating a series of legal actions around the world):

Ah, but if the company lose in *China*. Ah! You see, what then? Now they have nowhere left to go until they find little green women in space. What then?

El-e-na! Look around! Then there's another hundred companies here meanwhile all doing the same thing or something else like it, and another and another, streets and streets of them in Matamoros, Reynosa, Juarez, Nogales.

So, we do nothing?

[. . .]

Let's do something else. An occupation, *protesta*, *manifestación*, a general *maquilladora* strike, yes – but not the courts. *Their* courts. (Newman 2003, 63)

The description of these local disenchantments (and the complicities of the agents of injustice with larger multinational corporations and international alignments) and the formation of the desire for a new kind of more inclusive and wide-scale protest lead first to the description of a protest march, a *manifestación*, in the town of Calderon. The novel then sweeps towards the 1999 Seattle protests, mentioning some of the other such local disaffections and search for redress that get incorporated, thus creating, in its build up towards the climax, a sense of the enormous diversity of interests and gestures that converge in the 'movement of movements' concretized at Seattle.

There are other ways in which *The Fountain* coheres with discussions of real social movements and their convergence in 'anti-globalization' protests. For instance, the ostensible mirroring of apparently similar democratic norms on both sides of the globalization alignments, from above and from below, and yet the ineradicable difference between them, are registered neatly in the novel. This occurs by setting up a confrontation of and intellectual engagement between the brothers – between Chano, the representative of oppositional social movements, and Evan, the representative of establishment global capitalism – in a hotel in Seattle. Consider, for instance, the following bit of their exchange:

You're right. We're not clever enough, said Chano. None of us. That's why it's impossible for one human or a few humans to lead lots of other people. *Only* the people can run their own lives. One leader makes everyone else less human. Chano found that there was something about talking to his younger brother which lent him fluency and clarity. He was surer of certain beliefs than he'd thought, not in the sense of being sure those beliefs were right, but of being sure they were his. [. . .]
   [. . .]
Well, said Evan, I don't see the masses out on the streets calling for the revolution that you want. I see them buying Air Nikes, queuing for the multiplex and buying free-trade coffee with Big Mac and fries. (Newman 2003, 191)

The difference between Chano's progressive idealism and Evan's cynical realism is clear, but in a way it is borne on the reader that there is a certain common ground – the two are looking at the screen of people (the *demos* in democracy) from opposite sides. To put it as a crude and simplistic opposition: Chano wishes to give people what they deserve to have, some kind of self-possession, while Evan wishes to give people what they appear to want to have, to fulfil the desire for possessions and pleasure. The accord underlying the indelible discord, and vice versa, between the two brothers' ideological positions is underlined by the mutually enhanced clarity of conviction that they feel in this exchange.

Ultimately, though, the literary form of the novel proves to be particularly conducive to conveying the complexity of Seattle-like mass protest as a convergence of diverse social movements (local to global) because, as observed above, the momentary unity in diversity is to a significant extent a matter of presentation, a kind of linguistic performance as much as the performance of a material gesture and an image. The studied discussion of this depends on the suggestiveness of apt phrases, such as 'movement of movements', and an accounting of particularities which is always open-ended, whereas the fictional representation can be impressionistic and connected and whole at the same time. The sweep of disaffection and the will to protest for change that is captured in *The Fountain* by focusing on the specifics of a small Mexican town, Tonalacapan, and then building from there to the *manifestación* in Calderon, and from there finally to the WTO protests, conveys impressionistically but comprehensively something of the structure of social movements and convergences – in ways that are difficult to achieve in a theoretical or academic or journalistic exposition. This is demonstrated briefly in the description of the Calderon *manifestación* (Newman 2003, 123–5, 130–3), but that remains incomplete as the military move in to arrest Chano's son to entrap Chano. It is shown on a grand scale in the day-by-day account of the Seattle protests (occupying all of part 4, entitled 'The Battle of Seattle', chapters covering 30 November to 3 December 1999, pp. 245–311). The fluid and often truncated narrative here slips from protagonist to protagonist, from group to group, from action to action, weaving disparate scenes and conversations and events into a fictionally and realistically coherent whole.

Interestingly, what comes across powerfully in this attempt to give literary form to a (well-conceptualized) reality of global scale, focalized into a convergent period of protest, is in fact exactly the opposite of what is conveyed in DeLillo's anti-globalization protest of the imagination in *Cosmopolis*. If in the latter violence was somehow, obviously implausibly, concentrated on the protesters and activists, so that the anti-globalization activists seem to have a near monopoly on real violence, in *The Fountain* that monopoly is clearly the establishment's. It is in the hands of the US police and military, as the shields and agents of the most obvious global capitalist alignment, the WTO. *The Fountain* describes in visceral detail all the modes of crowd control and dispersal – concussion grenades, tear gas shells, CN gas shells, rubber bullets, arrests and beatings, cordons – unleashed by the police and paramilitary forces in Seattle against a non-violent mass. The effects of being tear-gassed on the first day of the protests set the tone:

Tear gas seared his skin, scorching every pore and blood vessel. He screamed out. Acid hooks pulled at the roots of his tongue, burning his throat and mouth. Screams broke all around him, bodies were heaving and tipping this way and that. He tore off his molten goggles and thrashed around on his back, legs lashing out. The pain grew worse by the breath. (Like missing the moment you snatch your scalded hand away from a pan. Instead the hand stays there, only it's your whole body, and the burning gas is everywhere.) Lava dribbled down his chin. He grabbed at his scalded eyes with scalding hands. He whimpered in terror and panic and tried to breathe but seized up, convulsed in a paroxysm of strangled airless panic. (Newman 2003, 254–5)

In the midst of a steady proliferation of such violence as the protest grows, Chano is described as symbolizing the spirit of the protest. Though protesters are subjected to these painful measures with ever-increasing intensity, they remain stolidly and non-violently resistant – their spirit immured and toughened by their sense of injustice and oppression. Chano significantly discovers that he has grown resistant to the effects of tear gas through prolonged chemical poisoning, and is able to move through it unaffected: 'Alone among the fifty thousand protesters Chano's long years of marination in sodium metabisulphite had rendered him immune to tear gas. [. . .] Now and then he coughed in the gas and his eyes stang a little, but only as much as someone standing downwind of a bonfire' (ibid., 259).

PEACE MOVEMENTS

The literary representation of anti-globalization movements/social movements is one among many threads that could characterize discussions of globalization. What such representations arguably convey is a sense of a coherent and dynamic social awareness that, while clearly located and contextualized, is not contained by immediate locations and contexts. In other words, a sort of social awareness is conveyed that understands its location and context in terms of world-embracing systems or global interconnectedness. This apprehension of interconnectedness has various levels – political, economic, communicative, organizational, etc. – which are naturally within the ken of literature, and must in some sense reconstitute ideas about literariness. Literary treatment of such a global social awareness is not seen simply in the meaningful event or gesture, such as a particularly large-scale or effective protest. The global social awareness in question, while effectively concretized and concentrated in such events, is ultimately dispersed in the everyday life of people. At any rate, some such dispersal of a global social awareness in the interstices of everyday life is often assumed and discerned by globalization theorists and registered in literary works – in, for instance, the contemporary British and North American literature to which this chapter is devoted.

By way of maintaining continuity with the discussion in this chapter so far, the dispersal of a global social awaresss can be traced in literary representations that deliberately delve behind such significant events as large-scale international protests. Perhaps the most globally effective protests in recent years, certainly in terms of scale and organization, have been not so much the December 1999 Seattle kind of 'anti-globalization' protest as the anti-war protests or peace marches after the Islamist terrorist attacks in New York and Washington of 11 September 2001 and the military actions against Afghanistan (immediately after) and Iraq (in 2003) that followed. In various ways the post 9/11 context has given globalization both from above and from below an edge that is distinct from perceptions in 1999 or 2000, which the novels by DeLillo and Newman cited here addressed. In terms of protest movements, some of the largest international mobilizations were evidenced during and following the US–UK led attack on Iraq, which was undertaken without United Nations sanction and on the unproven allegation that Iraq was harbouring weapons of mass destruction that were dangerous to international security, and which was later touted as a war for international democracy against tyranny. This military attack deposed the Saddam Hussein-led Baathist government in Iraq and unleashed a protracted period of internecine violence and instability in that country.

Of the many peace marches and anti-war protests that took place in this period the most memorable and enormous were undoubtedly those organized worldwide on 15 and 16 February 2003 (on this, see Gupta 2006, ch. 12), when the impending attack on Iraq was widely regarded as inevitable. Over that weekend it was estimated that more than 600 cities and towns around the world had witnessed protest marches (Conradi 2003), with about 30 million persons participating. A more cautious estimate later suggested that, for 15 February alone, 12 million worldwide, with 6 million in Europe, joined anti-war marches. All the newspaper and broadcast reports on these noted at the time that the largest rallies took place within those Western European countries whose governments were pushing for military action in Iraq most single-mindedly – particularly in London, Rome, Barcelona and Madrid. It was reported that the London rally of 15 February 2003 had (according to police estimates) 500,000 to 750,000 protesters or (according to organizers' estimates) between 1.5 to 2 million. The consensus now appears to be that there were at least 1 million protesters marching in London that day. According to a brief survey of protests in *The Guardian* (Chrisafis et al. 2003), rallies in Barcelona and Madrid were estimated as bringing together 1 million people, campaigners in Rome claimed 3 million people had converged (though police put the figure at 650,000), and organizers in New York counted 400,000 demonstrators marching in defiance of a court order. Though estimates of figures differed widely between police and organizer sources, it is generally accepted that these were the largest international protests ever seen. However, they had little effect on the plan for invading Iraq, which was initiated by US President George Bush on 19 March 2003.

Worth noting here is the difference of such international protest gestures from the anti-globalization or social movement protests, which reflect in effect another turn to the globalization/anti-globalization opposition. If anything, the peace protests brought together an even more diverse set of interests under the banner of a strongly defined anti-war objective. They were addressed not directly to an abstract system of global economic alignments and regulations but to a specific and contingent series of events that could be related to those; however, they also had an independent moral impetus. The main organizing groups, though aligned broadly with the left, clearly incorporated a wide ideological spectrum. Writing about the British Stop the War Coalition (STWC), a report in *The Guardian* (Vidal 2003) observed: 'More than 450 organisations, including such disparate groups as Greenpeace, Americans against the War and Britons versus Bush – a group of Bedford cabdrivers – have joined 11 political parties including SNP, the Liberal Democrats, Plaid Cymru and the Greens, and affiliated themselves to the STWC.' It was also observed that there were separate anti-war groups that had come together outside the STWC because of the predominantly left make-up of its steering group, such as Our World Our Say (which registered its protest by placing advertisements in major national dailies). The International ANSWER (Act Now to Stop War and End Racism), United for Peace and Justice and the Not in Our Name project, the main protest organizations based primarily in the United States, listed on their websites a range of endorsements from representatives of groups that embraced positions far outside the remit of left associations. A *New York Times* report (Clemetson 2003) mentioned a number of groups with no specific ideological position other than a humanitarian one (such as Win Without War and September Eleventh Families for Peace), church-based groups, and even Republican and business associations (Business Leaders for Sensible Priorities) coming together with an anti-war agenda.

Unsurprisingly the anti-war protests in the context of the 2003 attack on Iraq have been drawn into literary representation, but often interestingly not so much to present them directly (as in *Cosmopolis* or *The Fountain*) as to register the more dispersed and fraught global social awareness that enabled them. Two examples can serve to demonstrate the literary treatment of this: British novelist Ian McEwan's *Saturday* (2006), which follows the movements and thoughts of a London surgeon with the protests in the background; and American novelist Nicholson Baker's *Checkpoint* (2004), which records a fictional conversation between two men in Washington as the violence following the invasion of Iraq unravels.

McEwan's *Saturday* describes an eventful day, 15 February 2003, in the life of a London neurosurgeon Henry Perowne, through his eyes and thoughts. The novel begins with Perowne rising at dawn and witnessing from his window a plane crashing, then details his interactions with his immediate family and colleagues, his memories, his social and philosophical attitudes, and his professional activities, and is gradually structured around two events – an encounter with a gang of aggressive youths after a slight car accident and the reappearance of this gang at his home to wreck an evening family get-together. Perowne obviously belongs to the affluent professional middle class, lives in an up-market house in central London and drives an expensive car, and his view of the world and life – effectively conveyed through a sort of stream of consciousness (rather more formally and linguistically orthodox and less immediate than James Joyce's or Virginia Woolf's stream of consciousness novels) – is circumscribed by his circumstances. The two encounters with the gang of youths, particularly their leader Baxter, turn out to be encounters across a class chasm, infused with the desire and aggression that the less solvent Baxter feels towards Perowne and his family. Baxter's disadvantages are underlined by his having inherited a genetically transmitted disease, which Perowne discerns in their first meeting (thus establishing a kind of authority). The novel ends with

Perowne, the authority figure and devoted family man, overcoming Baxter, and then, as healer and humanist, saving his life by performing surgery on him (though unable to cure him of his fatal inherited disease).

The reader is tempted to read this sequence of events, especially the well-heeled London surgeon's overcoming and patching up of the diseased and disadvantaged criminal, as somehow related to the larger conflict that occupies the background – the invasion of Iraq by US–UK led forces on the pretext of overcoming tyranny and a threat to world peace, and the global protests against that. There is no attempt whatever in the novel to labour any such association – merely the juxtaposition of Perowne's experiences against the most momentous anti-war protest march in history as an intimation. An association is also suggested through the occasional foregrounding of Perowne's thoughts on the matter of impending war, inevitably lurking in his mind as on everyone's mind in London at the time, as he passes the anti-war march that takes over the city that day or as he debates the issue with his anti-war daughter. But mostly his preoccupation with the pros and cons of the coming war are in an almost subliminal stratum of his consciousness: he finds himself thinking of Saddam Hussein as he watches his sleeping wife, for instance. Despite qualms about the motives of the drive for war, Perowne is not against it. On the contrary, and largely due to a personal encounter with a professor who was tortured in Iraq, he rather thinks it might lead to desirable outcomes, albeit in a conflicted fashion. While watching the protesters from his car he lists in his mind all their arguments against war and recognizes their veracity, and yet 'can't feel, as the marchers themselves probably can, that they have an exclusive hold on moral discernment' (McEwan 2006, 73). Or, as he later explains in an argument with his daughter: 'No rational person is for war. But in five years we might not regret it. I'd love to see the end of Saddam. You're right, it could be a disaster. But it could be the end of a disaster and the beginning of something better. It's all about outcomes, and no one knows what they'll be. That's why I can't imagine marching in the streets' (ibid., 187). But more than these explicit positions it is in his passing reflections on the protesters themselves – redolent with Perowne's sense of individual scepticism against their collective certainty – that conveys his position:

There are ragged practice chants which at first he can't make out. Tumty tumty tum. Don't attack Iraq. Placards not yet on duty are held at a slope, at rakish angles over shoulders. Not in my name goes past a dozen times. Its cloying self-regard suggests a bright new world of protest, with the fussy consumers of shampoos and soft drinks demanding to feel good, or nice. Henry prefers the languid, Down With this Sort of Thing. A placard of one of the organising groups goes by – the British Association of Muslims. Henry remembers that outfit well. It explained recently in its newspaper that apostasy from Islam was an offence punishable by death. Behind comes a banner proclaiming the Swaffham Women's Choir, and then, Jews Against the War. (McEwan 2006, 71–2)

Perowne's view of the myriad of protesters is reductively contained (or conveniently selected by the author) in his two substantive observations there. He disparagingly associates the protesters as a whole, on the basis of misreading one of their slogans, with moral self-regard and self-gratifying consumption. And he homes in on the co-sponsoring group, the Muslim Association of Britain (MAB), whose conservative Islamic ideology and alleged links to the Egyptian Muslim Brotherhood were hotly debated by alignments within the anti-war coalition itself (the statement referred to here appeared in an article published in the MAB newspaper *Inspire* in 2002) – without any reference to the other sponsors (the Stop the War Alliance, incorporating an enormous number of differently located interest groups, and the Campaign for Nuclear Disarmament or CND) or the varied ideological interests which converged in the anti-war protest.

By sieving the protest, while keeping it tellingly in the background, through Perowne's overarching consciousness and suggestively juxtaposing it on the surgeon's carefully close-up humaneness and humanity, it could be argued, the book itself is positioned ideologically vis-à-vis the anti-war protests and the invasion of Iraq. But, equally, it may be argued that any reader's determination to find a position in this regard for the book, the novel's invitation to the reader to do so, itself makes a point. The book demonstrates deliberately how deeply embedded the matter of this war and these protests were in the routine consciousness of people in London (and presumably elsewhere), how enmeshed in the domestic, personal, everyday preoccupations of people such as Perowne (and others, presumably both all the protesters and all those who didn't protest). At the same time, a reader's interest in determining where the novel comes from in this regard, a reader's suspecting that every aspect of Perowne's day may be inextricably interlinked in a grand design (at least a fictional design) with the enormity of events and protests which, ultimately, spin out across the globe, draws that reader into a similarly engaged social-intermeshed-with-personal consciousness. It involves them in the complicity of taking the fictional Perowne and his attitudes to be as real as themselves and their own. The novel presents and plays upon, seemingly, a sort of global social awareness and mixes it up with individual private lives by evoking 15 February 2003 as a backdrop.

From a somewhat different ideological direction but with similar effect comes Baker's *Checkpoint*. This is set a bit over a year after the 15 February 2003 anti-war protests, in May 2004, in a hotel in Washington, DC, where two friends, Ben and Jay, meet after what appears to be a considerable period of time. Jay sets off the conversation by declaring that he has decided to assassinate US President George Bush 'for the good of humankind' (Baker 2004, 5). The entire novel is the conversation that follows, in which Jay lays out his reasons and Ben tries to dissuade him, and incidentally, amidst that, they reveal something of their personal circumstances and preoccupations. The conversation takes place well after the invasion of

Iraq and towards the end of the occupation period (the occupation-period government, the US appointed Coalition Provisional Authority supported by a puppet Iraqi Governing Council, was in place from May 2003 to June 2004), and Jay's decision derives entirely from his bitter disenchantment with the invasion, its US–UK leadership, and its results (constantly escalating civil violence and discord). To justify his decision, Jay recounts the various incidents of killings of civilians and torture of Iraqi prisoners (markedly the media-exposed photographs of torture conducted by American soldiers in the Abu Ghraib prison) that occurred in gruelling detail. Ben, though determined to dissuade Jay from any such rash step, shares his friend's sense of outrage, and, as a historian, is able to see the lines of complicity running from the Iraq invasion backwards into post-Second World War US foreign policy generally. Jay roots his decision to assassinate the president in his experience of joining an anti-war protest march in 2003 – not, as it happens, on 15–16 February, but one soon after the invasion started, on 19 March. Jay's view of this march is evidently diametrically opposed to that of Perowne in *Saturday*; where the latter was largely sceptical of the protesters' moral discernment and character, Jay felt both utterly convinced of the moral purpose of the march and completely deflated by its futility. His decision, it seems, arose from that conjunction of conviction and impotence:

But there I was with my fist in the air, I'm sobbing, I'm screaming with these people because we all sensed and we all knew, regardless of what we did or didn't have in common in other ways, we all knew that the war that the United States was waging on that patchwork country was, was – it was ushering in a new kind of terribleness into the world. And we knew we had to do something. So we marched and marched and marched, and we shouted till we couldn't shout anymore, and then we all went home and we put on our pajamas or our whatevers, and we went to sleep and woke up the next morning, and what? People were still getting their limbs blown off – families were still being killed. I'd given it everything I had. I felt like a lump of depleted uranium. (Baker 2004, 21–2)

As their conversation develops it becomes clear that Jay's and Ben's agreement on the character of the invasion and occupation of Iraq doesn't arise from shared ideological convictions, just as the protesters don't necessarily share an ideological platform. On the contrary, they hold opposed views on most matters. Jay turns out to be vehemently anti-abortion; Ben is firmly pro-choice and doesn't even wish to engage Jay on this. Jay's thinking tends to leap to wholly implausible conspiracy theories, suggesting at different times that President Bush's neoconservative Iraq policy deviously uses the anti-abortion lobby and is connected to the popularity of abstract art. Ben is more methodical and informed in his analysis of the Iraq invasion and its links to history.

Unlike *Saturday*, *Checkpoint* foregrounds the Iraq conflict and, insofar as they are presented, the anti-war protests. But like *Saturday*, *Checkpoint* also effectively conveys how people's engagement with this conflict is deeply enmeshed with their private and domestic lives, their experiences of the everyday, and derives from as well as devolves into a kind of global social consciousness. As the novel progresses it becomes apparent that Jay and Ben are very differently located in their personal and professional lives, and that this might have a bearing on Jay's passionate and Ben's relatively stoical response to their shared sense of outrage at the situation in Iraq. Jay is in financial difficulties, and has moved from a teaching job to working as a day labourer. He has consequently lost his intellectual interests and is unable to focus on books. He is also separated from his children, and has been unable to sustain relationships with a series of partners. Ben has a steady job as an academic, has a stable family life with wife and child, and has cultivated his research interests and developed new hobbies (photography). Ben suggests, and it seems increasingly likely, that Jay's vehement hatred of President Bush and his rage at the injustice being perpetrated in Iraq may be driven by the deficiencies of own personal and professional circumstances, and that he channels the frustrations of the latter into the broader political disquiet of his time. Likewise, if Ben is able to temper his sense of outrage it is because his personal and professional stabilities enable a more temperate disposition, or at the least a more cautious and restrained one. But in both cases what's established is an intermeshing of personal and domestic and everyday concerns with larger, indeed international, political events. Through whatever process, Jay's own vulnerabilities translate into an intense sense of empathy for a distant people and their suffering and a powerful will to protest – which arguably was to some degree what all those anti-war protesters felt – and perhaps even kill 'for the good of humankind'. It is forcefully expressed towards the end of the book by Jay, effectively undercutting Ben's somewhat parochial attempt to appeal to Jay's humaneness:

Ben: But don't you think that if you – I mean, you've seen the tape of when Kennedy was shot. You've seen the frames that were cut out of the film because all that blood was blasting from his head? A spray of brain? I mean it's a horrifying sight. It's a human being that is now just nothing. You want to be a part of that?

Jay: That's the thing. I have allowed myself to feel that feeling with the people in Fallujah, in Karbala, in Nasiriyah, in Basra, in Baghdad, in Mosul – all these cities. And Afghanistan before that. I've seen the pictures. And I feel that they – I mean Bush, any Marine sergeant, any soldier – all these guys are in the war business, one way or another. So they know that there's a certain risk involved. You can become a casualty of the wars you incite, or that you volunteer for. But these kids who are having their limbs blown off, they don't know what's going on. There's just a sudden sound of jet engines. (Baker 2004, 108–9)

At the end Ben accepts this but still prevents Jay from carrying out his assassination attempt – presenting Jay with a picture of Bush instead on which to vent his rage in a ritual fashion. This is not so much a resolution of anything, simply an assertion finally by the successful and stronger personality over the vulnerable and weaker personality.

Both *Saturday* and *Checkpoint* appear to convey, in the context of disquiet about the Iraq war in 2003, a sense of a continuum between global politics and oppositional movements, their immediate collective manifestations in local contexts (in specific images of protest marches, for instance), and individual preoccupations with/engagements in these within the flow of ordinary individual lives. Events spanning different nations and cultures seem to have a bearing on individuals in their specific locations leading their everyday lives. In both novels the central protagonists are not involved in immediate strife, and nor are their thoughts guided entirely by narrow self-interest or entirely circumscribed by their own national or cultural allegiances. And in both novels the everyday lives of the central protagonists, their personal and professional concerns, are impinged upon by those larger events and oppositions in a more or less continuous fashion, as a continuous prickle to emotion and intellect. It is this intermeshing between the macro- and micro-levels of awareness which gives weight (whether for a detached sceptic such as Perowne or a passionate participant such as Jay) to the collective materialization of these anti-war protests and gestures towards the ubiquity of a global social awareness (especially since most readers would know that the specific protest described is but one amidst a global phenomenon).

These novels present this global social awareness as naturally and obviously given: there already, but heightened and crystallized by the pressures of the Iraq war period. They do not attempt to analyse or highlight the means through which this consciousness has come about or how it is fed. But the primary means are written as incidental and unquestioned facts of contemporary living: the presence of distant realities as selectively presented realities, but immediate, even personal and visceral, through mass media. To a significant extent these are realities in various parts of the world sieved through the conventional media channels – newspapers, television and radio broadcasts – into London and Washington drawing-rooms. The conventional media channels are clearly at the heart of Perowne's stream of consciousness in *Saturday*, constantly revolving and returning to arguments and bits of information that have passed the television screens. It is interesting both how visually affective these media images are and how seamlessly they are woven in with Perowne's daily occupations. Thus, it is while thinking about sex with his wife Rosalind that his thoughts first stray towards Saddam Hussein, an image of Hussein's face in fact, as vividly etched in his mind apparently as if Perowne has seen him in the flesh:

It's only children, in fact, only infants who feel a wish and their fulfilment as one; perhaps this is what gives tyrants their childish air. They reach back for what they can't have. When they meet frustration, the man-slaying tantrum is never far away. Saddam, for example, doesn't simply look like a heavy-jowled brute. He gives the impression of an overgrown, disappointed boy with a pudgy hangdog look, and dark eyes a little baffled by all that he still can't ordain. (McEwan 2006, 38)

The closeness of this evocation of Hussein's image resonates later with Perowne's memory of a not dissimilar sense of uncertainty in Tony Blair, drawing upon a meeting and exchange in the flesh, as it were. When Perowne is later described watching the television news while preparing dinner, the two activities weave news images and domestic preoccupations together into an indiscriminate whole (ibid., 176–80). But it isn't just the conventional media channels which contrive in the moulding of a global social awareness; it is as importantly the resonance of distant voices brought into close communion with individuals in their private reveries through the internet that plays a part. This is particularly picked up in *Checkpoint*, when Jay speaks of his growing obsession with blogs (or web logs – diaries of various sorts kept for public access by individuals in different web servers):

Jay: [. . .] I told myself you're not going to read blogs all day. Because I'd been reading Daily Kos and the Agonist, Talking Points Memo, Checking Google News twenty times a day.

Ben: I don't read blogs so much.

Jay: I said to myself, No more, because where does that get you? You've got to detach. (Baker 2004, 22)

The ability of distant voices and images to impinge upon domestic as well as public spaces through conventional and new media is undoubtedly one of the key features of contemporary lives. That these media are a key battle-ground both for establishment forces of globalization from above and for dissenting and oppositional global social movements from below is a well-recognized and much researched area. To a great extent global fissures and tensions are fought in specific living quarters in the contemporary world. This feature of the current world is not merely reflected in the kind of global social awareness remarked in the literary works discussed above; it also impinges upon the conception of literature and literary form – in ways which are taken up in the next chapter.

V-DAY

To conclude this chapter on literary representations of global protests and social movements, I turn to an unusual possibility that is relevant to the above arguments. Under the conditions of some kind of widely dispersed global social awareness, a literary work may itself provide, very rarely, the impetus of something like a social movement that crosses boundaries. Arguably, something like this has been generated by Eve Ensler's play *The Vagina Monologues* (first published in 1998, and modified in 2001), in the V-Day activities that have grown around and through performances of it. Performances of the play (initially primarily in the United States and thereafter in various locations in Europe and elsewhere) have provided a structure and channel for mobilizing opposition to violence against women, and building coalitions with organizations devoted to that, on an international scale. Karen Obel's 'The Story of V-Day and the College Initiative', published along with the revised text of the play in the V-Day edition (2001), describes how a celebrity benefit performance in 1998 in New York on Valentine's Day led to a college initiative programme whereby the play was performed on that day in 1999 and 2000 in a large number of universities: 'Based on figures reported by the participating schools it is estimated that about 65,000 people attended V-Day 2000 College Initiative events and that, through these events and the associated publicity, more than 1.5 million people were introduced to *The Vagina Monologues* and V-Day around the world' (Obel 2001, 138). The V-Day website (http://www.vday.org) now describes itself as 'a global movement to stop violence against women and girls', and observes that:

The V-Day movement is growing at a rapid pace throughout the world, in 120 countries from Europe to Asia, Africa and the Caribbean, and all of North America. V-Day, a non-profit corporation, distributes funds to grassroots, national and international organizations and programs that work to stop violence against women and girls. In 2001, V-Day was named one of Worth Magazine's '100 Best Charities' and in 2006 one of Marie Claire Magazine's Top Ten Charities. In nine years, the V-Day movement has raised over $50 million.

Eve Ensler's play is regarded as the inspiration for and as providing the founding drive behind V-Day, and performances have been central to the planning of events and publicity for its cause.

There is no doubt that this extraordinary initiative has been enabled by the energy of the activists who have used *The Vagina Monologues* as a vehicle for defining the cause of violence against women and girls, and building a movement around it. The question that arises is: to what extent are the intrinsic features of the play, its form and content and performative qualities, responsible for the kind of global mobilization that has grown around it? A response to that question involves, it seems to me, engaging with the following points, most of which are germane to the relation of literature to globalization and social movements and evidence of some level of (however mediated) global social awareness with which this chapter is concerned.

The dynamics of the play derives from the different sorts of cultural and social expressions (mostly of anxiety) that are invested in enunciating the word 'vagina', and attitudes towards such enunciation. Ensler introduces the monologues as follows: 'I was worried about my own vagina. It needed a context of other vaginas – a community, a culture of vaginas. There's so much darkness and secrecy surrounding them – like the Bermuda Triangle' (Ensler 2001, 3–4). There's a collision of linguistic senses in that statement of an overarching motif: it operates both as a biological and inevitably gendered signifier and as a socio-cultural (within communities and cultures) referent. The switching back and forth between the biological signifier and the socio-cultural referent is playfully emphasized in the metaphor of the Bermuda Triangle (both a place and a trope for mystery) and in the adjectives 'darkness and secrecy' (vaginas are literally covered/vaginas are figuratively silenced). In fact this collision of senses, playful though it is, is also central to the politics of the play. The vagina is enunciated in the play as a biological fact and as a purely gendered *possession*: that would explain why Ensler 'decided to talk to women about their vaginas, do vagina interviews, which became vagina monologues' (ibid., 4). Otherwise, vaginas often have something to do with men also, and the latter may have been asked to contribute a few interviews. The enunciation of 'vagina' is meant to establish a common denominator among women, an essentialized common denominator which is biologically fixed outside socio-cultural discourses. Only once that biological signification is understood as given is 'vagina' then drawn into socio-cultural discourses – all women from all sorts of backgrounds are invited to talk about it: 'older women, young women, married women, single women, lesbians, college professors, actors, corporate professionals, sex workers, African American women, Hispanic women, Asian American women, Native American women, Caucasian women, Jewish women' (ibid., 4–5). Despite this reminder of the echo of other women's voices and experiences in Ensler's play, however, it is clear that *The Vagina Monologues* is presented as a single text emanating, being performatively presented, through a single authorial consciousness. This is obvious in its carefully moulded and aesthetically trimmed language and in its formal disposal as a series of monologues.

This ploy of focalizing gender as an essential factor, preceding all socio-cultural discourses, through the enunciation of 'vagina' is emphasized in other ways too. The 'vagina' is often, again playfully and deliberately, given as a biological signifier that arraigns all other socio-cultural references around itself – the vagina becomes, so to speak, a super-signifier that is centred vis-à-vis socio-cultural discourses. Thus, one monologue lists how the vagina could be dressed; another what the vagina may say; another how the smell of a vagina may be described; a Jewish women describes dreaming that her vagina releases a flood; an English voice describes her experience of an orgasm in a 'vagina workshop' with the words 'My vagina is a shell, a tulip, and a destiny' (Ensler 2001, 50); a Bosnian woman raped by soldiers in 1993 says, 'My vagina a live wet water village. They invaded it. Butchered it and burned it down' (ibid., 63); and so on.

Insofar as violence against women features as a theme in the play, it is structured in accordance with the exigencies of enunciating and essentializing 'vagina'. Some monologues describe anxieties about having periods, about having pubic hair, about vaginal fluids, about commercial products to control these, all deriving from the attitudes of men or of patriarchal social attitudes; two monologues describe violent rape of women by men;

two describe reasonably happy heterosexual relationships where the man takes a voyeuristic pleasure in the vagina; four dialogues describe the pleasures of sex with other women who understand vaginas; and one describes the visceral tearing of the vagina in giving birth. Insofar as violence is identified as gendered violence, and portrayed as an assault on the vagina, the source of that violence can only be located in the other of what the vagina embodies and stands for here: conventional heterosexual men or patriarchal social discourses which silence the vagina are the locus of such violence. Just as the 'vagina' as an essentialized rhetorical device allows for the universalization of female or feminine anxiety and the object of violence against women, so too it conveys a univerzalisation of that violence as emanating from its gendered other – an equally essentialized 'penis'. The two monologues that describe a harmonious heterosexual relationship do not mention the penis. On a related matter, it has been variously noted that the 1998 version of the play and the V-Day 2001 version had significant changes, notably in the monologue entitled 'The Little Coochi Snorcher that Could'. This monologue describes the sexual awakening of a thirteen-year-old girl at the hands of a 24-year-old woman, and in the 1998 version the monologue contained the following words from the girl: 'Now people say it was a kind of rape. : . . Well, I say if it was rape, it was a good rape . . .' In the 2001 version these words were erased, probably to remove any suggestion of rape or violence as possible between women.

As that last observation indicates, *The Vagina Monologues* has been in some ways a fluid text, accommodating itself to different contexts and circumstances. It is also more or less fluid in the sense of being preeminently a performance text, and thus open to a performer's interpretive devices (inflection of voice, pauses, gestures, etc.) according to their audience. To that may be added the fluidity that every text acquires in crossing cultural and linguistic boundaries as *The Vagina Monologues* has – it has been translated, according to the V-Day website, into forty-five languages.

These features of the play arguably have a bearing on its success as the basis of the V-Day global movement. The slippages between biological signification and socio-cultural reference in enunciating 'vagina', the rhetorical ploy of centring 'vagina' as an essentialized and universalized gender signification around which socio-cultural discourses are arraigned, the tacit binaristic positioning of the 'vagina' as the object of violence and its other (patriarchy/the 'penis') as the source of violence – these features enable a curious decontextualization of the idea of violence against women even while presenting contextually specific instances of women's (all too often victimized) experiences. That decontextualized focus on women's experiences, that attention to essentialized and universal gender identities and violence, arguably enables the play to move across specific boundaries and accommodate itself to different contexts and realities. In fact it allows the frictions of different contexts and realities to be reoriented to a focus on gender and violence in apparently meaningful ways. This could explain why the play provides such an effective anchor for feminist activism of various sorts and in various contexts, and why it could act as a frame for political solidarities or the scaffolding of a 'global movement'. The rhetorical practice of the play – its accommodative performances – allows for a reduction of complexity that gives coherence to a widely dispersed set of political interests with a few basic common denominators (i.e. for women and against violence). It may be surmised that such a reduction of complexity is an essential aspect of global social movements, for the mobilization of diverse interests around specific issues. It may, however, also be observed that such a reduction of complexity, a playing down of contextual realities and overdetermination of abstract factors (gender identity, acts of violence), opens up uncomfortable questions and politically invidious claims. Is violence against women somehow more important or distinctive than other kinds of violence – violence against men and boys, or against some racial or ethnic or religious or national group, or against the poor and dispossessed, or against ordinary human beings anywhere? Is violence against women linked to those other or wider targets of violence (in a condition of war, for instance, women are not necessarily particular victims but part of a general violence directed against whole populations)? Should all sorts of violence against women (rape during war, domestic violence, female circumcision, communally sanctioned violence) be indiscriminately painted with the same brush, or should they be rigorously examined in terms of the social/political/economic/cultural circumstances that underlie them? That is tantamount to asking whether it is possible to oppose such violence in a meaningful fashion with a superficial unifying sweep or whether it can really be meaningfully addressed only in terms of the specific causes and the particular social injustices and proclivities of its specific contexts. Is the suggestion that such gender-specific violence is perpetrated by its other (patriarchy, men, the penis) necessarily true?

Finally, this discussion of *The Vagina Monologues* as an impetus for a global movement also draws attention to a more general feature of many political alignments and activities that may be regarded as global social movements. Just as this play encourages solidarities and convergences by focalizing gender identity in general, a large number of oppositional social movements revolve around and focalize concepts of identity (religious, ethnic, indigenous, racial, etc.). Indeed, it is often averred that globalization from above has released an oppositional agglomeration of diverse local and identity-based interests, and pushed their political expression and activities across boundaries to a globalization from below. And, at the same time, it is also often observed that the processes of globalization from above (international economic regulation, multinational capitalist enterprise, utilization of global labour markets, and exploitation of global consumer markets, transnational political alignments, etc.) co-opt such identity-based politics into its structures. Thus, for instance, the rhetoric of multiculturalism and diversity is assumed by transnational political alignments, commodities targeted towards specific identity groupings are produced and promoted by multinational corporations, international economic regulatory bodies often work through indigenous interests and local alignments. In many ways, thinking in the current ethos is powerfully structured from all directions along the lines of identity, not least in literary studies. The claims and necessity for maintaining parity between different identity-based groups form a strong strain in literary pedagogy and the academy – a matter that is taken up later in this study. It could be meaningfully observed, for instance, that this chapter itself suffers from unevenness in considering literary representations of globalization in relation to social movements by looking closely at four male-authored books and only one female-authored book. Whether that renders this chapter itself, or the field to which it attends, patriarchal or partisan is a question that is worth considering seriously.

3 Global Cities and Cosmopolis

GLOBAL TEENS

It is obvious in the previous chapter that literary representations of globalization from above and below stretch across geopolitical boundaries. Nevertheless, it does seem reasonable to assume that these are registered as aspects of globalization more continuously within the urban British (and such Western European) and North American environments depicted in the novels discussed above than in many other contexts. In these locations, in other words, a global consciousness is underlined both by the visible occurrence of protest and regulation and by an everyday sense of the world being within reach. The latter obviously has something to do with the concentration of images and information and commodities that are available in such spaces. The everyday global consciousness also derives from a continuous acceptance of the fluidity of cross-border movements, of people (relatively affluent) travelling to different parts of the world, or people from different parts of the world (looking for affluence) appearing and living there. It further incorporates a sense of the cultureless ubiquity of certain spaces – corporate offices, supermarkets, multinational chain stores, etc. – which increasingly map the patterns of daily life (the sort of space that anthropologist Marc Augé [1995] had described as 'non-places'). And the global in the everyday could simply be recognized in a certain kind of cosmopolitan behaviour, gestures and attitudes that are somehow redolent of capitalist efficiency and impersonality. Such an apprehension of the global in the everyday of the United States is pithily captured as a late twentieth-century generational trait by Douglas Coupland in his novel *Generation X* (1991) – not so much for the 'generation X' protagonists who are centre-stage in the novel as for their younger siblings, the 'Global Teens' ('though most are in their twenties'):

They're nice kids. None of their folks can complain. They're *perky*. They embrace and believe the pseudo-globalism and ersatz racial harmony of ad campaigns engineered by the makers of soft drinks and computer-inventoried sweaters. Many want to work for IBM when their lives end at the age of twenty-five (*'Excuse me, but can you tell me more about your pension plan?'*). But in some dark and undefinable way, these kids are also Dow, Union Carbide, General Dynamics, and the military.

And I suspect that unlike Tobias, were their AirBus to crash on a frosty Andean plateau, they would have little, if any, compunction about eating dead fellow passengers. Only a theory. (Coupland 1991, 122)

It is a revealing passage, that. It conveys the complexity of the corporate capitalist construction of globalization as it is popularly understood and experienced in the everyday. It is the everyday experience of those who are subsumed by the ideological attitudes, and personal and professional ambitions, which are manufactured for global consumption – and who are thereby themselves manufactured, in some sense, as persons. But all that is conveyed mainly to those who will recognize the allusions and references in that passage. This includes those who have watched the Coca-Cola multiracial advertisements since 1971, when the 'hilltop advertisement' featuring peoples of the world singing 'I'd like to buy the world a Coke' first appeared; and those who are familiar with the United Colours of Benetton advertisements since 1982, when photographer Oliviero Toscani's images associated the colours of Benetton's clothing range with a 'multiracial' theme. This would resonate with those who readily recognize that the Dow is the Dow Jones Industrial Average, the oldest US stock market index; that the Union Carbide Corporation is the oldest chemical and polymer corporation in the United States and its Indian pesticide plant was responsible for one of the largest industrial disasters in history (the 1984 gas leak in Bhopal which killed more than 20,000 people and left numerous others afflicted with debilitating ailments); and that General Dynamics Corporation is one of the largest defence contractors in the world. Readers of that passage would find it helpful to be aware of the Hollywood film *Alive* (1993), which was based on the true story of the 1972 crash of the Uruguayan Air Force flight 571 where some of the survivors stayed alive by resorting to cannibalism. This range of cultural references would be recognized by large numbers of readers outside the United States and Britain, as would the thrust of this observation of the 'Global Teens'. But these cultural references are rooted and pervasive in the Anglophone West in a way which is self-evident. That nexus of Coupland's address in this passage, and the addressee who is likely to unpack the nuances thereof, gestures to the aptness of the British and North American literary context for a discussion of globalization as a literary theme.

GLOBAL CITIES

Relevant to the manner in which North American and British (and broadly Western European) contexts harbour an everyday global consciousness is the kind of representations of cities often found therein. Large North American and Western European urban spaces are often signified as being greater than their ostensible geopolitical and cultural locations. New York, Chicago, London, Paris, for instance, are often presented as more than American or British or French cities. They are understood and presented in media, political, sociological, and also literary narratives as microcosms of the world at large, as 'world cities' or 'global cities'. There are several ways in which such a super-signification of these locations seems plausible: as noted already, the centres of regulation and finance and enterprise with a global reach have a larger concentration here than elsewhere; there is greater availability of non-place-like corporate capitalist neuterness in the everyday of such cities; these are hubs of international media and communications conglomerates and agencies which collect global information, and consequently likely to be attuned to what may be regarded as a global consciousness. But perhaps most importantly, these are cities that are simply enormously cosmopolitan – these are nodes of immigration and global movement, so that they present an extraordinary mosaic of diverse populations coexisting and cohabiting.

Let me return to DeLillo's *Cosmopolis* for a bit. In a self-evident way this is a novel about New York and those who inhabit New York (the polis that is defined by its people). It constantly evokes the peoples of New York collectively, in all their heterogeneity, to convey the textures of the polis: the drivers 'talked, in accented voices, some of them, or first languages, and they waited for the investment banker, the land developer, the venture capitalist, for the software entrepreneur, the global overlord of satellite and cable, the discount broker, the beaked media chief, for the exiled head of state of some smashed landscape of famine and war' (DeLillo 2003, 10); 'Hasidim walked along the street, younger men in dark suits and important fedoras, faces pale and blank [. . .]. He saw a woman seated on the sidewalk begging, a baby in her arms. She spoke a language he didn't recognize. He knew some languages but not this one. [. . .] Black men wore signboards and spoke in African murmurs' (ibid., 64–5); 'They saw the cockney selling children's books from a cardboard box, making his pitch from his knees. Eric thought they were the same thing, these two, and the old Chinese was the same, doing acupoint massage [. . .]' (ibid., 83); and so on to the description of the funeral procession for musician Brutha Fez which seems to bring together and hybridize an extraordinarily diverse set of influences and followings into a harmonious whole. The mourners include women 'in headscarves and djellabas, hands stained with henna, and barefoot', bodyguards in 'Western dress, dark suits and ties, polished oxford', 'the mayor and police commissioner in sober profile, a dozen members of Congress, and the mothers of unarmed blacks shot by police, and fellow rappers in the middle phalanx, and there were media executives, foreign dignitaries, faces from film and TV, and mingled throughout were figures of world religion in their robes, cowls, kimonos, sandals and soutanes', 'A line of elderly Catholic nuns in full habit recited the rosary', dervishes 'in tunics and long flared skirts, with topaz caps, brimless, cylindrical, tall' (ibid., 133–6).

The textures of New York life evoked here are composed of its parti-coloured population, which flows through the urbanscape in an *accustomed* fashion, without disorientation, habituated to its streetwise togetherness and its manifold segregations and fissures. Behind this definitive condition of New York lies a history of accumulating cultural influences and popula-tions, so that variegation becomes the quality of the city. Fiction centred on New York sometimes captures the early transitions that lead to this contemporary variegated feel of the world in a city, the cosmopolis. Chester Himes's *The End of a Primitive* (1990), which traces a criss-crossing line of black–white racial and gender tensions reminiscent of Richard Wright's *Native Son* (1940), is placed within 1950s New York to evoke an awareness of racial and ethnic complexity that lies alongside, interacts with, and goes beyond the black–white binary and ghettoized populations. The transfor-mation of a strip of Madison Avenue describes here, briefly, the process of that awareness:

For more than twenty years this strip of Madison Avenue had been relinquished by the city fathers to old ladies of the Arsenic and Old Lace variety as a reservation in which to walk their cats and dogs. Then came the apocalyptic day when the quiet, genteel atmosphere of the reservation was shattered by house wreckers and team shovels excavating for the foundation of the new, modern aluminium build-ing which, later, was to house the Ford Foundation. [. . .] They [the old ladies] considered the clean, shining, bright building a profanation, a veritable tower of Babel. [. . .] But when the old stone Godwin Mansion was given over to the India Institute, and the reservation was invaded by its rabble employees, Jews from Brooklyn, Italians from the Bronx, Irish from Hell's Kitchen, blacks from Harlem, foreign Americans from such outlandish places as Akron Ohio, Gary Indiana, Tulsa Oklahoma, that was the bitter end. (Himes 1990, 43)

Interestingly the passage describes an awareness of New York not so much as an accumulation of extra-American immigration or as a patchwork quilt of discrete ethnic and racial ghettos, but as a space within which the dif-ferent populations of New York itself, and of the United States at large, interlace and mesh together into a more complex brew. This complex brew doesn't dissolve the racial fissures or the ghettos, but they do introduce in them a dimension of complexity. Behind that 1950s focus lies a longer story of how the different populations of New York came to become New York, the history of populations within New York. This is rapidly sketched out, for instance, in the three stories of Patrick McGrath's *Ghost Town: Tales of Manhattan Then and Now* (2006). The three tales work through the anti-colonial war and cholera epidemic of 1832 ('The Year of the Gibbet'), the late nineteenth-century gilded age and the eponymous figure's love for an Irish model ('Julius'), and the immediate aftermath of 9/11 and the curious obsession with a Chinese prostitute of the main protagonist Danny Silver, and his psychiatrist's even more curious obsession with this relation-ship ('Ground Zero'). The process in these stories of eliding the defining racial black/white frame of American history, literature and culture nevertheless locates the history of New York as a shifting and blurring play of ethnic and racial boundaries, defining its population historically against the British, then refracting its ebbs and flows through different lenses of identity – class and race. As the successful businessman Noah reflects from the vantage point of the nineteenth-century *fin de siècle* in 'Julius':

He had recently read that the coming of the great cosmopolitan city marked the beginning of the last stage of civilization, the city being a sure symptom of imminent degeneration and decay. [. . .] More shipping lay at anchor out in the river and the Upper Bay beyond, among them his own clipper ships, narrow, high-masted vessels which crossed the Atlantic faster even than the steam-driven packets; and seeing all this he knew that what lay ahead was not the first stage of decay but the last preparation for greatness, or more than greatness, for New York's triumphant assumption, rather, of the mantle of distinction of being not only the pre-eminent city of America, but of the world. (McGrath 2006, 120–1)

The other side of this complex texture of contemporary New York as a site of parti-coloured and variegated populations meshed into each other, and yet held apart and opposed to being placed as the culmination of a historical process, is when it acquires a timeless and ahistorical quality as cosmopolis. This is arguably best captured in Colson Whitehead's *The Colossus in New York* (2003), the thirteen parts of which are timeless vignettes of the city, somewhere between essays and prose poetry. Each of the parts is addressed to either a typical New York location (Central Park, Broadway, Coney Island, Brooklyn Bridge, etc.) or a New York atmosphere (in the morning, when it rains, at rush hour, etc.). The book begins by observing, 'There are eight million naked cities in this naked city – they dispute and disagree' (Whitehead 2003, 6), and ends with the affirmation that, 'Talking about New York is a way of talking about the world' (ibid., 158). This New York is peopled by men and women who are anonymous, described only by pronouns ('he', 'she', 'they'), without details such as names, appearances, colour, clothes, etc. It is not the people who are the protagonists here; only the city which contains them is a protagonist. Their personalities are so subject to the city, so overwhelmed by it, that sometimes they almost wish for the city to recognize them and give them a more distinct identity – as for the person walking along Broadway:

Everybody remembers the city. Some people the city remembers. He is disappearing with every step. Who is he among that crowd. Pick him out among the great unwashed. Wouldn't it be funny if the city actually gave a damn about you. If you made your mark despite odds, if all this step-taking was actually alms-giving and in one unlikely moment after all these years this place smiled upon you. (Whitehead 2003, 80)

Much of the New York view of the cosmopolis, consisting in fluid and variegated populations which are stratified nevertheless, is found in literature about London too. The intermeshing of racially and ethnically defined populations alongside segregated spaces is described variously for London's historical accruals, and on London's peripheries and in its centre. From the city's fringes, for instance in *Londonstani* (2006), Gautam Malkani's exploration of the ghettoized mindset of South Asians (Indian, Pakistani, Bangladeshi) in London's Hounslow area, one encounters the following description of the audience for a duel between two gang leaders, the Sikh Harjit (known as 'Hardjit') and the Muslim Tariq:

> It weren't just Muslims and Sikhs who'd showed up. Eddie Bishop was here, this black kid who lived near Brentford an had been tight with Hardjit since before school. He'd even brought some other guys I'd never seen before. [. . .] Wai Qwok-Ho, who was top a Hardjit's ju-jitsu class, had come down too an brought another Chinese face with him. Respect to Oriental kids, it's their turn now. Those guys are coming the way a black kids an desis, I in't lying to you. [. . .] There were other people with fuck all to do with the fight out by the track that after-noon. Random people who worked at random offices, takin random fag breaks to soak up the sunshine. [. . .] That's London for you. All different kinds a people bringin all their different kinds a weather. Even a group of Somalians who nobody knew had wandered in from the streets to see what was going down. (Malkani 2006, 99–100)

The boundaries of the ghetto and the crossings over those boundaries are part of the same pattern, held together by the logic of a marginal language. The narrator Jas's deliberately 'roughboy' voice announces its segregated narrowness and its cosmopolitan accommodations at the same time. It is typically marginal London, more immediately recognizable than and yet as jarring as the Slavic jargon of Burgess's *Clockwork Orange* (1962). Eschewing a distinctive voice altogether and close to the heart of the city, Geoff Ryman's *253* (published in book form in 1998 and developed as a website at http://www.ryman-novel.com/home.htm) effectively encapsulates the interweaving of London's variegated populations. The novel sets the scene on 11 January 1995 on a London Underground train, travelling on the Bakerloo line from Embankment station to Elephant and Castle station, in which all 252 seats are occupied, no one is standing, and the driver is in his place. Carriage by carriage, each person on the train is described in terms of 'Outward appearance', 'Inside information' and 'What they are doing or thinking'. There are occasional links between them, some ostensible and some hidden, but the total effect is of presenting the enormous intermeshed complexity of backgrounds and identities and subjectivities that converge in London – so complex that this has to be a novel without any beginning or middle or end or progression and which can be read in any direction from anywhere. The only structure that is possible is a superficial and momentary imposition of order enabled by the device of the London Underground train, which is itself, with the tube map and 'roundel' logo, iconic of London. The device of the train is transient and the citizens' containment within it temporary; all must finally meld into the different strata of London. The formal fluidity of *253* obviously has something to do with the dual media in which the novel is made available, as an internet website and as a printed book – a matter of some interest here to which I return soon.

In brief, through the literary peopling of such cities as London and New York in late twentieth- or early twenty-first-century fiction, a super-signification of these cities seems to make sense. They become more than their locations and boundaries and physical geographies; their populations flow over definitions and constitute a sort of world-in-itself. They represent the accruals of history which are not understood through any limited progression of history, which push such cities into an apparently unhistoricizable complex present. They offer boundaries of ethnic and racial conflict, of segregation and stratification, of marginality and centrality, only so that all these are criss-crossed and interpenetrated even while being reified in the process. The city simmers in such representations somewhere in the aggregation of the urban mass, the numerous divisions and subdivisions therein, and the innumerable individual lives that unravel there. This seething variegated parti-coloured complex is somehow textually concretized in literature into the 'world city' or the 'global city'.

GLOBAL CITY TRANSACTIONS

These surface literary representations of people in these cities, often no more than impressions, capture something of the superlativeness of such metropolises as London and New York, of their 'world city' or 'global city' character. It is arguably not the task of literary representation to offer explanations and analyses for that which is figured, more to make it vivid and concrete through figuration. It seems to me that what is rendered vivid in such representations of people in the city, what concretizes the global character in such representation, is that they fit in various ways with both analytical and intuitive apprehensions of the relationship of such cities to globalization.

The relationship between global economic regimes and particular metropolitan centres has been considered in terms of socio-economic relations and urban spatial dispositions (Hall 1966; Castells [1972] 1977; Harvey 1973) since the late 1960s. The place of these à propos the lived experience of cities was picked up in an interesting fashion in Jonathan Raban's *Soft City* (1974). The city life that Raban charted out, largely drawing upon observations as various as with regard to shifting populations and literatures and images and fashions and architectures and crimes and enterprises and anecdotes of particularly London and New York, is as protean and resistant to definition as the twenty-first-century metropolis:

The city, our great modern form, is soft, amenable to a dazzling and libidinous variety of lives, dreams, interpretations. But the very plastic qualities which make the city the great liberator of human identity also cause it to be especially vulnerable to psychosis and totalitarian nightmare. (Raban 1974, 8)

Raban's soft city was implicitly visualized *against* sociological and economic attention to cities of the time, envisaged against the pull of ideologically mapped cities. In a Cold War context the pull of ideological polarizations, the possibility of concretizing ideological aspirations (whether of corporate capitalism or of socialist planning), was what Raban felt his perception of the soft city resisted and undermined. He therefore presented his soft city as naturally resisting the straitjackets of ideologically led conceptions of cityscapes through history – and is as scathing of Campanella's City of the Sun in *Civitas solis* (1623) as of Le Corbusier's *La Ville radieuse* (1935) and as of 1950s–1960s council housing in Britain (his example is the Millbrook estate in Southampton) and elsewhere. According to Raban the character of the soft city, with all its freedom, allure and danger, derives from the following observation:

There is no single point of view from which one can grasp the city as a whole. [. . .] For each citizen, the city is a unique and private reality; and the novelist, planner or sociologist (whose aims have more in common than each is willing to admit) finds himself dealing with an impossibly intricate tessellation of personal routes, spoors and histories within the labyrinth of the city. (Raban 1974, 222)

Raban's sense of the everyday life of the metropolis simply eludes, even undermines, the urban planner's and sociologist's reckonings.

The everyday life of the cosmopolis – the even more variegated and complex global or world city – that is presented three decades later in literature (as cited above) is, however, less resistant to the possibilities of sociological mapping. DeLillo's cosmopolis does not defeat the theorist; its visualization is enhanced by the participation of the theorist. This is not because the experience of the city had changed dramatically in the interim. It has actually grown more complex, more compressed, but it is still very like Raban's soft city. What has happened, though, is that the sociology of the world city has developed accounts of globalization that can contain the variegated and plastic quality of such cities, or, rather, that has made space for that complexity. Whereas in the 1970s it seemed that this complexity defied sociological charting, by the 2000s it seems that it is coeval with sociological reckonings with globalization.

This has something to do with observable changes in global cities in the course of the 1980s and 1990s and with the manner in which sociologists have taken account of these changes. Saskia Sassen's influential sociological account of New York, London and Tokyo presents the 'new ways' in which such cities function as follows:

first, as highly concentrated command points in the organization of the world economy; second, as key locations for finance and for specialised service firms, which have replaced manufacturing as the leading economic sectors; third, as sites of production, including the production of innovations, in these leading industries; and fourth, as markets for the products and innovations produced. [. . .] Cities concentrate control over vast resources, while finance and specialised service industries have restructured the urban social and economic order. Thus a new type of city has appeared. It is the global city. (Sassen 1991, 3–4)

To gauge the complexity of these developments Sassen finds that it isn't enough to trace ideological consistencies that place global cities within the international political economy, or even (in a conventional manner) to approach such cities as the centre for large multinational corporations and transnational banks and global political alignments/regulators. Delineating these cities involves, she observes, both marking the homogeneities that such formations and products bring to the global economic space and taking account of the increasing dispersal and differentiations of multiple layers of small industries and micro-enterprises. The economy of the global city, thus, acquires the conceptual complexity that derives from a paradox of engendering both increasing homogeneity and increasing fragmentation and variety:

On the one hand, there has been a world wide standardization of consumer goods and decreasing differentiation among places in terms of feasibility of producing a whole range of items for the world market, from apparel to electronic components. On the other hand, the dispersion of economic activity has contributed to the reproduction of structurally differentiated labour supplies and labour markets in the otherwise homogenised economic space. (Sassen 1991, 31)

It is also important, it is further observed, to account not only for the formal features of production and labour that are concentrated in global cities but also for the informal aspects. Instead of homogeneities character-izing the agents and processes involved in the processes that define the global city, there is a balance of homogenizing and differentiating tenden-cies, each holding the other together, each exacerbating the other. In a visible sense, the global city is therefore the site of formal structures and agents constituting their regimes, but also, and in a far more dynamic and protean way, of informal structures and agents which are part of the same frame. It is the energy of the informal which increasingly realizes the formal:

We need to distinguish two spheres for the circulation of goods and services pro-duced in the informal economy. One sphere circulates internally and mostly meets the demands of its members, such as small immigrant-owned shops in the immi-grant community that services the latter; the other circulates throughout the 'formal' sector of the economy. In this second sphere, informalization represents a direct profit-maximizing strategy, one that can operate through subcontracting, the use of sweat-shops and homework, or direct acquisition of goods and services. (Sassen 2000, 124–5)

The conceptual complexity of the global city at the hub of globalizing processes sits more coherently with contemporary visualizations of the cosmopolitan urban space than Raban's soft city did with the city sociology of the 1970s. There are in fact other dimensions of complexity which contribute to such sociological perspectives of global cities, and which concretize the reality-imaginary of the contemporary cosmopolis in litera-ture. There are proliferating differentiations and homogeneities which, as Sassen observes, are not only internal to global cities but are also overlaps and distinctions between global cities to keep in view. For instance, Anthony King's close study of the development of London as a world city (his preferred phrase) presents a complex mapping of its transition from colonial to postcolonial centre of world capitalism, with an attendant dynamic of policy adjustments and a consequent series of demographic and architectural-spatial changes. All these, King observes, contribute to Lon-don's intermeshed global–local character, which is manifested in the inter-dependence between the life of the city and of the wider world ('dependent metropolis' is the phrase King used) and a simultaneous 'unhook[ing] from the state where it exists, its future decided by forces over which it has little control' (King 1991b, 146). While this character as a generic world city ('a microcosm of the world itself') develops in London, he observes, it con-tinues to maintain, as each world city does, 'its own distinctive history, its own very distinctive social and cultural composition and its own distinctive locations within a particular culture and state' (ibid., 153). This perception coincides rather well with the sense that London novels and New York novels as urban genres have both a relation and a discreteness. The effer-vescence that is manifest in the representation of global cities, of the twenty-first-century cosmopolis qua cosmopolis, could be regarded as coherent distillations and concretizations of the internal and comparative variegations that are charted in recent sociological studies of global/world cities.

It is seldom the task of literature to provide explicit sociological or economic explanations, or even to take account of them. The surfaces of the global cities that simmer in the works of Don DeLillo, Martin Amis, Ian McEwan, Greg Ryland, Brett Easton Ellis, Colson Whitehead and others gesture towards implicit social relations, underlying economic pro-cesses, ideologies at work, tacitly. Very few works of fiction attempt to address the economic processes that actuate the immense dynamism and variety of the global city; insofar as this does occur, the tendency is to follow the inequities and iniquities of large multinational corporations and transnational banks. This occurs in DeLillo's *Cosmopolis*, which, after a fashion, picks up the trend set in the 1980s by Tom Wolfe's *The Bonfire of the Vanities* (1987) and Oliver Stone's film *Wall Street* (1987). A simpli-fied understanding of global cities as socio-economic spaces is available in these, focusing on the formal structures of multinational corporations and transnational players that are usually centred in such spaces. This focus comes at the expense of the informal and micro-sectors of production and consumption that are also constitutive elements of such spaces. Interestingly, Malkani's *Londonstani* (2006), with its deliberate interest in the economics of contemporary urbanity, is a rare instance of a fictional work that doesn't merely register the surface of the global city but also tries to get under its skin – in ways which are reminiscent of Sassen's or King's studies.

For the youthful members of the Hounslow gang who are the main protagonists of *Londonstani*, and particularly for the narrator Jas, meeting the well-heeled and well-educated economist turned mafia don Sanjay is a turning point in their lives. Until they met him, the gang had sustained itself by acquiring stolen mobile phones, unblocking them and selling them on. Sanjay offers to take four times the number of stolen phones off the gang and pay them five or six times the price so long as they don't bother unblocking them. He doesn't offer an explanation for this extraordinarily generous offer, and instead persuades them by delivering a lecture on what he calls 'Bling Bling Economics' ('bling' is the slang term for shiny desirable commodities). He pegs them as typical urban youth consumers who cannot do without excessive consumption, without an overwhelming desire for bling, and suggests that this is an indelible and neglected aspect of contemporary urban economics. The idea is that all official economic measures, such as inflation, are given in terms of some notion of an average or typical family's needs, whereas in the contemporary urban sphere such measures should take account of the alternative consumer indexes arising from superlative consumption, the desire for bling:

Sanjay's argument was that more an more people couldn't live in the official economy when more an more people's inflation rates were runnin at double digits. That meant wages, interest rates, investment yields, everything was off. For example, suppose you was workin for a company that din't recognise the gap between the inflation rate in your urban scene an the inflation rate in the official economy, then even if they gave you an annual pay rise a 7 per cent above the official inflation rate, you'd still be an impotent mug takin a fuckin pay cut an probly needin to borrow money from the bank. (Malkani 2006, 171)

This argument seems so reasonable to the gang members, accustomed as they are to their marginal London lifestyle and their part in the immigrant informal economy and their desire for bling, that they go along with Sanjay's offer. It eventually turns out that this small-scale incorporation of an informal business enterprise, in tune with a particular form of marginal cosmopolitan lifestyle, is for the benefit of a scam that involves a possible corporate takeover (of Jas's father's mobile phone company) and a fraudulent operation of international proportions (involving VAT fraud exploiting a loophole in European Union laws). In effect, *Londonstani* makes an intelligent set of links between marginal urban youth culture and large-scale corporate activities in the city and global financial regulatory mechanisms. The chain of fraudulent operations that links a microcosmic aspect of the urban informal economy to the macrocosmic operations of international financial regimes is reminiscent of the holistic conceptualization of Sassen's global city. In spirit, at any rate, Malkani's *Londonstani* concretizes the sociological connectedness and complexity of Sassen's sociology of global cities such as London, and places at the heart of the modern global city something suggestively plausible and yet intractable such as 'Bling Bling Economics'.

COSMOPOLITAN ORDER AND COSMOPOLIS

There are other inflections to the term 'cosmopolis', so effectively employed by DeLillo, which go beyond concrete representations of global cities. In political theory the term is now firmly associated with the adjective 'cosmopolitan' and the cultivation of a cosmopolitan view of the world, or 'cosmopolitanism'. Cosmopolitanism has a particular resonance with theories of globalization and gestures towards the determination and cultivation of political and ethical and social principles that are consistent with a globalized world, or with the world in the process of globalization. This contemporary view of cosmopolitanism is therefore distinct – though related in various ways – from conventional notions of cosmopolitanism in the conservative/liberal Eurocentric mould of modernists such as T. S. Eliot or James Joyce, or in the socialist internationalism of Jean-Paul Sartre or Lu Xun or Bertolt Brecht. Introducing a collection of papers on what the implications of cosmopolitanism are in contemporary social and political theory, Steven Vertovec and Robin Cohen are thus able to discern six distinct perspectives on the term, none of which cohere entirely with conventional notions: i.e. cosmopolitanism as the determination of an emerging socio-political condition, as a philosophy or world-view, as a political project for creating effective transnational institutions, as a political project for enabling people to act upon their multiple subject positions, as the cultivation of an attitude or disposition, or as an ability or competence to deal with others and the world (Vertovec and Cohen 2002, 9–14). The philosophical or world-view aspect of cosmopolitanism in relation to globalization is perhaps most broadly and yet succinctly delineated by Seyla Benhabib:

> Cosmopolitanism [. . .] is a philosophical project of mediations, not of reductions or of totalizations. Cosmopolitanism is not equivalent to a global ethic as such; nor is it adequate to characterize cosmopolitanism through cultural attitudes and choices alone. I follow the Kantian tradition in thinking of cosmopolitanism as the emergence of norms that ought to govern relations among individuals in a global civil society. These norms are neither merely moral nor just legal. They may best be characterized as framing the 'morality of the law,' but in a global rather than a domestic context. They signal the eventual legalization and juridification of the rights claims of human beings everywhere, regardless of their membership in bounded communities. Membership in bounded communities, which may be smaller or larger than territorially defined nation-states, remains nevertheless crucial. (Benhabib 2006, 20)

In a less abstract and future-gazing way, the cultivation of contemporary cosmopolitanism frequently impinges upon pressing and immediate and all too material issues that have a bearing on ongoing globalization processes. In recent years this has been an especially fraught matter in contemplating the global security regime – in, for instance, the arguments that could justify so-called humanitarian military interventions in conflict-ridden Kosovo or Somalia, or military interventions in Afghanistan or Iraq to counter an alleged threat from 'international terrorism'. The gradual realization of a cosmopolitan ideal or of cosmopolis as a, so to speak, realizable space – the world as polis or the polis as world – has also given rise to debates about concrete contemporary realities. Thus the possibility of giving flesh to cosmopolitan ideals in the transnational arrangements of the European Union is a much discussed and optimistic area of thinking (most optimistically in Beck [2002] 2005 and Beck [2004] 2006). More ambitiously, theorists of cosmopolitan democracy have turned their attention to modes of embedding cosmopolitan principles in international governance. The broad idea has been that a global democratic regime of some sort can be evolved through a systematic restructuring of existing international bodies, such as the United Nations, both by evening out the current inequities of power in such bodies and by making them adhere more stringently to normative concepts of democracy (rather than pragmatic multilateralism) – the arguments are most clearly available in the collection edited by Archibugi and Held in 1995, *Cosmopolitan Democracy*. A large number of political and social theorists have invested in exploring such cosmopolitan aspirations, including (apart from those mentioned) Martha Nussbaum, Jürgen Habermas, Kwame Appiah, Richard Falk, Mary Kaldor and Will Kymlicka.

Such contemporary attempts to envisage a political realization of cosmopolitan principles, or to realize cosmopolis in that sense, often causes justifiable disquiet. Perhaps the term 'cosmopolis', suggesting the achieved existence of a political space in which cosmopolitan ideals are embedded, is most immediately resonant with such disquiet. Unsurprisingly the term 'cosmopolis' has appeared as the title of works which take issue with attempts to draw cosmopolitan norms into political practice. Stephen Toulmin's *Cosmopolis* (1990) evokes the term, for instance, with misgivings. In this history of ideas, Toulmin traces the concept of the cosmopolis back to a Newtonian world-view wherein science, politics and theology merge into a whole: 'We are here concerned, not with "science" as modern positivists understand it, but with a *cosmopolis* that gives a comprehensive account of the world, so as to bind things together in "politico-theological", as much as scientific or explanatory, terms' (Toulmin 1990, 128). According to Toulmin such a global order ambition was nurtured in a variety of ways as a modernizing mission between the seventeenth and early twentieth centuries, whereafter for a while it was abandoned in favour of more diverse or variegated approaches to the world, but disquietingly: 'Since the 1960s [. . .] both philosophy and science are back in intellectual postures of the last generation *before* Descartes' (ibid., 168). The post-1960s context is, of course, characterized by the gradual recognition and con-solidation of globalization processes through concordant ideological and political economic structures and technological innovation. In a similarly critical spirit appears another book entitled *Cosmopolis* (1997), by Danilo Zolo, largely a critique of those who seek to institute global cosmopolitan democracy. From a politically realist standpoint, Zolo carefully demon-strates how cosmopolitan principles have been deployed in various contexts (the first Gulf War, the Kosovo War) to further the self-interests of Western powers and to extend their imperialist economic and military domination. His conclusion, diametrically opposed to the cosmopolitan one, is that:

Far from being reformed and empowered in the cosmopolitan direction of 'world government', existing international and economic institutions – such as, in par-ticular, the United Nations, the World Bank and the International Monetary Fund – will instead need to be subjected to substantial functional reduction. (Zolo 1997, 169)

Timothy Brennan's 'Cosmo-Theory' (2001) gives a succinct account of current understandings of cosmopolitanism and the problems with them.

For both Toulmin and Zolo the term 'cosmopolis' – the world as a city, the city as world – is evoked ironically to flesh out misgivings about idealistic aspirations of a global order. It marks both an idealistic longing for global order and a realistic reckoning with that longing. DeLillo's *Cosmopolis*, in being so titled, clearly has an ironic ring. What slips through Eric's global financial speculations and Kinski's eulogistic theorizations from that, through the hectic violence of the anti-globalization protests, through the multi-ethnic unity of musician Britha Fez's funeral procession, is ulti-mately the sad loneliness of Eric's death. But that opposition between individual loneliness and cosmopolitan togetherness has also been presented in literary works in ways which are less overtly critical and more ambigu-ous about the contemporary cosmopolitan world. The idea is that where, say, DeLillo's *Cosmopolis* shows individual loneliness as somehow exacer-bated and rendered tragic within and because of the logic of cosmopoli-tanism's diverse and dynamic togetherness, it is possible to present loneliness as imposed by anti-cosmopolitan ideology – as a violent removal of the cosmopolitan citizen from their environment. However, and this is ironic too, even this removal of cosmopolitan citizens by enemies of cosmopoli-tanism is usually disturbingly presented as within the structure of cosmo-politan aspirations and systems. Something of this paradox can be discerned in literary images of kidnapped Westerners in the hands of alignments that oppose West-dominated cosmopolitanism (Islamic alignments in Lebanon are the obvious choice) – such as in Richard Powers's *Plowing the Dark* (2000) and DeLillo's *Mao II* (1991).

Of course, there is an obvious question mark over reading the Western man abroad, out of place and sequestered, as representative of cosmo-politan citizenship, and over reading their anti-Western captors as anti-cosmopolitan. But that suggestion is itself part of the ambiguity of cosmopolitan idealism (as evidenced in Toulmin's and Zolo's critical takes), and is contained in the literary exploitation of the image of the kidnapped Western European or American in Lebanon. What gives that image its particular resonance is that the victim is presented, in the eyes of the captors, as 'Western man' in abstract rather than as a specific person, and the captors are presented as opponents of Western power and global ambition – which may be thought of as a cosmopolitan one. In both *Mao II* and *Plowing the Dark*, divided as they are by a decade, the image of the kidnapped Westerner in Lebanon is exploited in similar ways, and leads to similarly complex realizations of what being a cosmopolitan citizen is and what the current global order consists in. In both novels, the kidnap victims are citizens of the world, crossing boundaries, trying to acclimatize them-selves amidst cultural shifts, perceiving themselves or being perceived through the larger than nationalistic lenses that come with their cosmo-politan backgrounds. In both instances, on being kidnapped and imprisoned the victims gradually withdraw into their minds amidst utter isolation and a pared-down physically tortured, rigidly constrained condition, and grad-ually understand their place in the cosmopolitan world. It is between their withdrawal into themselves and their sense of what they have been with-drawn from that a view of the contemporary world emerges.

Hostage Jean-Claude Julien in *Mao II* tries to visualize how the news of his kidnapping would have been registered out there, in the world:

In the beginning there were people in many cities who had his name on their breath. He knew they were out there, the intelligence network, the diplomatic back-channel, technicians, military men. He had tumbled into the new culture, the system of world terror, and given him a second self, an immortality, the spirit of Jean-Claude Julien. He was a digital mosaic in the processing grid, lines of ghostly type on microfilm. They were putting him together, storing his data in starfish satellites, bouncing his image off the moon. He saw himself floating to the far shores of space, past his own death and back again. But he sensed they'd forgotten his body by now. (DeLillo 1991, 112)

What Julien realizes vividly in his isolation, in fact, is that his absence would be acknowledged primarily in terms of being registered and placed on a global information network. This network is controlled by intelligence officers, diplomats, technicians, the military, and consists in a reduction of all living reality into a referential system, into data to be assimilated or dispersed. There is something disheartening in Julien's realization that out there, where his captors are also charted in a grid of 'world terror', he ceases to have a concrete individual presence. There is even some kind of mutual confirmation in how he is placed between the ideology of his captors and the ideology of the cosmopolitan West – between them Julien is constructed into something abstract, constructed as something other than his physical self, given 'a second self, an immortality'. Similarly, kidnapped

American teacher Taimur Martin in *Plowing the Dark* has a growing realization of his place in the world from which he has been removed. In fact, it's a realization that grows not only vividly in the silence of complete isolation but also in complexity across the experience of his captivity. Thus, at the beginning of his captivity he has the following vision:

Hand between your head and the infested mattress, your free leg slung across the manacled one, you force your two column inches of captivity to materialize on the crazed plaster ceiling. And along with it, you summon up the whole front section of today's *Tribune* – World's Greatest Newspaper – the first image of any resolution to grace your private screening room. The blue banner and the hedging headlines. The weather for Chicago and vicinity. Metroland meanderings, carping columnists, gridiron second-guessers: pages scroll across your field of view on microfiche of your own devising. And tucked away, make it page 12, safe where the news will spare Des Moines and hurt only those whom hurt will benefit, you put a black-and-white reduction of your college yearbook photo, a face so saddled with goofy impatience for the future that even you no longer recognize it. (Powers 2000, 101)

And after a protracted period of being imprisoned, tortured, maltreated, just when he gives up hope, the vision recurs as follows:

He waves a scrap of newsprint under your blindfold. Eternity's long-sought armistice. Page 6 of the *Herald Tribune*, and there is the old man's photo, identified as you. Someone has been duped, either you or the world at large. And you don't care anymore, just who. (Powers 2000, 369)

Like Julien, Martin in captivity sees himself transferred and recorded in the world of news media, the grid of information that criss-crosses and characterizes cosmopolis. His physical presence is surrendered to the virtual presence of being registered in the news. In a *Dorian Gray*-like turn, the virtual presence in the news absorbs his physical reality – he feels that the entire trauma of captivity, his aging, has been misguidedly appropriated by the news media. The inconsequentiality of that reduction of self is a kind of complicity between his captors and the news world: his captors physically contain and torture him, and the news world reduces him to inconsequentiality, sticks him deep inside the information surfeit that is the news (page 12, or page 6 at best), of less consequence than the insurance corporations of Des Moines who profit from fear of loss of human life and property.

In brief, on the one hand, there is the suffering of being removed from the Western cosmopolitan world by those who oppose it, of being sucked into anti-cosmopolitan hatred. On the other hand, there is the despair of realizing that the mediatized, digitized grid that is ultimately cosmopolis somehow works in concert with, rather than against, its enemies. To be removed from the cosmopolitan West is unbearable suffering, it is suggested, but the production of enemies and victims is part and parcel of the network or grid that is the cosmopolitan order. Literary treatments of the idea of cosmopolitan order are seldom, unlike philosophical or theoretical treatments, unambiguous or partisan. Perhaps in this they come closer to the bone of the complexity of systems and agencies that operate in the name of cosmopolitan principles.

VIRTUAL COSMOPOLIS

The access to ideas or experiences of globalization that are available through literary treatments of global protests/anti-globalization protests, world cities, cosmopolitan principles and their discontents, a global consciousness, etc., are all powerfully associated with the growing centrality of technologically enhanced information and communication networks and grids. The images of captured Westerners just discussed gesture towards these, and in fact these are of particular moment in a study of globalization and literature such as the present. Up to this point I have discussed globalization insofar as it is thematically treated in literary works, in relation to various relevant issues. But the effects of technological enhancement of information and communication networks, the drivers of globalization forces, are not merely represented *within* literature; they also comprehensively *act upon* literature. Reckoning with globalization changes the very way in which literature is thought about, disseminated and consumed, and even constituted. This change is so dramatic that some literary critics, notably J. Hillis Miller, regard the emerging age of the internet as portending the 'end of literature' (Miller 2002, 1). It is, however, possible to see instead a potential re-energizing and transformation in literature and literary studies which is nevertheless organically and closely linked to the past practice of these. Subsequent chapters discuss how globalization impinges upon the manner in which literature is thought about (literary criticism/theory and globaliza-tion) and the manner in which literature is disseminated and consumed (literary circulation and globalization, or the globalization *of* literature).

I have noted in passing that technological enhancement of information and communications networks impinges on the manner in which literature is constituted. I meant thereby that it is not merely that literature represents the effects of such global connectedness, but that it is itself affected by that connectedness in its expressive modes, its textual forms, its receptions as literature. Such concepts as literary authorship, readership and textuality themselves are stretched and tested in new ways, so that arguably literature, so to speak, grows in scope. One may say that the cosmopolis is not merely something that literature sometimes talks about; literature gradually begins to perform cosmopolis within itself in its new media and environments. Literature increasingly performs within itself some of the characteristics of that realized but virtual space of cosmopolitan connectedness: the cosmopolis of the World Wide Web.

What I mean by that will, as I said, become clearer in subsequent chapters, and I therefore do not discuss the substantive ideas and observations involved here. Instead, I use the remainder of this chapter to read some literary texts which appear in such new media and environments with a view, before *discussing* them, to *demonstrating* what sorts of radical changes are becoming possible for literature and literary studies.

I have already mentioned the internet novel by Greg Ryland, *253* (to be found at http://www.ryman-novel.com/home.htm, and also published in book form in 1998), and given a brief summary of its contents. Relevantly here, *253* encourages different approaches in the two forms in which it is available, as a website and as a printed book. Both forms carry substantially the same material. The printed book naturally falls in with the convention of linear reading, and therefore follows a person-by-person and carriage-by-carriage progression, according to the layout of the underground train, with ancillary material intervening. Cross-references – between characters, to footnotes, etc. – are indicated on the pages where they appear. Checking them out is a matter of physically conforming to the linear structure of reading, by the movement of the eye or the act of shuffling pages backwards or forwards. The range of reading experiences can be as varied as one wishes to make it (one can skip pages randomly, for instance), but all variations are departures from a physically structured norm of linearity that is the shape of the book as a material object. The internet novel allows for more varieties of reading experiences, following different chains of connections and associations, and, importantly, without being constantly predicated on (departing from or adhering to) the normatively linear disposition of the physical book. By simple clicks of a button on hyper-referenced words or phrases, within any text or menu or image in the novel, the reader can construct different progressions of reading without being constantly reminded of departing from a physically maintained norm – the reader can, so to speak, construct different progressions naturally and effortlessly. These different progressions are not randomly or arbitrarily constructed; they are implicit in the logic of computer-mediated reading. The website novel, in other words, invites reading along a range of associational chains (e.g. character to similar character to explanatory footnote to another character to author/website advertisement, and so on), whereas the printed book invites reading along a linear structure, and if the reader departs from this they are consciously going against the grain of the book.

As a fiction-reading experience the website *253* is an unusual one. In printed book terms it has few analogues – *253* as a printed book is a fairly conventional matter. Normally, the idea of the literary text, the understanding of literary form, is powerfully predicated on the physical printed object, the directionally read page and book. So strong is this complicity between print culture and literary culture that their mutual dependence is scarcely noted; literary texts and forms are simply tacitly premised on their physical manifestations in print. One deliberate and somewhat laboured attempt to interrogate this complicity *within* conventional print culture that comes to mind is B. S. Johnson's novel *The Unfortunates* (1969). This was published as a loose sheaf of papers in a box which the reader could arrange in any way they chose, and could thus have a different novel at every reading. In a similar way, as a *fiction-reading* experience the website *253* might be an unusual one, but, and entirely unlike reading *The Unfortunates*, as a straight-forward *computer-mediated reading* experience it presents no difficulties and falls into now familiar reading practices. At least for those who are accus-tomed to surfing the net (undeniably a constantly increasing constituency), dealing with any range of websites (news, institutional, search engines, blogs, etc.), associational reader–constructed directions of reading are part of everyday life. It is simply that many are still not wholly accustomed to associate fiction – or broadly reading literature – with the habitual patterns of reading websites. Literature is still too strongly associated with print culture. *253* manages to bring these together in a reasonably coherent way. It seems to work as a work of fiction and as a website, and it is at this conjuncture that a symptom of the radical possibilities of technologically enhanced information and communication networks for literature can be discerned.

As a website novel *253* does unexpected things to literary preconcep-tions and concepts of reading and text; received notions of both are dispersed in a manner that isn't wholly anticipated in or contained by the various theoretical interrogations of these. The given structures of the fictional text along the expected lines of formal structure (e.g. beginning, middle and end; chapter and part divisions), generic structure (a novel nar-rating time, space, protagonists) and even syntactic structure (the integrity of sentences and paragraphs, or a deliberate playing with these) are each poten-tially and systematically undermined by the associational reader-constructed reading that the website invites. This potential undermining is not constructed within the text itself (James Joyce's *Finnegans Wake* is a text which constructs its own undermining of readerly expectations; the *253* website doesn't), but is at the whim of the reader's habitual website reading practices. The reader may jump off from any part of a text to another, may stray outside the fictional text into an advertisement or footnote or explana-tory text, may be drawn away in mid-sentence. This may appear to be a particularly liberating reading experience, but that's only insofar as reading is predicated on the directions embedded in print culture. What happens here is a layering of the web-design logic of providing associational linkages in the programme with the literary print-based logic of following/departing from material linearities. The reader is, so to speak, constructed somewhere between the presumptions of print culture-based literary reading and the presumptions of the website programme. Or perhaps, more appropriately, the agency of the reader shifts to a wider range of exploitations of the two sets of presumptions. However one looks at it, *253* symptomatizes poten-tially radical shifts in concepts of literary text and literary reading in a technologically enhanced information and communication environment.

Complicit with these, Greg Ryman also deliberately uses the *253* website to gently interrogate concepts of readership. He does this, of course, after firmly establishing his own authorial claim: 'About this site' on the home-page menu comes with a set of unambiguous authorial attributions, beginning with, 'The concept, structure and text of *253* are by Geoff Ryman', and posting author information and a list of his other works. Having done that, though, he sets up a couple of games on the *253* website which prod at conventional notions of authorship. From the 'advertisements' page there's a link to an 'another important announcement' page where one finds the following:

Every passenger in *253* has a number that is his or hers alone. And every section has 253 words. This means that:
    each character
    has his or her own word
    in *every* section.
Put all these words together – and you have made a monument to your favorite *253* character.
[. . .]
Do that for each of the seven cars, and you will have a new 253-word section in honor of Mr Keith Olewaio. In the privacy of your own home, you will have:
    treated words as things,
    moved them into place
    and counted them.
That is all that writers do! That's all there is to it. Try it next time you want to write a business letter or instructions for the general public. Write a poem and see if it really is any different from the *253* method. You'll have a fun hobby and will impress your friends. But remember, the one thing you will not do is
Earn big £££££ !!!!!
(http://www.ryman-novel.com/car2/ad2.htm)

This is obviously a sarcastic take on a familiar functional view of writing, often found in advertisements for commercial ventures selling packaged creative writing courses or guides. This can also, however, be read as a warning against assuming a reductive and mechanical concept of authorship which is relevant within the electronic context where it appears. That literary reading has been layered with a website programming logic, or that the habitual practice of website reading has been dislocated on the fiction-reading experience, should not be understood as a mechanization of the authorial function. If, however, this seems to leave the sanctity of literary authorship intact, it isn't for long – also tucked away in *253* is a serious and plausible invitation, on the 'another one along in a minute' page:

Immediately behind this train is another. It is stalled in a tunnel, like so many of us are in life. The passengers wait, wondering why the train is not going forward. No one can leave, no one can enter. It sits still for five minutes.
[. . .]

Another One along in a Minute pays tribute to stalled time by describing each character in 300 words, one for each second of time.

Together, we are inexhaustible. Populate Internet with people you imagine. Click here to email your 300-word contribution to *Another One along in a Minute*.

What will your characters do in that five minutes? Talk to neighbours? Read their papers? Complete their crosswords? Imagine that there has been a nuclear attack?

No money will be made from this sequel. Copyright will rest with you. The editor reserves the right not to publish, or to suggest amendments. You must undertake that no one will be slandered by your text and accept full responsibility for the material you submit.

(http://www.ryman-novel.com/info/one.htm)

This, in a logical progression from opening up readerly expectations on the basis of computer mediation, lays a programme for opening up authorial contribution or for, in a sense, dispersing authorship into a participatory conglomeration of multiple voices. This is analogous to a multiple-author academic volume with an editor, but still likely to result in an unusual and yet coherently discrete *literary* work with an unprecedented polyvocal authorship. If realized, it can raise searching questions of what it does to the concept of literary authorship.

It may be argued that *253* is more a one-off innovative juxtaposition of literary convention upon web-based communicative practice than a symptom of wider potentialities for literature arising from technologically enhanced information and communication networks. Anyone with a slight acquaintance with the scale of such networks – as special interest e-groups or e-discussion forums, blogging networks, user/consumer communities of various sorts, topical discussion site participants, e-activism alignments, etc. – would know that, even if a literary work such as the *253* website is an unusual instance, the kinds of potentialities it gestures towards are far from unique to it. The vast cross-boundary reading–writing networks in question are naturally, to some extent, already impinging on literary production and consumption, and thereby on concepts of literariness. It is mainly a sort of institutional and establishment inertia, the conservativeness which is ingrained in how literary value is attributed and how literary industries and markets are shaped, which has impeded serious reckonings with them. But that the implications of activities in technologically enhanced information and communication networks for the presumptions of literature and literariness are wide-ranging is easily apprehended by giving cursory attention to even a small element of it. Consider, for instance, the growing cyber-world of blog-writing and blogging communities.

Whether this world could be regarded as one that is devoted even in part to literary production and reception is a moot question only because its circulations of reading and writing are not carefully policed as literary, and occur outside the domain of institutional and corporate sanction.

Dismissive sentiments range from complaints about lack of discrimination, to doubts about superlative unchecked production, to scepticism about the inchoate character of the e-communities within which such productions circulate and perpetuate further production. Very occasionally, the verve of literary production therein is brought under the aegis of literature by the usual literary sanctions – approval by some institutional authority (an established author, an academic, the media) and corporate sanction through conventional publication (inculcation into print culture). Thus, for instance, novelist Dennis Cooper has collected fiction through the use of a blogging website and published it with the title *The Userlands: New Fiction from the Blogging Underground* (2007). In his introduction Cooper sees in this a challenge to the gate-keeping of conventional print-culture literature, which would be exemplified by the self-evident and cutting-edge literary quality of the collected writing:

The contemporary fiction known to the majority of book buyers and reviews readers is a highly filtered thing composed for the most part of authors carefully selected from the graduating classes of the university writing programs that have formed a kind of official advisory board to the large American publishing houses. To read that allotted fiction and look no further, it would be easy to believe contemporary English-language fiction has become a far less adventurous medium than music or art or film or other forms that continue to welcome the young and unique and bold. *Userlands* offer one alternative to the status quo, one unobstructed view of contemporary fiction at its real, unbridled, vigorous, percolating best. (Cooper 2007, 13)

Rather subjectively, it seems to me that some of the pieces in the anthology do have a fizz, an unexpected energetic quality, which is rare in the more staid stylistics of contemporary fiction in print. But it is impossible to determine at present whether creative writing in an electronic environment is coming up with distinctive literary styles – a great deal more research needs to go into that issue than is there at present. Ultimately, Cooper's anthology reads as another collection of unknown 'new' fiction, somehow contained and tamed by the printed pages within the book covers. It gives little scope for understanding the shifts in presumptions about literature and literariness to which blogging (for instance) may give rise. For that, I suspect, blogs have to be read as blogs, within their electronic medium, with the logic of writing, textualizing, reading that is conditioned or enabled by that medium.

There is another way of approaching the matter. If we continue with a focus on blogs, instead of looking for the literary qualities of blog fiction as if the 'literary' is an abstract normative measure which may or may not apply to this neglected realm, we may consider whether the blog could be thought of as a literary genre. Blogs incorporate a wide field, and may come as theme-defined (business blogs, news blogs, cookery blogs, music blogs, etc.) or more generally as personal blogs (the life, times and thoughts of an individual). Insofar as epistolary narratives, diaries or notebooks can be regarded as making up a distinct literary genre (an aspect, or structurally presenting an illusion, of 'life-writing'), personal blogs could be understood as a development of that genre in a technologically enhanced information and communication environment. Seen thus, the blog as a literary genre presents several critical differences from the conventional diary genre, and these differences, again, symptomatize the radical potentialities of the technologically enhanced environment for literature.

The obvious difference is in the disposition to audience in diaries and blogs. Whereas diaries (say those of Leonardo da Vinci, Samuel Pepys, John Evelyn, Alexis de Tocqueville, Franz Kafka, Virginia Woolf, Anne Frank, Anaïs Nin, etc.) are generally written or kept, at least initially, as a private record, and become accessible as public texts after the fact, blogs are from their inception maintained as public texts. Diaries are usually composed within a closed circuit of writer as reader (or writer and a closed circle of readers), and the impetus behind them is accordingly a limited one – as a mnemonic aid, as an exploration of self, as a notebook of observations and ideas to be developed in a more sustained fashion, as a desire for secret archiving, etc. In becoming drawn into print culture and literary reading, that impetus is comprehensively overturned: the diary comes to be read as a performance/construction of a particular personality, a type of character, an age, a place, etc. As a literary form, the diary is interpretively received as a literary text apparently against the grain of its form and style. A blog appears in cyberspace as a public document, and moreover as a public document which is amenable to maximum exposure, with a sense of being potentially available to an inchoate and uncharacterizable global information and communication network. It appears with its claim to being a literary form imbued within it, irrespective of the discernment or selectivity of interpretive reception, and the impetus for blogging is usually the autoconstruction/autoperformance of a blogging identity, its locations, its times, etc. Compared to the privacy, the closed circuit, of writing–reading that ostensibly subsumes the textual form of the diary, blogging reduces privacy, if at all, to the singular paradox of secreting the real-world author (say, by assuming a pen-name or constructing a fictional self) while presenting the text to maximum exposure. When, rarely, a blog rises through the surfeit of blogs that occupy cyberspace to be *received* as a particularly recognized literary text, this comes as a confirmation of its original claim and impetus. The process behind that is usually not immediately a matter of entering print culture and interpretive reception, but one of percolating through a hierarchy of blogging links. Essentially, a large percentage of blog readers– writers–watchers follow a few blogs which keep track of what relevant, topical, interesting, 'hot' stuff appears on the internet, and a reference in these guarantees a spurt of global interest (Peter Kuhns and Adrienne Crew's *Blogsphere*, 2006, conveys a sense of the blog-tracking mechanism). If that spurt can be turned into a sustained interest, the blog in question may rise through the ocean of blogs, and, by hitting a few corporate mea-sures of saleability, even seep into print. Typically, this happens if a blog emerges as a contribution to a significant and unusual ongoing debate – thus Salam Pax's and Riverbend's Iraq blogs covering the 2003 invasion of Iraq and its ongoing violent aftermath have become books entitled, respec-tively, *The Baghdad Blog* (2003) and *Baghdad Burning: A Young Woman's Diary from a War Zone* (2005). Sometimes, as seen above in Cooper's anthology, blogs are collected into published volumes – another example is Wendy Attenberry and Sarah Hatter's *The Very Best Weblog Writing Ever* (2006). And this could happen if blogs seem able to tap into a universally marketable interest. The sex industry occupies the largest part of the com-mercially viable sector of cyberspace and a significant part of the material cultural industry, and unsurprisingly blogs which are marketable within that circuit have also appeared as books, e.g. Belle De Jour's *The Intimate Adven-tures of a London Call Girl* (2005), Abby Lee's *Diary of a Sex Fiend* (2007) or Maxim Jakubowski's edited *The Mammoth Book of Sex Diaries* (2005).

Even those cursory observations on the differences between diaries and blogs as representing a shift within a literary genre gesture towards poten-tially radical changes in concepts of literature and literariness. This goes beyond the kinds of shifts that have been remarked for the fiction-reading experience between Ryland's novel *253* as a book and as a website. The shift between diaries and blogs obviously conforms to those shifts too. Like *253* on the website, the blog-reading experience is one that overlaps a conventional linear reading direction (usually structured by the calendar) with a computer-mediated associational-reading habit (following links of various sorts, and investing those links with various kinds of nuances – referential, informative, humorous, visual, etc.). As a text the blog appears with a more dynamic surface than is usual in books, composed usually with an attention to visual design and effect within the text, and with a range of intrinsic and extrinsic matter (e.g. advertisements) in the margins, than would be the case with published diaries – in this the layout of blogs bears some resemblance to that of magazines. The kind of participatory polyvo-cal authorship towards which Ryland gestures in his *Another One along in a Minute* plan is in fact shadowed constantly in the authorship of blogs. Most blogs invite comments from readers, and bloggers often devote parts of their blogs to responding to comments. In blogs which intervene or are located within areas of heated topical debate, such as those of Salam Pax or Riverbend, large sections are devoted to bloggers responding to such comments from readers. To an extent, therefore, readers become authorial agents and authors reading subjects in an interlinked process. Further, blog-gers also read blogs, link to other blogs, exchange technological information and assistance with other bloggers, and copy and paste from other blogs in a kind of ongoing conversation. But beyond and underlying these features, the blog as a literary form simply disperses notions of authorship and reading and textuality into an intricate mesh which invites reconfiguration of received literary concepts. The kind of play of identity that is noted above, the manner in which blogs enter a blogging circuit to ripple or rise or drown, the manner in which blogs exist in a blog-referential network, the potential of maximum exposure which goes into their composition/appearance, the kind of participatory and polyvocal authorship and readership within which blogs locate themselves and are located, the disregard for geopolitical and cultural boundaries which are implicit in each of these (irrespective of declared culture-specific sentiments within specific blogs) – all these place the blog as a literary genre which, unlike any print-culture literary production and consumption, is in a seething continuum of writing–textuality–reading.

If the potentialities of web novels such as *253* or of personal blogs are anything to go by, especially when seen as developments over conventional literary genres such as printed fiction or diaries, technologically enhanced information and communication networks seem to enable something like a dispersal and blending of the received categories of literary critical concepts. The optimistic may regard these potentialities as a kind of democratization of literature, a performance of global cosmopolitan dynamism within literary processes and forms themselves which radically interrogates conventional literature. The pessimistic may think of them as a failure of literary discernment and value, an irreversible challenge to the recognizable (conventional, institutional, industrial) practice of literature, and a portent of a – yet distant – end of literature itself. The reader won't have failed to notice that the above discussion of literature in relation to technologically enhanced information and communication networks has referred almost exclusively to electronic texts which have, in fact, been published in book form. This could be taken as an indication of this author's limitations as a student of literature, or of his compliance with still powerfully maintained establishment norms of literary respectability, or perhaps as an indication of the constraints of the academic form and institutional spaces within which this book itself appears.

4 Literary Studies and Globalization

LITERARY ENTANGLEMENTS

In introducing a special issue of the *South Atlantic Quarterly* (2001) on 'The Globalization of Fiction/The Fiction of Globalization', Susie O'Brien and Imre Szeman present the question underlying the various contributions as follows:

[This special issue] seeks to understand a [. . .] fundamental entanglement between literature and the phenomena most commonly associated with globalization – transculturation, the various forms (from cultural to economic) and periods (from the time of Columbus to the present) of imperialism and colonialism, the violent and uneven impact of socio-cultural and economic systems on one another as they came into contact, the eclipse of traditional ways of life, the temporal (moderniza-tion) and spatial (nationalism-internationalism-transnationalism) demands of Euro-pean modernity, the global spread of capitalism and Western liberalism, and so on. To [address this] is to think not just about how globalization is reflected themati-cally in fiction, for example, but also about literature's role in the narrative con-struction of the numerous discourses or 'fictions' of globalization. One of the first things to realize about globalization is that its significance can only be grasped through its realization in a variety of narrative forms, spanning the range from accounts of the triumphalist coming-into-being of global democracy to laments about the end of nature; literature no doubt has a role to play in how we produce these often contradictory narratives about globalization. (O'Brien and Szeman 2001, 604)

The quotation makes a move in precisely the direction in which I hope to take the present study at this juncture, away from consideration of 'how globalization is reflected thematically in fiction' and towards understanding a 'fundamental entanglement' between literature and globalization. Interest-ingly the quotation not only *states* an approach for making this move, but also *performs* that approach. In considering that conjunction of stating and performing, some of the imperatives underlying the approach of this study to the 'fundamental entanglement' are clarified.

At the level of statement, O'Brien and Szeman assume that (perceivably or constitutionally) literature and globalization do not have an immediately self-evident relationship (apart from globalization being thematized in literature in various ways). Literature and globalization are not, evidently, fields that are obviously implicated in each other, are not understood as being fields that feed into each other or contain each other in given ways. That is why any 'fundamental entanglement' has yet to be understood, is opened to question here. In making this explicit O'Brien and Szeman are doing no more than noting a given institutional disposition which certainly obtained at the time, and still obtains: 'globalization' as a term, and as connoting a cluster of concepts, has been located primarily in social studies disciplines and, until recently, relatively neglected in the humanities disciplines (especially in literature and art). At the level of statement, too, O'Brien and Szeman chart a particular way in which literature and globalization may be considered as being entangled. They insist that the significance of globalization 'can only be grasped through its realization in a variety of narrative forms', in 'the narrative construction of the numerous discourses or "fictions" of globalization'. By highlighting this aspect of globalization – its narrativizations, its discourses, its 'fictions' – an obvious link with the concerns of literature is discerned. It is, of course, understood that terms such as 'narrative' and 'discourse', not to mention 'fictions', are of the discipline of literature in a given institutionally recognizable way.

The emphasis on 'narratives of globalization' is, however, not really a matter of highlighting an important aspect of the phenomenon of globalization which is relevant to literature – and that's where the performative aspect of the quotation comes in. What happens in the quotation is not really the identification of an aspect of globalization (apart from as a theme) that is arguably entangled with literature; rather O'Brien and Szeman perform a literary taming (so to speak) of globalization and translate globalization into a register that is literary and is amenable to literature. This involves several implicit steps. First, there is an ostensible registering of the complexity of the 'phenomena most commonly associated with globalization'. The listing of some of these phenomena that follow, from which closure is carefully withheld, is heavily weighted towards directions with which literature students would be comfortable. The contextual specificities of the term 'globalization' are elided in precisely the way charted in chapter 1. The concrete economic and political nuances of that term's travels and accrual of meaning are underplayed in favour of broad abstractions such as 'transculturation' and 'spatial and temporal demands of European modernism', which are well ensconced in literary theory and criticism. The extension of a retrospective embrace for the term to incorporate histories of colonialism and imperialism (a field where 'globalization' would have been largely meaningless before the 1980s) is overplayed because, obviously, of the central institutional position that postcolonial theory enjoys in the literary academy. The advantages of these almost off-hand manoeuvres are evidenced in the essays in the special issue the quotation introduces. Second, in identifying narratives or discourses or 'fictions' of globalization as key,

O'Brien and Szeman do something that few economists or sociologists or political scientists would recognize as being relevant to the area. They assume, in other words, that globalization is constituted in how it is talked about or narrated rather than in, say, material and technological and social processes and arrangements. By presenting 'narratives of globalization' as globalization, O'Brien and Szeman manage to bring globalization *within* the ken of literature (some might argue that regarding *all* narratives as being entangled with literature over-endows the ken of literature anyway).

The third, and perhaps most significant, step in the performance whereby globalization is tamed for the approach from literature is in O'Brien and Szeman's inattention to their own discourse. The above steps are taken silently, without elucidation of their presumptions, without explication of their context and location. These steps are performed *within* literature and *for* literature. O'Brien and Szeman speak where literature is a given and understood field; literature, that is, speaking to itself. Their observations issue and are recorded within that distinctive part of literature where literature institutionally speaks itself and perpetuates and reproduces itself even while addressing things outside itself − usually demarcated as the institutional practice of academic literary studies, literary theory and criticism, and text editing and bibliography.

In this and the next chapter, I look at the entanglement of literature and globalization insofar as it figures in or is relevant to this distinctive area of academic literary studies. Unlike O'Brien and Szeman, I do not feel that this is an entanglement which can be engaged by simply rendering globalization amenable to the existing proclivities and institutional comfort zones of literary studies. Both the meeting points and the departures between globalization as an area of study and literature as an area of study, the fissures and overlaps between their institutional and disciplinary and discursive constructions, the amenabilities and discomforts involved in examining literature and globalization in relation to each other, need to be registered. This cannot simply be a matter of seeing how far debates about globalization are relevant to debates in literary studies, or how far existing ideas of interest in literary studies can be fitted with notions of globalization. This has also to take account of unexpected, or at least relatively unfamiliar, directions that are opened up for literary studies in coming to grips with debates about globalization. In other words, this entails taking account of the directions that literary studies may be pushed resistantly towards. That means that in this discussion I attempt not only to consider the relevance of globalization *within* literary studies, by performing a literary discourse, but also to discern the locations/relocations/dislocations of literary studies *within* globalization, by putting some of the discourse of literary studies and its presumptions into perspective. What that involves becomes, I hope, clearer as this chapter progresses.

TURNING TO LITERARY STUDIES

By way of approaching literature and globalization within literary studies, some stocktaking of the ways in which literary studies has evoked globalization provides a useful platform for the following discussion. There are several broad directions discernible here. First, the kind of exercise that has been conducted in the previous two chapters, and described in the above quotation as 'about how globalization is reflected thematically in fiction', represents one of the significant ways in which literary studies has engaged globalization. Second, in a related fashion, occasionally literary texts and the interpretation thereof have been recruited to support or elucidate conceptual positions taken by political and social theorists about globalization. Third, there have been some attempts to find accommodations between terms and formulations (such as 'text', 'culture', 'identity') in literary studies and in globalization studies (or discussions of the political, economic and cultural processes of globalization). Fourth, a number of studies have attempted – like O'Brien and Szeman above – to fit ideas of globalization with developed and familiar fields of literary studies. In particular postcolonial and postmodern literature and literary theory have proved fruitful ground for literary scholars to seek to embrace or draw in discussions of globalization. Fifth, noteworthy attempts have been made to understand globalization as a process that implicates the institutional or disciplinary pursuit (particularly at the level of pedagogy) of literary studies itself. This is available in some of the rethinking to which the disciplines of English studies and comparative literature have been exposed. And finally, sixth, some scholarly attention has been devoted to the industries that mediate the production, circulation and consumption of literature outside academic precincts, or more broadly in the buying and selling of books in the world. These industries – which implicate particularly the publishing and media industries – are at present understandably as subject to globalization processes as any industrial sector. The impact of globalization on these industries has considerable knock-on effects on literature and literary studies, which have also received some scholarly attention.

These six broad areas in which literary studies has evoked globalization suggests a structure for the remainder of this study. So far, in the previous two chapters I have examined some contemporary British and American fiction in which different aspects of globalization processes and debates are thematized or represented. Insofar as this chapter turns to *literary studies*, a retrospective look at what the exercise conducted in the previous two chapters implies in terms of literary criticism is called for – it is incumbent upon me not just to *do* literary interpretation but to explore my practice in doing that in a literary critical spirit. This retrospection can be usefully informed by reference to other criticism in a similar direction. The first two of the six areas just mentioned would be effectively covered in this. That, in turn, puts this study in a position to undertake what I have stated above as an ambition: not only to consider the relevance of globalization *within* literary studies but also to discern the locations/relocations/dislocations of literary studies *within* globalization. That is appropriately attempted with reference to the four remaining areas remarked above, and best begun with the third. This has to do with formulations which occur in both globalization and literary studies. The latter part of this chapter is accordingly devoted to this – especially to exploring notions of 'text', 'identity' and 'culture'. In the following two chapters I pick up the next two areas in question: i.e. chapter 5 discusses globalization in relation to postcolonial and postmodern literature and literary theory, and chapter 6 examines globalization in relation to the institutional spaces of English studies and comparative literature. The final chapter focuses on the globalization of industries implicated in the production, circulation and consumption of literature.

To keep sight of specific literary texts within a discussion that might otherwise feel rather abstract at times, this and the following chapter will often (but not exclusively) revolve around two literary texts. James Joyce's *Ulysses* (1921) and Salman Rushdie's *Midnight's Children* (1981) offer some peculiar advantages for this study. These two texts have been at the heart of most significant literary critical debates and movements in and since the twentieth century.

GLOBALIZATION THEMATIZED

The kind of exercise to which the previous two chapters have been devoted is not without precedent. Two books which, in similar ways, have tried to approach ideas of globalization through fiction are *The Novel and the Globalization of Culture* (1995) by Michael Valdez Moses and James Annesley's *Fictions of Globalization* (2006). Moses's book recruits a selection of European and Third World fiction to intervene in a contextually specific political debate about globalization, while Annesley's is an attempt at examining a range of issues associated with globalization through contemporary American novels. The decade that separates the two has something to do with the difference in approach. Examination of these two approaches can inform a retrospection of the previous two chapters.

Moses's book is a literary intervention in a debate conducted primarily by political theorists and sociologists in the early 1990s, arising from Francis Fukuyama's *The End of History and the Last Man* (1992). The latter wedded a strand of Hegel's philosophy to comparative democracy studies to argue that a global convergence on liberal democracy is in progress, and that a future of global political, social and cultural homogenization could be foreseen which would effectively be an end of history. In this instance the idea that history would end does not imply that human beings would cease to exist, but that the manner in which history has been conceived so far, the manner in which we are accustomed to thinking about history, would cease to apply. According to this argument, at the bottom of our current thinking lies that notion that history has a progressive direction or is teleological, and that this direction is maintained through conflicts and contradictions of various sorts within and between societies. Hegel envisaged an idealistic direction for history, whereby what he regarded as increasing degrees of 'self-consciousness' would be manifested in increasingly rational social organization through history, and could lead to an end of history where world society would have achieved complete 'self-consciousness'. Hegel's *Phenomenology of Spirit* ([1807] 1977) conceptualized this process, and his posthumously published lectures on the *Philosophy of History* ([1837] 1956) attempted a factual fleshing out of the idea by presenting a world history which ostensibly charts different levels of self-consciousness in different societies. Fukuyama recalled Hegel's view of history's direction and culmination, sieved through the work of philosopher Alexander Kojevé, significantly *in the early 1990s*. This period is now indelibly associated with what is regarded as the end of the Cold War. Fukuyama's declaration of an imminent Hegelian 'end of history' couldn't but have been received as the crowing of victorious North American capitalism and an announcement of its global ambition. To some extent the conceptual generality and argumentative quality of Fukuyama's book raised it above the level of a party-political manifesto. And yet, Fukuyama's inspiration from the Cold War-rooted comparative democratization studies, the unquestioning complacency with which he assumed that capitalism and democracy (as *a priori* good) are coeval, and his own Republican political allegiances in the United States placed the book fairly clearly for his audiences. A debate on the nuances of the book followed: neoconservatives and neoliberals were suspiciously congratulatory of the book; liberals of various other hues were uneasy about its universalist assertion; political realists observed that liberal democracy is not without debilitating contradictions; leftists worried about the impetus thus given to North American neocolonial ambitions (passing as globalization); and those with investments in neonationalisms and identity politics observed that the post-Cold War period is marked more by fragmentation than homogenization. In many ways, this debate encapsulated the myriad conceptual positions and ideas that have come to be associated with globalization – that have both constructed and interrogated globalization – in the course of the 1990s. Much more than the content of Fukuyama's book, it is the specific debate surrounding it that connects it to globalization. Moses's book is a somewhat unusual intervention in that debate, and needs to be placed accordingly.

Moses starts off by proclaiming himself persuaded by something like Fukuyama's Hegel–Kojevé inspired 'end of history' thesis, and by seeking to persuade his reader of it by distancing it from controversies:

A less controversial way of stating that history has come to an end is to suggest that a homogenizing worldwide process of modernization has become irreversible. All human communities are gradually but inexorably coming to resemble one another, exhibiting the same salient characteristics of a modern society. [. . .] A modern society accepts and exploits the technological achievements of modern natural sciences. [. . .] Modern society is consequently one that at least implicitly embraces the secularization of human society. [. . .] Intimately connected to the spread of modern sciences and the secularization of society is the simultaneous advance of trade and commerce. The market economy, especially the advantages it produces from the division of labour, leads to an ever-increasing accumulation of capital. (Moses 1995, 6)

Even this briefest of quotations checks the markers of Fukuyama's thinking: it carries a recognizable sense of an autonomous agency-free process in human history. This process has a direction (modernization), it is understood as evidenced in the present and as being progressive in a normatively positive sense, and it consists in universal acceptance of liberal democratic political and advanced capitalist economic arrangements. To underline the plausibility of this perception, Moses covers the Hegel–Kojevé–Fukuyama ground in some detail, thus emphasizing the philosophical basis of his argument and leaving the sociological and political empirical evidence that is usually cited in support of that argument aside. Instead of the latter kind of evidence, Moses, interestingly, chooses to use works of literary fiction to a similar purpose. He picks up two works of European fiction (Thomas Hardy's *Mayor of Casterbridge*, 1886, and Joseph Conrad's *Lord Jim*, 1900), as representing moves towards social and political values that are espoused in the globally dominant West, and novels by two authors from the so-called Third World (Chinua Achebe's *Things Fall Apart*, 1958, and *No Longer at Ease*, 1960, and Mario Vargas Llosa's *The War at the End of the World*, 1981) representing views from the periphery. His reading of these is meant to demonstrate that, irrespective of their geopolitical origins and concerns, these chart a uniform vision of what modernity consists in, and what human aspirations should be. Having done this to his satisfaction, Moses observes modestly that the conformity of a handful of novels to an 'end of history' direction can hardly be regarded as proof of that thesis, examines some of the objections that have been raised to that thesis, and concludes by reiterating that the global homogenization that portends an 'end of history' advances despite evidence of exacerbated nationalism, religious communalism and particularist ideologies.

The point here is not to examine the extent to which Moses's readings of the chosen novels confirm an 'end of history' view. Rather, what is of interest here is the thinking underlying his methodology. In this methodology, clearly, literature and literary criticism are *instrumentalized* in the service of a debate of political and sociological and philosophical moment. The debate rages out there irrespective of literature, disregardful of literature, and Moses pushes his way in unexpectedly by drawing upon his literary resources – to take a position in the debate. It is a modest position, mainly giving the thumbs up to proponents of the 'end of history' without affecting the contours of the debate particularly. Nor does it specifically impinge upon the practice of literature and the pursuit of literary criticism: the range of literary reference is too limited. Using some literary fiction as exemplary for a general ideological position does not allow for reflection on the literary to a sufficient degree to feed back into literature and literary criticism. And yet there is a grain of an interesting idea in there. It is in the presumption that literary fictional texts can serve as evidence in a similar fashion as empirically based political or social observations. It is presumed that the processes represented within and implicit around fictional works, which can be discerned by a reader or interpreter, convey a reality or veracity about their geopolitical locations that is as germane as, say, statistical data or sociological field work or political reports. Moses obviously believes that, if one is looking for evidence to support a sociopolitical theory, one may call upon literature.

Appearing a decade later, James Annesley's *Fictions of Globalization* (2006) also treats globalization as a theme in a range of contemporary American fiction – touching on works by Don DeLillo, Paul Beatty, Chuck Palahniuk, Sandra Cisneros, Dave Eggers, Brett Easton Ellis, William Gibson, Jhumpa Lahiri and Bharati Mukherjee. Annesley's approach to this task and methodology are, however, substantially different from that of Moses, reflecting shifts in the connotations of 'globalization' in the interim. Annesley introduces his project in the following manner:

> The aim [of the book] is not [. . .] to read these novels in terms that evidence the reality of globalization, or to present them as homological expressions of the specifics of these material conditions, but to use the analysis of different texts to refine ways of knowing globalization's discourses. [. . .] The suggestion is that the examination of recent American fiction and a consideration of the ways in which globalization's processes are represented offers an insight into the shape and character of concerns that have a key bearing on the interpretation of contemporary culture, social and political life. In these terms the aim is neither to celebrate nor condemn globalization, but to finds ways in which it might be possible to read contemporary fiction in terms that add to knowledge about, and understanding of, its discourses. (Annesley 2006, 6)

The idea here is not to instrumentalize literature to be able to contribute to an ongoing debate about globalization, but to become part and parcel with a more dispersed (than a specific debate) and familiar set of narratives of globalization. The latter implies that acts of literary reading will both register globalization's appearances as literary theme and seek to develop or extend narratives of globalization. Debates about globalization and literature, thus, are not held apart with merely the possibility of the latter being able to represent something of the former, but are meshed together so that they merge in a conjoined field that processes globalization in literature and the literariness of globalization.

Again, the point here is to examine not how far Annesley succeeds but the presumptions of his methodology in relation to that of Moses. Annesley's mid-2000s context, and the now somewhat different sense of the term 'globalization', is material. I had observed in chapter 1 that by the turn of the millennium the term had become almost ideologically neutral, and was gradually abstracted from specific histories and cultures, as a markedly protean and thickly connotative word. These shifts indicated a move from a disciplinary axis for 'globalization' in sociology, economics, politics, culture and media studies to application with regard to issues or topics relevant to almost any disciplinary frame. Something of this move is marked in the difference between the two authors' attitude to the term. For Moses globalization is primarily a conceptual matter, to do with a debate that is usually perceived as non-literary, a debate that is in the process of unfolding, and moreover one that is inevitably ideologically loaded. Moses could only intervene from outside, as it were, to take a definite position within the debate. For Annesley, however, the positions in this debate are already largely thrashed out (which doesn't mean they have been resolved – far from it), and the ideological commitments invested in debating globalization are not pressing. In fact he deliberately decides 'neither to celebrate nor condemn globalization', but to treat it as ideologically neutral. And this is possible for Annesley because globalization is not merely a conceptual field, but one that is manifest in a widely dispersed fashion in a range of issues or topics which are as literary as they are political or sociological or philosophical, etc., issues which *include* the 'globalization debate' itself: he addresses, in his words, 'the connections that tie ethnicity, identity and consumption together; the representation of globalization and the globalization debate; dreams of escape from, and rebellion against, consumer society and the forces of globalization; and the impact and consequences of tourism and migration' (Annesley 2006, 8). Consequently Annesley's engagement of globalization in fiction draws upon something like Moses's conviction in literature's ability to give access to contextually concrete reality and veracity. But, pace Moses, fictional texts are not instrumentalized as sociological evidence for globalization debates. Rather, Annesley reads his chosen texts as giving access to a field which constitutes the processes of globalization, and which can therefore inform ongoing discussion about globalization, inform its narratives. As he says at the end of his book:

It is the understanding that globalization must be read in relation to the ordinary transactions of ordinary people that underpins this analysis of the representation of leisure, technology, consumer-culture, the market *and* migration in recent American fiction. [. . .] Instead of asking what the understanding of globalization can do for literary studies, this book has asked what the study of literature can do for the understanding of globalization. (Annesley 2006, 163)

The thematization of globalization that I have attempted in the previous two chapters is close in spirit to that in Annesley's book. That is, it is close in methodological approach and intention, rather than in themes addressed – which are obviously different. And, in contrast to Annesley's work, the previous chapters come with no attempt at maintaining an ideology-free attitude towards the term and its connotations. Ideological baggage and normative proclivities have accrued in a variegated fashion among the connotations of the term and cannot really be overlooked. Any treatment of themes associated with globalization in literature inevitably releases ideological nuances which are impossible to be neutral about, which immediately provoke evaluative attitudes. This is, I think, self-evident in the treatment of the fictional themes of globalization in the previous two chapters.

LITERARY TEXT

Moses's and Annesley's conviction, brought out in different ways, that literature concretizes a kind of reality or truth about a given geopolitical context, environment, everyday existence, about given people, ordinary lives and transactions, is noteworthily at the heart of both their methodologies. Moses and Annesley test respectively a conceptual debate about globalization and a specific set of issues associated with globalization in terms of fictional reality or veracity (which has long been a meaningful oxymoron). For Moses such testing informs a definite position in the debate, and for Annesley it feeds into thinking about globalization itself. Both work on the understanding that literary texts, with their themes and rootedness in the world, with their authorial inputs and readerly constructions, are always larger and deeper than their specific references and ostensible content. Such a conviction has certainly guided readers of two texts around which I structure my next set of observations – on the shifting concept of literary text amidst globalizing processes: James Joyce's *Ulysses* (1921) and Salman Rushdie's *Midnight's Children* (1981).

Both *Ulysses* and *Midnight's Children* seem to stand somewhat behind the period when 'globalization' – with the specific connotations covered in chapter 1 – became the characteristic defining term of our Zeitgeist. Both, in different halves of the twentieth century, seem to be intensively focused on the antithetical conceptual space of the national rather than the global. *Ulysses* details a specific day in Dublin so vividly through the minds of its protagonists and an omniscient arranger that it is often regarded as representative of a juncture in Irish history. *Midnight's Children* uses magical realist devices to convey the complex plethora of the life of a nation too, reborn, so to speak, with independence from colonial rule. And yet, a little reflection indicates that these novels belie their obvious national remits. The authors seep out of the constraints of their spatially located themes: Joyce signed his book off as written in Trieste, Zürich and Paris, and Rushdie's migrant imagination is often written within the text. More importantly, the readers of these cut across national boundaries in extraordinary ways, and have been able to read the world in their all too obviously *located* words. Literary texts, readers, authors are, in a way, uncontainable; they travel or can travel without warning and in unpredictable ways. It is unsurprising then that, when a term such as 'globalization' comes into vogue and becomes thickly connotative and seems to define a world-embracing condition, literature would appear to be almost predeterminedly imbricated with it. Both Joyce and Rushdie have been gradually absorbed into thinking about globalization, especially in the ongoing receptions and transmissions of their writings. The Irish locus of Joyce's works thus negotiates with their global assimilations in various ways. This occurs in terms of how they are read now and accommodated in our time – as, e.g. Joseph Valente does:

the undeniable anti-nationalism of Joyce's Irish years and the budding nationalism of his early period in Italy dialectically resolved themselves into an idiosyncratic cultural *transnationalism*, in which localized attachments of and to the ethnos coincide, productively, with their cosmopolitan negation. (Valente 2004, 73)

This also occurs within the self-reflections of the ever-growing Joyce critical industry, so that in his study of that industry Joseph Brooker observes that:

The circuits of the contemporary Joyce industry are emphatically international. Yet at this moment of globalization, national questions are apt to reappear in unexpected ways. [. . .] Academics within and outside Ireland have accused the critical tradition of an insidious de-Irishing of Joyce, at the same moment that Joyce's posthumous image has become not only safe but lucrative in Dublin. (Brooker 2004, 7)

In a similar fashion, Jaina C. Sanga sees the following in the pattern of Rushdie's reception and fame, career and controversies (especially the so-called Rushdie affair, or the debate following the issuing of a *fatwa* calling for his death on the publication of *The Satanic Verses*, 1988), and ongoing productions:

The Rushdie Affair, and the continued enthusiastic reception of his literary work have spiralled him into the status of a celebrity, and internationally known superstar; in fact, as we consider the trajectory of Rushdie's writings within various metaphoric frameworks, what is notable is the extent to which Rushdie himself, as a representative example of the many interrelated polemics of migration, translation, hybridity, and blasphemy, has become a metaphor of globalism. This globalism is articulated not only in Rushdie's notoriety but also in his erudition, and in his responsibility as author to write the current historical and political moment. (Sanga 2001, 131)

Few literary texts have been subjected to more searching explorations in the quest for self-understanding in literary studies, and both are ideally placed to continue that quest in the context of globalization.

The key notion of the literary text, obviously the constitutive element of literature and literary studies, has already been exposed to comprehensive reconsideration in relation to processes associated with globalization. I have touched on this briefly in the previous chapter in considering Greg Ryland's internet novel *253* and such literary forms as personal blogs. Unsurprisingly, a considerable and diverse body of critical and theoretical writing has been devoted to the implications of such developments, which rebound with radical implications into not only the production and reception of literature but also the very practice of literary studies. Coming to grips with that entails coming to grips with at least a received or a conventional notion of the literary text, itself a tricky business. The problem lies with delineating what makes a literary text *literary*. One sort of conventional recourse has been to find some formal description general enough to capture the myriad variety that is recognized as literary, encapsulating all the fluid generic and sub-generic categories and rhetorical/linguistic possibilities that can be plausibly registered as such. Examples in this direction are too numerous to throw up any dominant view. And in any case, the very *raison d'être* of attempts of this sort has been questioned so insistently – as being ahistorical, insensitive to socio-political contexts and ideological leanings, indifferent to readerly or interpretive constructions, simply philosophically untenable, etc. – that such characterizations of the literary text have largely been abandoned. A relatively rare and recent effort to present a formal-linguistic theory of literary texts by Antonio García-Berrio can be cited to convey briefly the ambition of such an enterprise (this is a simplistic initial statement which is thereafter complicated at considerable length):

The literary or poetic text establishes, effectively, certain more precise and even conventional fixed limits for the creator of literary or poetic types of expression, which are unknown in the elaboration of the standard communication text. From the very start, the author of a sonnet works under the pressure of a closed textual space. He accepts a pre-set dimension for his discourse, which artistically specializes each of his operators and decisions regarding thematic invention, structural arrangement and elocution at every level [. . .]. Without knowing such stringent limits, the constructor of a theoretical piece or novel is similarly aware of the existence of relatively conventional boundaries, experienced, adopted and patterned for the communicative-aesthetic efficacy of said discourses. (García-Berrio [1989] 1992, 64)

This sounds like a rather restrictive description of literariness, but could be adjusted to allow for considerable flexibility. The generic closure of textual space with reference to which authors' work could include, for instance, testing and even subverting the limits and thereby constantly changing the parameters of that closure. That could bring a work as challenging to literary critical preconceptions as Joyce's *Ulysses* to be regarded as clearly literary, testing the dimensions of the novel form and literary style itself. Joyce, of course, did this quite deliberately – going through a variety of rhetorical tropes in the 'Aeolus' episode, and then working through an extraordinary range of English prose styles from Anglo-Saxon to Victorian in 'Oxen of the Sun'. He ends there with a slangy language that is almost derisively antithetical (teetering between malapropisms and neologisms) to the elite literariness of literature, and yet crafted with an aural quality that is reminiscent of his own yet to be written *Finnegans Wake*: 'Will immensely splendiferous stander permit one stooder of most extreme poverty and one largesize grandacious thirst to terminate one expensive inaugurated libation' (Joyce [1921] 1993, 405). In the 'Circe' episode (or '*Walpurgisnacht*' section, alluding to the inspiration of Goethe's *Faust*) Joyce, in fact, abandons the prose conventions associated with the novel form altogether to adopt something like the form of a play, and even the various conventions of that are systematically flouted as the section unfolds (rather like *Faust* part 2 itself) – a sort of layering of recognitions, testings, breakings, reinstatements of received textual spaces which both demonstrates a comprehensive awareness and extends the parameters of literariness. All these or such manoeuvres could be regarded as within the purview of the quoted statement, or broadly of a formalist text-centred approach to literature.

The usual objections to the formalist text-centred approach dwell on the productive and receptive dimensions surrounding the text, sometimes even at the expense of the text in itself. Thus, the productive aspect could start by observing what happens within the text of *Ulysses*: an authorial consciousness is constructed which is expressed, say, as the agent who chooses to present the 'Oxen of the Sun' episode in a series of literary prose styles. This is distinct from the interior monologue of the final 'Penelope' section, which gives the impression that direct unmediated access is being given to Molly Bloom's semi-somnolent thoughts. The authorial agent is, as often noted, available at another level within the text of *Ulysses* as an 'arranger', one who chooses where to place the sequence of happenings/narrations in the order in which they appear in the text. In a broader sense, one may feel an authorial presence in the opaque quality of *Ulysses*, which seems deliberately to draw attention to the performance of its language, as opposed to an instrumentalist narration where the language transparently doesn't draw attention to itself and simply tells what happens. Even Molly Bloom's interior monologue is not really an apparently unmediated entry into a mind, but, as John Spencer had observed, a linguistic performance that the author enacts: 'By giving each movement of the mind separate and equal graphological status as a sentence, whatever its syntactical structure, Joyce provokes for the reader a raw immediacy' (Spencer 1965, 389). But beyond these manifestations of authorship as a performance within the text, there's the presence of the biographical person identified as author – James Joyce for *Ulysses* – whose intentions can be discerned in the text. In the case of *Ulysses* this could involve the discernment of what Joyce as a person might have had in mind when writing the work, by looking at such evidence and accounts of that as are available – and indeed there is an enormous mass of bio-critical writings about Joyce in relation to *Ulysses*. But, unusually in this instance, that is complicated by the fact that Joyce evidently influenced perceptions by retrospectively exercising his authority as author to tell readers what he intended – he, so to speak, constructed his authorial intentions for the benefit of readers after writing *Ulysses*. He provided the scheme of the structural analogue with Homer's *Odyssey* in a letter dated 21 September 1920 to his friend Carlo Linati; he was in discussion with the writers of the first extended works of criticism on the novel, his friends Stuart Gilbert (*James Joyce's Ulysses: A Study*, 1930) and Frank Budgen (*James Joyce and the Making of Ulysses*, 1934); he even oversaw the construction of his biographical persona as author in Herbert Gorman's authorized life story (*James Joyce: A Definitive Biography*, 1941). But beyond the individual author and their intentions – after all, authorial intentions would always be uncertain retrospective reconstructions and speculations, even when it's the authors themselves who spells them out – lies the question of whether the individual author really matters. After all, all individuals are products of social and political and cultural circumstances, the text attributed to them a derivation from these, the language attributed to them a crystallization from their linguistic context. The literariness of the text arguably cannot be teased out by looking at the text in itself or at the biographically constructed individual author; literariness is probably more appropriately understood as an emanation of a socio-political ethos, a historical period, within which the author and his text are located. Thus, *Ulysses* could be thought of as emerging from the overlapping socio-political contexts of Ireland/France/Italy/Switzerland through which the author and text evolved; it represents the literary modernist impulse of the first three decades of the twentieth century and expresses the ideological field of its production. The 'death of the author' that Roland Barthes so influentially announced (Barthes 1977) is implicit in this dispersal of the individual writer; and yet the idea of an author is so powerful a convention of literary studies that his 'return' (as Sean Burke, 1992, was to phrase it) is always portended after the announcement of his demise.

On another side, consideration of the receptive aspects of literature also produces substantial challenges to the formalistic text-centred approach. This too could be constructed within the text at one level, as Wolfgang Iser's understanding of the 'implied reader' did. For Iser the text is disposed to make space for its implied reader's predispositions, which gives an indication of how specific readers may realize a range of different readings by bringing their different ways of filling in blanks or gaps in the narrative, by bringing their sense of relevant associations and selections, etc.: '[The implied reader] embodies all those predispositions necessary for a literary work to exercise its effect – predispositions laid down, not by empirical outside reality, but by the text itself' (Iser 1978, 34). Unsurprisingly, one of Iser's examples was the implied reader of *Ulysses*, the mythic parallels and multiplicity of styles in which presses the reader, so to speak, to 'create' the novel, or forces the conception of the 'implied reader' to assume a critical presence. However, this is still too text-centred for some reception critics. In a series of influential formulations starting with the 'informed reader' and moving towards a concept of 'interpretive community', Fish – in a book aptly entitled *Is There a Text in this Class?* – firstly 'challenged the self-sufficiency of the text by pointing out that its (apparently) spatial form belied the temporal dimension in which its meanings were actualized' (Fish 1980, 2), and secondly suggested that literary texts are actually constructed even before they are read, in terms of pre-agreed strategies of reading that exist in 'interpretive communities': 'Interpretive communities are made up of those who share interpretive strategies not for reading (in the conventional sense) but for writing texts, for constituting their properties and assigning their intentions. In other words, the strategies exist prior to the act of reading and therefore determine the shape of what is read rather than, as is usually assumed, the other way around' (ibid., 171).

The history of the reception of *Ulysses* appears to lend credence to this view. Since the beginning of serious *Ulysses* criticism, critics have been uncharacteristically unanimous in acknowledging that its appearance undermined extant interpretive strategies comprehensively. It led to a kind of bewilderment or terror, so that critics had to engage with it extraordinarily energetically to produce 'reconceived' and new interpretive strategies. Paul Armstrong, noting this bewilderment effect both among his students and in a general way across the history of *Ulysses* criticism, puts the matter succinctly:

> The novel both welcomes and undermines our attempts to discover hermeneutical constructs that would adequately organize its seemingly inexhaustible variety and complexity. The inability of any single construct [. . .] to assimilate all the novel's parts into a consistent whole denies the assumption that meaning is simply 'there' to be uncovered. (Armstrong 1987, 2)

If meaning has to be brought to the text, then the text, of course, doesn't mean in itself – as Fish suggests. *Ulysses* is a textual event which makes this extraneousness of literary meaning clear, forces it to consciousness. The result is that *Ulysses* has come to be constructed as literary not just within the engagements with its words but in an almost autonomous attention to the history of critically engaging with it. This has been charted variously and regularly since the 1960s, recently in Brooker's *Joyce's Critics* (2004), Gillespie and Gillespie's *Recent Criticism of James Joyce's Ulysses* (2000), and Gillespie and Fargnoli's *Ulysses in Critical Perspective* (2006).

This brief excursus into the idea of the literary text – and digression from literature and globalization – conveys the complexity of it. The idea of the literary text, the notion of literariness in a text, is somewhere at the juncture of the above considerations to do with formalistic text-centredness, the production and authorship issues, the readership and critical reception issues. All are implicated in what McGann describes as the 'perceptual and conceptual event' that is a literary text (McGann 2001, 178).

Complex as these familiar reflections on the literary text are, further dimensions of complication are introduced when considered in relation to globalization, particularly in relation to that medium which appears to concretize processes of globalization most immediately: hypertext and the internet. The development and gradual democratization of the internet have coincided with the late twentieth-century passages of the term 'globalization', and to a large degree the conceptual underpinnings of the term and the realization of the possibilities of the internet have fed on each other. The impact of the internet is considered in a succinct but wide-ranging fashion in Manuel Castells's *The Internet Galaxy*:

The Internet Galaxy is a new communicative environment. Because communication is the essence of human activity, all domains of social life are being modified by the pervasive uses of the Internet [. . .]. A new social form, the network society, is being constituted around the planet, albeit in a diversity of shapes, and with considerable differences in its consequences for people's lives, depending on history, culture, and institutions. (Castells 2001, 275)

Castells discusses both the range of cultures that coalesce to lead towards the still developing form of the internet and the various ways in which the internet has modified the conduct of human activities. The latter include processes of business and finance, social and communal organization (from individual to familial to institutional functioning), sense of space and place, mainstream and marginal political communication and action, and the cultures of information and media. Castells also ponders the implications of the digital divide, i.e. the prospects for those who are unable to access the internet for various (mainly economic) reasons. In the midst of these he briefly touches on the possible development of hypertext as an integration of all media. However, his understanding of hypertext is a rather future-gazing one – at present, the notion of hypertext is commonly understood as that which obtains in reading and writing when general (i.e. not necessarily technologically savvy) users surf or contribute to the internet, or the kind of reading and writing that occurs in *using* the internet. This is precisely the kind of text that I have considered briefly in the context of personal blogs and Ryland's internet novel *253*. This commonly understood sense of hypertext, and the processes of writing and reading that apply, is of immense importance for the reckoning of literary studies with the notion of the literary text – and indeed for its self-reckonings as a discipline concerned with literariness and textuality.

The impact of the internet on literature and literary studies has been assessed with both trepidation about passing conventions and excitement about new possibilities. As I have observed already, J. Hillis Miller, for instance, found reason to feel anxious about the manner in which literary texts are placed in cyberspace. He felt that the ensuing dislocation of texts from historical contexts, the distracting juxtaposition with various auditory and visual texts, and the consequent dissociation from the culture of the book could well portend an inevitable 'end of literature' (Miller 2002). In a more optimistic vein, careful early studies of modifications in concepts of reading and writing in relation to hypertexts (such as Bolter 1991 and Landow 1992) foretold promising developments for literature and literary studies. For Jay David Bolter the development of electronic texts opened up the possibility of 'interactive fiction': 'a nonlinear fiction, which invites the reader to construct a dialogue with the text' (Bolter 1991, 121). In this writers would be called upon to think of their work not as 'a closed and unitary structure' but 'as a structure of possible structures' (ibid., 144), and readers would cultivate the ability to become a 'second author, who can then hand the same text to other readers for the same treatment' (ibid.). Similarly, Silvio Gaggi observed that hypertext entails an empowerment of the reader in that they can construct their own paths of reading and even interfere in the text by creating new links and inserting comments (Gaggi 1997, 103); that hypertext thereby challenges the concept of the author as a unitary presence and leads to 'encouragement of collaboration in the creation of knowledge and their capacity for a free, rapid, and unimpeded dissemination of knowledge' (ibid., 106); and that consequently hypertexts could lead to the development of an 'interactive literature', untrammelled by mediating authorities and industries (ibid., 122). Though Gaggi identified a range of problems in each of these steps of his argument, his generally upbeat tone is unmistakable. By the early 2000s textbooks charting the various ways in which the internet could be used in literary pedagogy and research were becoming available, thus suggesting increasing institutional respectability for the area within literary studies. A good example is *Literature and the Internet* (2000), by Browner, Pulsford and Sears, which also expounded in its final section comparable arguments to Gaggi's in a similarly upbeat fashion.

Attempts to come to terms with the development of hypertext within literary studies have followed broadly two directions: 1) reflecting on hypertext reveals practices and proclivities that are already implicit in literature and literary studies but as yet insufficiently understood; and 2) hypertext opens up new possibilities which can comprehensively change current understandings and practices in literature and literary studies.

There are several interesting ways in which the development of hypertext has been seen as bringing to consciousness, as it were, proclivities implicit but hitherto understood in a limited way in literature and literary studies. Jerome McGann's notion of 'deformative' rather than 'interpretive' reading is relevant here. The idea is that, since literary texts do not simply narrate in a linearly progressive direction but are also organized as 'rhetoric and poiesis' (McGann 2001, 113), critical readers are always pushed towards or drawn into apprehending several layers of non-linear features in such texts: features that 'are alphabetical and diacritical; [that] are the rules for character formation, character arrangement, and textual space, as well for the structural forms of words, phrases, and higher morphemic and phone-mic units' (ibid., 115). These various levels of reading that every literary text demands are effectively deformative reading. However, the convention of linearity in print culture has coalesced with the convention of construc-tive interpretation, so that the inevitable deformative steps in reading are relegated to the position of being pre-interpretive and pre-critical, and interpretation constructs a linear and stable and singular mode of under-standing a literary text. The fact that literary texts are amenable to a mul-tiplicity of interpretive readings is because of their deformative nature, though each interpretive reading shrouds that deformative nature by an assertion of stability and integrity. This implicit and constantly available deformative nature of the literary text could be regarded as that which makes a text literary, but in a hidden way. Literature in hypertext renders immediately visible the always available but usually hidden deformative quality of the literary text: the possibilities of hypertextual reading and writing brings to the surface, so to speak, and exposes the deformative nature of literature. In working with hypertext, the limitations of an inter-pretive reading are evidenced and the multiplicity of deformative possi-bilities foregrounded. The very manipulability and fluidity of hypertext becomes a clarification of the always implicit deformative nature of literary textuality.

That the development of hypertext allows for a realization of something that has always been implicit in literature and that, in some sense, the literary text has been constitutionally inclined towards the development of hypertext are significant perceptions in recent literary studies. Though conceptually these ideas apply to the literary text *per se*, they have been exploited more in relation to a certain kind of literary text – those which are, in Umberto Eco's terms, more 'open' than 'closed', though all literary texts are to some measure both: 'A work of art [. . .] is a complete and *closed* form in its uniqueness as a balanced organic whole, while at the same time constituting an *open* product on account of its susceptibility to count-less different interpretations which do not impinge on its unadulterable specificity' (Eco 1979, 49). Eco's example of an exemplarily open text was *Ulysses* and examples of exemplarily closed texts Ian Fleming's James Bond books. In fact, Joyce's *Ulysses* and *Finnegans Wake* have been seen as ame-nable to the perceptions enabled by and possibilities contained in hyper-textuality to an extraordinary degree. In a typically prescient way, Derrida had gestured towards this in 1984:

[Joyce was] in advance, decades in advance, to compute you, control you, forbid you the slightest inaugural syllable because you can say nothing that is not pro-grammed on this 1000th generation computer – *Ulysses, Finnegans Wake* – beside which the current technology of our computers and micro-computerfied archives and translating machines remain a *bricolage* of a prehistoric child's toy. (Derrida 1984, 147)

One of Bolter's examples of early 'interactive fiction' that naturally lends itself to hypertextual features is *Ulysses*:

Joyce places his reader. The superstructure of the final text alone is taxing: the layers of genesis are even more so. For that reason it is not quite right to claim that Joyce is seeking to reproduce in his text the quality of print. It is true that Joyce employs most of the technique available in the repertory of print [. . .]. But Joyce's narrative strategy is too complex and too dynamic for the medium to print.

   Joyce could not have anticipated the electronic medium, but his works would be a rich source of experimentation for writers in the new medium. (Bolter 1991, 137)

Now that efforts have been afoot for a considerable time to harness the Joycean text in hypertextual form, the particular amenability of his writing for this purpose seems a foregone conclusion. Thus, with reference to *Ulysses*, Donald F. Theall observes:

The unremitting 'intertextuality' of the redrafting of 'Cyclops,' followed later by the complex multiphonic allusiveness of 'Oxen of the Sun' began Joyce's sophisticated experimental transformation of the mechanics of the text.

   This transition fully launched his role of becoming the prime explorer of the place of the book in the post-electronic world – a road which was to permit him to explore poetically the accelerating modes of synaesthesia, the orchestration of the arts and contextual fluidity which would provide a new language, a new sense of structuring and probing of the depths of the social as well as the individual unconscious in dreams that had always already provided the sense of art as virtuality. (Theall 2004, 28)

Joyce has obviously moved from the pre-electronic location given him by Bolter to the post-electronic location where Theall receives him.

   The openness of Salman Rushdie's *Midnight's Children* has been constantly noted by literary critics too. The manner in which Rushdie uses various textual devices and schisms, tests the limits of the mechanics of the text, has often been noted. The metaphor of the 'crumbling, over-used body' (Rushdie 1981, 11) from which the narrative voice of Saleem Sinai issues, plumbing memories from well before that body was born; the metaphor of 'chutnification' (especially ibid., 443); the juxtaposition of various lines of time (personal, national, clock, mythological) – these are all obvious references to a deeply self-conscious structuring of the literary text. What seems to be less often remarked is that *Midnight's Children* throws up some of the most trenchant metaphors for the performance of hypertextuality as the underlying principle of the novel. Saleem's becoming aware that he has telepathic abilities ('I became a sort of radio'), whereby he can hear the thoughts of those around him and further afield, is presented in the linear narrative with a sense of overwhelming simultaneity of apprehension that undercuts that linearity at the self-same moment:

Telepathy, then: the inner monologues of all the so-called teeming millions, of masses and classes alike, jostled for space within my head. In the beginning, when I was content to be an audience – before I began to *act* – there was a language problem. [. . .] I only understood a fraction of the things being said within the walls of my skull. Only later, when I began to probe, did I learn that below the surface transmissions – the front-of-mind stuff which I'd originally been picking up – language faded away, and was replaced by universally intelligible thought forms which far transcended words . . . (Rushdie 1981, 166)

This is suggestive of a hypertextual field, which can barely be conveyed in printed text, in several ways. There is the simultaneity of a plethora of widely dispersed voices/sources/discourses being brought at one's behest at a portal. There is the understanding that negotiating this field is an act of reading in a particular way, and of being able eventually to intervene in the field as author – to be both audience and actor. There is the discernment of an underlying unity, the 'universally intelligible thought forms', which may be suggestive of the digitization that makes hypertextuality possible. More interestingly, this metaphor of hypertextuality, if we look on it as such, stretches further in a plausible way in the text. When Saleem Sinai begins to act upon this telepathic field, he does so on his tenth birthday by establishing a telepathic club with the midnight's children:

On my tenth birthday, abandoned by one set of children, I learned that five hundred and eighty-one others were celebrating their birthdays, too; which was how I understood the secret of my original hour of birth; and, having being expelled from one gang, I decided to form my own, a gang which was spread over the length and breadth of the country, and whose headquarters were behind my eyebrow.

And on my tenth birthday, I stole the initials of the Metro Cub Club – which were also the initials of the touring English cricket team – and gave them to the new Midnight Children's Conference, my very own M.C.C. (Rushdie 1981, 203).

In the hypertextual field this could be a metaphor for organizational mode of interactiveness: the formation of or becoming participant in a virtual cyber-community at the expense of real communities, the crucial act of naming the formation of virtual communities.

Perhaps more of the moment than the literary text's anticipations and amenabilities to hypertext are the new possibilities opened up for literature and literary studies by the development of hypertext. This is powerfully felt in that field of literary studies which attends to literary texts most closely: text editing and textual criticism. In a way, this kind of impact also revolves around the notion of making visible something which is, so to speak, always implicit in literary texts. John Bryant's understanding of the specific sort of 'fluidity' that is a condition of all literary texts has a bearing on the matter at hand:

The textual condition – encompassing processes of creation, editing, printing, and adaptation – is fundamentally fluid not because specific words lend themselves to different meanings or that different minds will interpret the words fixed on the page in different ways, but because writers, editors, publishers, translators, digesters, and adapters change those words materially. Moreover, these material revisions can attest not simply to localized fine tunings but to new conceptualizations of the entire work. Thus, a literary work invariably evolves, by the collaborative forces of individuals and the culture, from one version to another. If we want to know the textual condition, we must get to the versions of a text, and there we will also find an even deeper condition of creativity within a culture. (Bryant 2002, 4)

What this recognition of the fluidity of texts does is dislocate strongly embedded conventions of trying to identify and work with an authentic or definitive single version of a literary text, which has substantially guided the practice of textual criticism and editing until recently. Conventionally, textual criticism and editing have been devoted to arguing for and giving material presence to the most authentic or definitive version of a literary text, usually according to notions of what the author intended as available in a copy-text (e.g. Tanselle 1989, 1990) or in terms of what collaborative and material processes a text goes through before appearing in print (e.g. McGann 1983). Bryant's notion of textual fluidity introduces a considerably greater degree of complexity into the notion of the literary text in that it not only brings together and yet makes distinct within the idea of a text all its material forms and processes before appearing in print but also thereafter, including adaptations and translations. The convention of an authentic or definitive text, according to Bryant, is mainly a commercial invention. The realization of fluid text editions, with all their fluidity made visible, would require a reorientation not only of concepts of text and literature but also of reading habits at a more basic level, and of the manner in which literary archives are kept and literary studies conducted – in fact, a transformation of the field of literature and literary studies in all its aspects. In 2002 it seemed to Bryant that such a realization of fluid texts made visible had become possible because of the development of hypertext, and that this could place the print form into a new horizon of use (because it could be threatened):

The principles outlined above can best be realized, perhaps *only* realized, through the extraordinary hypertextual features of the electronic medium; but it would be imprudent to reject the codex out of hand. Fluid-text editions should attempt to create a dynamic coupling of book and computer screen. (Bryant 2002, 145)

In a similar direction, theorizing from the practical experience of building the Rosetti Archive in electronic form at the University of Virginia from 1993, Jerome McGann also anticipates radical changes in the pursuit of literary studies. I have cited above his perception of the deformative nature of literary texts, which also appears in this context. In fact McGann discerns from 'the *scholar's* point of view' the 'immense, even catastrophic significance' of moving from print to electronic texts, both in terms of implications for how we think about textuality and literariness and in terms of how we organize knowledge itself – into archives, categories, in relational ways, etc. (McGann 2001, 55). In a prophetic spirit, McGann observes that:

We are entering a period when the entirety of our received cultural archive of materials, not least of all our books and manuscripts, will have to be reconceived. The initial stages of this reconception, which is well underway, have been largely confined to work with archives and libraries, whose holdings are being digitally repossessed in many new ways. (McGann 2001, 169)

But beyond the current efforts he feels that:

As digital books and environments develop, we grow increasingly aware of their aesthetic functions and of the importance of those functions. We appear to be passing from a bibliographical to an 'Interface Culture'. Indeed, the aesthetic resources of digital tools appear so vast and synaesthetic that our bibliographical anxieties might grow more acute in face of them. (McGann 2001, 171)

To grasp the implications of such observations, the study of *Ulysses*, again, provides a useful arena. I have observed already that the text of *Ulysses* has a polyvocal and multilayered quality, densely allusive in form and substance, which can easily be seen to pose particular difficulties for anyone trying to, say, annotate it. From a textual editor's point of view, the work's process of composition, its various published versions and its ever-expanding afterlife as a text present particular challenges. The time period of its composition marked at the end by Joyce, 1914–21, is a fairly extensive one, and understandably consists in a complex process of notings, collations, draftings, redraftings and authorial editing – one that has preoccupied scholars since (a detailed account is available in Groden 1977). A number of episodes, heavily edited by Ezra Pound, were published serially in the *Little Review* before the whole was published by Shakespeare and Co. in 1922. This version had numerous errors, according to Joyce, some of which were corrected by him in subsequent prints, and trying to correct it has thereafter remained an ongoing preoccupation. It was pirated by publisher Philip Roth in New York, and some of it was serialized in Roth's *Two Worlds Monthly*. In 1961 an ostensibly corrected edition by Random House was found to have 4000 corruptions. In 1984 Hans Walter Gabler and his team used computers to go through all the available urtexts of *Ulysses* and come up with a definitive 'critical and synoptic edition' (Gabler 1984) – which led to the 'scandal of *Ulysses*'. Gabler's edition followed editorial principles which gave rise to a text substantially changed from any previous version and was vociferously attacked by critic John Kidd. An acrimonious public debate followed which was unresolved and remains a test area for working out the principles and practices of text editing. Subsequently popular editions of *Ulysses* have been reprints of the earlier ones

– Jeri Johnson's Shakespeare and Co. 1922 version published by Oxford University Press (1993) and Declan Kiberd's 1960 Bodley Head version published by Penguin (1992) come to mind.

What that brief outline of the textual history of *Ulysses* conveys is its extraordinary fluidity, in Bryant's terms (and for *Finnegans Wake*, the fluidity is arguably even more complex) its superfluidity. *Ulysses* could be regarded as a literary text which, by dint of the intricacy of its textual fluidity meshed with its superlative deformative potentialities, does not merely call for hypertextual realization, but can really only be satisfactorily accessed as a hypertext edition. Unsurprisingly Joyce's work has attracted electronic resources from an early stage. After Gabler's controversial use of computers to produce the 'synoptic edition', in 1990 a section of *Finnegans Wake* was subjected by Fritz Senn and the Zurich Foundation to one of the earliest attempts at computer presentation of a literary text, entitled *HyperWake* (for a discussion, see Armand 2004a, 12–17). In 1996 Michael Groden initiated the enormous 'James Joyce's *Ulysses* in Hypermedia' project (since 2002 the 'Digital *Ulysses*' project in collaboration with SUNY; for Groden's thinking on this, see Groden 2004). The various ways in which James Joyce scholarship in all its multifacetedness is being consolidated and integrated into the effort at digitizing his works, and the manner in which that effort is feeding back into the modalities of exploiting hypertext for literary studies, is charted to some degree in the essays in Armand 2004b.

Contemplating these developments in the single field of Joyce studies clarifies some of the implications of hypertext for literary studies generally in the context of globalization, and gives flesh to the enormity of conceivable and imminent changes in the field. So far these changes are outlined only very sketchily in critical works such as those of Landow, Gaggi, Bolter, Bryant and McGann. The following points are worth noting. First, the enterprise of having *Ulysses* in hypertext – hypermedia – edition presents the possibility of a resolution of such impetuses to scholarship as trying to find the truly author-sanctioned or definitive or authentic or flawless text, not so much by achieving any such thing but by rendering such aims redundant. The prospect is of having *Ulysses* as a plethora of related and interwoven and yet discrete textual performances within a syncretic space. Inevitably concepts and practices of textuality, authorship, reading attached to Joyce will be altered in the contemplation of and engagement with this syncretic space. Second, that doesn't mean that the painstaking textual-editing productions that *Ulysses* has engendered would cease to matter. They would become integrated as nodal points within the hypertext, as annotations to the hypertext itself. What may be affected is their status as discrete productions in an academic process of exchange; instead they may come to be regarded as the material strata of the hypertext to which literary studies attends. Third, to some extent, scholarship that derives from and feeds back into textual editing and further scholarship would also become a node within the syncretic space of the hypertext, related and differentiated with reference to the hypertext as much as within a free-flowing field of Joyce scholarship. The discrete boundaries of *Ulysses* and of *Ulysses* scholarship in print culture – as tangible editions, libraries, archives, and the products of individual energy and learning – may come to be gradually dissolved in favour of thinking of all these as aspects of processes. *Ulysses* and *Ulysses* scholarship could then be understood more as a process of continuous accretion and reorganization, which can be materialized as hypertext. Fourth, this possible dissipation of boundaries for *Ulysses* and *Ulysses* scholarship is likely then to attach to the institutional apparatus of the relevant literary studies. The boundaries of specifically located universities and departments and research centres and libraries, of the prerogatives of national and disciplinary resourcing, could themselves grow more fluid. *Ulysses* in hypertext, and further in hypermedia, could turn any literary studies that accrue around and within it into a continuous multilocational and collective endeavour. That doesn't necessarily mean that individual quirks and inspirations would be subsumed by some kind of mass scholarship mechanism – the anxiety that has attached to contemplation of mass culture and 'mechanical reproduction' (to use Walter Benjamin's 1936 phrase) – but would operate as syncopations in the syncretic space. This, in turn, has significant implications for the manner in which academic institutions and careers are gauged and in which resourcing for scholarship and pedagogy is allocated.

Many of these possibilities may seem to be rather fanciful at present, but their very enunciation has a point. In brief, the literary interaction with hypertext, hypermedia, the internet, even in its very nascent current form, has within it the features of a field that performs simultaneously dispersed and connected processes that are understood often as akin to globalizing processes.

CULTURE AND IDENTITY

Shifts in conceptualizing and exploiting the literary text are undoubtedly key aspects of literature's relationship with globalization processes, but far from being the only ways in which that relationship is moderated. Literature's testing and traversing of boundaries through the latter half of the twentieth century – both within itself and across conventional linguistic, regional, cultural and disciplinary contexts – are also pertinent here. This has involved revisiting literary textuality as often as reconsidering ideological and social environments in ways that resonate with the preoccupations of sociologists, economists and political analysts – or of those avowedly engaged in globalization studies. Indeed, literary studies and globalization studies have fed off and into each other in increasingly productive ways since the 1980s, especially in jointly irrigating the nuances of related concepts such as 'culture' and 'identity'.

'Culture' has distinct connotations in the disciplinary traditions rooted in anthropology and sociology and in the humanities, including literature. The manner in which these distinct connotations have played against each other can be briefly conveyed by looking at an exchange at a crucial (for literary studies) moment in the late 1980s to early 1990s. This exchange occurred in a one-day symposium in the State University of New York, Binghamton, on 1 April 1989, of which the proceedings were published in 1991 (with some additions) as *Culture, Globalization and the World-System*, edited by Anthony King. It was part of a debate on globalization and localization that developed in the course of the 1980s in the journal *Theory, Culture and Society*, and culminated in Mike Featherstone's edited volume *Global Culture* (1990). The 1989 exchange revealed a schism between recent sociological reckonings with cultural studies (associated in the UK with the establishment in 1964 of a Centre for Contemporary Cultural Studies [CCCS] at the University of Birmingham) and the even more recent turn towards culture studies in the humanities (more soon on the implications for literary studies). In this event three extended presentations laid out in complementary ways the perceived cultural effects of globalization processes from a sociology/anthropology perspective. These were by sociologist Stuart Hall, sociologist Roland Robertson and anthropologist Ulf Hannerz. Each tried to take account of recent developments in the humanities; indeed Hall observed that at a grassroots level globalization had released a powerful space of marginal self-expressions against dominant regimes, 'a space of weak power but [. . .] a space of power', especially 'in the contemporary arts' (Hall 1991, 34). Immanuel Wallerstein's contribution to the published proceedings summarizes the sociological perspective of culture while taking account of the humanistic perspective – this is useful in the present context since it both captures the various conventional nuances of culture and conveys the thrust of the three presentations (which had to do with the balance of the global and the local):

On the one hand, culture is *by definition* particularistic. Culture is the set of values or practices of some part smaller than some whole. This is true whether one is using culture in the anthropological sense to mean the values and/or practices of one group as opposed to any other group at the same level of discourse (French vs. Italian culture, proletarian vs. bourgeois culture, Christian vs. Islamic culture, etc.), or whether one is using culture in the belles-lettres sense to mean the 'higher' rather than the 'baser' values and/or practices within any group, a meaning which generally encompasses culture as representation, culture as the production of art-forms. In either usage, culture (or a culture) is what some persons feel or do, unlike others who do not feel or do the same things.

But, on the other hand, there can be no justification of cultural values and/or practices other than by reference to some presumably universal or universalist criteria. (Wallerstein 1991, 91)

These three presentations were followed in the afternoon session by responses and a discussion which revealed some unexpected differences.

Unlike the above-mentioned *Global Culture* (Featherstone 1990), to which all contributors were sociologists or anthropologists, in this exchange some of the respondents came from a humanities background. Among these was art historian Janet Wolff, who both summarized the afternoon discussion and responded herself to the three main presentations by way of a conclusion. One of her objections to the three main sociological/anthropological papers was worded as follows:

the papers are 'pre-theoretical' with regard to developments in cultural theory. None of them is able to recognize the nature of culture as *representation*, nor its constitutive role with regard to ideology and social relations. They operate with the notion of 'culture' as an identifiable realm or set of beliefs, objects or practices, more or less determined by social and economic relations, with more or less independence from and effectivity on the social process. Cultural theory, however, has stressed the 'materiality' of culture, by which is meant the 'determinacy and effectivity of signifying practices themselves'. Codes and conventions, narrative structures, and systems of representations in texts (literary, visual, filmic) produce meaning and inscribe ideological positions. (Wolff 1991, 170–1)

Wolff's is recognizably a contemporary (as opposed to Wallerstein's 'belles-lettres sense') humanities perspective on culture. According to this, culture, i.e. cultural discourses and representations and texts, *constitutes* ideology and social relations rather than appears as a by-product or an expression of ideology and social relations. This is a matter of emphasis: from the sociological/anthropological perspective culture arises as a result of prevailing ideologies and social relations, whereas from the humanistic perspective culture makes possible and moulds ideologies and social relations.

The distinct emphases placed on culture from the two disciplinary perspectives needs to be grasped to understand subsequent debates on culture and globalization and the place of literary studies therein. On the one hand, the humanistic assertion that cultural texts and discourses *constitute* ideology and social process occasionally impresses sociologists and anthropologists, who then seek to incorporate the humanistic emphasis within their disciplinary pursuits. In this attempt literature and literary studies have been significant points of reference. On the other hand, confidence about cultural texts and discourses *constituting* ideology and social processes has to a great degree emerged particularly from literary studies. This leads literary studies to open up – some would say, encroach upon – areas conventionally addressed in sociology, anthropology, political studies, etc. It even leads to literary studies moving away from a definitive commitment to literary texts and encompassing a broader field of cultural texts. Thus, through the 1990s, in discussions of culture there is a sort of convergence – despite different disciplinary emphases – between the humanistic field, where literary studies is placed, and the sociological/anthropological field, where globalization studies usually figures. The relationship of literature and globalization has developed along the twists and turns of this convergence on culture.

The incorporation of a humanistic, and particularly literary, emphasis on culture into the sociological/anthropological approach to globalization is evidenced in Arjun Appadurai's work. In his contribution to Featherstone's *Global Culture* he had proposed understanding globalization through a juxtaposition of the metaphor of landscape on several discursive areas, which he denoted in a fairly self-explanatory fashion as ethnoscapes, technoscapes, financescapes, mediascapes and ideoscapes. These were meant to convey fields of overlapping cultural flows and to indicate that 'these are not objectively given relations which look the same from every angle of vision, but rather they are deeply perspectival constructs, inflected very much by the historical, linguistic and political situatedness of different sorts of actors' (Appadurai 1990, 296). It is possible to think of Appadurai's '-scapes' as being close in spirit to what literary studies scholars may think of broadly as 'texts', presenting deformative possibilities and being constitutive of social processes as texts might appear from a literary perspective. His main thesis was that, under globalized conditions, where global cultural flows are evidenced across these fields, 'growing disjunctures between ethnoscapes, technoscapes, financescapes, mediascapes and ideoscapes' are manifested and can be perceived (ibid., 301), because of deterritorialization of cultural flows and transnational movements. In his book *Modernity at Large* (1996) he expanded on these ideas by emphasizing the humanistic inspiration underlying this view of cultural flows and globalization, and suggesting that sociology should attend to the 'work of the imagination' *as* social processes and relations rather than regarding products of the imagination as deriving from existing social relations and processes. In particular, when he turned to reconceiving cultural studies within his home discipline, anthropology, he gestured towards the assertiveness of literary studies already in the direction he contemplates:

At the epicentre of current debates in and about culture, many diverse streams flow into a single, rather turbulent river of many poststructuralisms [. . .].

In this postblur blur, it is crucial to note that the high ground has been seized by English literature (as a discipline) in particular and literary studies in general. This is the nexus where the word *theory*, a rather prosaic term in many fields for many centuries, suddenly took on a sexy ring of a trend. For the anthropology in the United States today, what is most striking about the last decade in the academy is the hijack of culture by literary studies [. . .]. Social scientists look on with bewilderment as their colleagues in English and comparative literature talk (and fight) about matters that, until as recently as fifteen years ago, would have seemed about as relevant to English departments as, say, quantum mechanics.

The subject matter of cultural studies could roughly be taken as the relationship between the word and the world. I understand these two terms in their widest sense, so that *word* can encompass all forms of textualized expression and *world* can mean anything from means of production and the organization of life-worlds to the globalized relations of cultural reproduction discussed here. (Appadurai 1996, 51)

This admission of the centrality of the *word* – of textualized forms – is in keeping with Wolff's humanistic emphasis above and especially with the emphasis that literary studies places on textuality. Appadurai has unsurprisingly been a popular reference point in literary studies. Interestingly, in a similar direction the work of sociologist Jeffrey Alexander from the later 1990s also seeks integration between a humanities and a sociological approach to culture by developing a method of 'cultural sociology' at the expense of the methods of 'sociology of culture' – a method that is both theorized and demonstrated lucidly in the book that brings together this work, *The Meanings of Social Life* (2003).

That process of literary studies 'seizing the high ground' to which Appadurai grudgingly pointed is, in fact, the process through which literary studies has reconstituted itself and its own understanding of culture, even to the extent of losing its disciplinary focus on the literary text. If Appadurai and Alexander (and many others) bring anthropology/sociology to absorb something of the humanistic emphasis in culture, it is because, as observed here, the approach of literary studies to culture has itself undergone a transformation that has allowed it to encroach upon erstwhile sociological/anthropological preoccupations. This convergence is useful for understanding globalization in relation to culture, and emerges from the impact of globalization on culture. In the present study the process within literary studies is naturally of some moment.

As Appadurai observes in that quotation, the renovation of *theory* – or Theory, as it is often designated – in the 1960s and 1970s has something to do with the reconsideration of culture in literary studies. To a large extent, the blossoming of Theory in late twentieth-century literary studies could simply be regarded as an importation of ideas from certain disciplinary fields – particularly from linguistics, philosophy, psychoanalysis and politics – to inform understandings of the literary text, of reading and writing, and of the implications of studying literature in institutional settings. Why these importations took place, and more importantly why Theory came to have such a powerful drive within the literary academy and became institutionally embedded therein are moot and much discussed questions which do not need immediate treatment here – I touch on some of the causes and effects as this study progresses. In the course of the 1980s, when the debate on globalization was just beginning to occupy social scientists and anthropologists, Theory became ensconced in literary studies in increasingly institutionalized ways. The late 1970s and early 1980s saw the appearance of several scholarly attempts to come to grips with Theory as something that is *in* literary studies already, i.e. not as something that literary scholars simply engage with in criticism but as an area of literary studies which can be contemplated and taught in itself (especially Graff 1979; Hartman 1980; de Man [1980–81] 1986; Lentricchia 1983; some essays in Said 1983). De Man's and Said's formulations can be dwelt on momentarily to convey the rather specific thrusts that Theory carried at the time.

Inspired particularly by Jacques Derrida's philosophical deconstruction of language, de Man's understanding of Theory was closely connected to the relationship of language and literary text:

Literary theory can be said to come into being when the approach to literary texts is no longer based on non-linguistic, that is to say historical and aesthetic, considerations, or, to put it somewhat less crudely, when the object of discussion is no longer the meaning or the value but the modalities of production and of reception of meaning and of value prior to their establishment – the implication being that the establishment is problematic enough to consider its possibility and its status. (de Man 1986, 7)

Or, as he put it briefly, Theory 'occurs with the introduction of linguistic terminology in the metalanguage about literature' (ibid., 8). The philosophical complexity of de Man's observations on Theory is self-evident in that quotation: it recommends a focus on language in literature and literary studies that goes, so to speak, deep *into* and *behind* the literary text and at the expense of the surrounding extrinsic factors, 'historical and aesthetic', that could attach to the literary text. Edward Said, whose own theoretical approach to literary texts and literary studies was derived largely from the work of historian and discourse analyst Michel Foucault, philosopher Louis Althusser, and a range of left-wing political theorists and literary critics, including Georg Lukács and Raymond Williams, was less than impressed by the inward-looking and abstract formulation of Theory exemplified here by de Man. He felt that the latter had rendered Theory too abstract and centred on 'textuality', and too disengaged from the political and social world within which literature is produced and received. He therefore reviewed its past 'travels' to evoke its constant engagement with 'worldly' social and political concerns, and recommended that Theory should enable politically effective, socially aware, contextually located, historically informed and intellectually responsible criticism (especially in the essays 'Traveling Theory' and 'Reflections on American "Left" Literary Criticism' in Said 1983).

In the course of the 1980s the apparently contrary directions of de Man's and Said's kind of understandings of Theory paradoxically joined up, and Theory came to be regarded as both a highly abstract set of insights into literary texts and literary studies and a means, sometimes preponderantly so, whereby literature becomes politically relevant and socially responsible. In the latter vein, the extent to which literary texts reveal how social processes and ideologies are constituted through discourse – how they are moulded and constructed within the ways they are talked and written about – was persuasively explored. Much of the 1980s and 1990s was devoted to agonizing about what this impact of Theory was doing to the conventional study of literature, to literary studies. Camps for and against Theory were formed, and impassioned arguments were undertaken about its political efficacy – in, for instance, Goodheart 1984; Cain 1984; Felperin 1985; Parrinder 1987; Berman 1988; Eagleton 1990; and Donoghue 1992. Also in the course of the 1980s and 1990s Theory became inexorably institutionalized in the literary academy. Textbooks were written to teach Theory to students of literature – beginning influentially with works by Catherine Belsey (1980) and Terry Eagleton (1983) – and Theory courses were introduced systematically in literature departments across the higher education sector, literary studies curricula were debated and revised to reflect the political realizations and agency released by Theory, and the literary classroom itself as a politically affective space was considered. These moves enabled literary studies to constitute itself as central to understanding culture with all its social and political nuances, as embodying cultural processes in a particularly self-reflexive fashion, so that some of the prerogatives of sociological/anthropological investigation seem to become relocated within it. Conversely, these moves also enabled in some instances a rebirth of cultural studies, with a humanistic emphasis, from within literary studies and yet away from both literary studies and sociology/anthropology. This rebirth of cultural studies was most cogently declared by Anthony Easthope (1991). He felt Theory had initiated a paradigm shift in literary studies which undermined the hegemonic ideology that is at the heart of literature itself, and recommended a renewal of cultural studies within which the political direction of Theory could be more meaningfully realized:

Cultural studies should situate its pedagogic subject not primarily in relation to truth but rather to the textual structures within which he or she is actually constituted [. . .] Confronting textuality not just cognitively – as generalisable meaning – but experiencing the work/play of the signifier and to move secondarily to criticism and analysis may disclose for the subject something of his or her own actual determinacy and situatedness. (Easthope 1991, 180)

In this renewed Theory-informed breakaway cultural studies Easthope called for attention to texts of mass and popular culture broadly understood (not just written media but in others too).

Interestingly Easthope's announcement of Theory-informed cultural studies was made precisely at the time when the predominantly sociological/anthropological debates about globalization and culture cited above were being conducted. And it foreshadowed clearly the kind of incorporations from the humanities that are found in Appadurai's work on global cultures. Conceptions of culture provide a locus around which the humanistic and sociological/anthropological approaches have gradually converged. Globalization studies have drawn the threads of this convergence into its exploration of global transnational cultural flows – but, ironically, without an explicit impact on the institutional pursuit of literary studies itself. Literary studies has drawn its reformulated sense of culture and political efficacy in moves that are analogous to those in globalization studies, but with distinct emphases and terminologies. I come to these in the next couple of chapters in addressing first the literary approach to postmodernism and postcolonialism and then the institutional spaces of English and world literature. Literary studies has been deeply complicit in the development of discussions of globalization and culture, has moved synchronously with those discussions, but while marginalizing and largely eschewing globalization studies within its perspectival field – until much later. That is, until Theory was not only squarely institutionalized in literary studies, but so much so that it appeared to be superseded: a process marked in the plethora of 'after Theory' or post-Theory studies that eventually appeared (e.g. McQuillan 1999; Butler, Guillory and Thomas 2000; Strauch 2001; Eagleton 2003; Payne and Schad 2003; Callus and Herbrechter 2004; Leitch and Williams 2005).

The complicity of literary studies with globalization studies (with a sociological/anthropological orientation) in contemplating culture is also expressed with regard to concepts of identity. In fact this is closely embroiled with the travels of Theory in literary studies briefly described above. The period of the advent and institutionalization of Theory in literary studies, especially of the politically aware and agency-seeking strand within the discipline, coincided with several socio-political occurrences of international significance. In the 1950s and 1960s a large number of African and Asian countries became independent from their colonial rulers and began a process of decolonization and postcolonial national consolidation. In Western Europe and Northern America, the 1960s and to some extent the 1970s were marked by anti-Vietnam War protests and a widespread left-wing student movement which overlapped and found common ground with a surge of identity-based movements. Particularly noteworthy among the latter were the political activism and intellectual productions of the African-American civil liberties movement, second-wave feminism, and the gay and lesbian movement. The 1980s in the United States (Ronald Reagan took office as president in January 1981) and United Kingdom (Margaret Thatcher became prime minister in May 1979) brought to power governments which systematically instituted government deregulation and privatization measures. There was also a perceivable hardening of conservative attitudes towards the minorities in these countries. Privatization and deregulation were adopted as international economic strategies in the 1980s and 1990s, mainly through the operations of the International Monetary Fund and the World Bank. These often undermined or limited state-led poverty alleviation and economic stabilization measures, which in turn gave rise to a range of social movements, often identity-based, against such policy changes around the world. In the course of the 1980s a series of communist governments, following single-party and strongly centralized systems, collapsed after mass demonstrations. This process was attended by growing disenchantment with the concept of class as the locus of the left movement, or with the international working-class movement as the structure on which left politics was centred. The attention of both left and liberal political alignments shifted gradually from class as the centre of emancipative political movements to identity as the fulcrum of political mobilization and social movements.

As it happened, identity-based political positions, exemplified by feminist, gay, ethnic and racial movements, had considerable traditions of being expressed through literature or in terms of literary studies. Understandably the travels of worldly (in Said's terms) Theory through a period characterized by the above occurrences consolidated the political awareness and agency of literary studies by becoming the ground upon which identity and identity-based political aspirations could be constructed and discussed. In specific terms the politics of gender, sexuality, race and ethnicity, and in general terms the politics of difference, multiculturalism, pluralism, marginality and postcolonialism, were all hotly debated in literary studies. As literary studies provided, through Theory, a field in which the politics of identity could be performed and clarified, so too Theory aspired to both rejuvenate and modify the undertaking of identity-based political activism and thinking. As Theory gradually came to be institutionalized in the literary academy in the course of the 1980s and particularly in the 1990s, it also substantially came to be structured around identity-based positions. Literary Theory textbooks broke the dynamic travels of Theory into schools, which now multiplied along identity lines: feminist theory, gay/queer theory, African American studies, postcolonial theory, etc. Literary anthologies along these identity-based lines marked the introduction of concordant courses or curricular reform in keeping with those moves. Appointments and research projects to concretize the institutional inculcation of identity in the literary academy were undertaken. In fact, much of the Theory debate variously and repeatedly revolved around the political ambitions centred on identity which were becoming characteristic of literary studies. Thus Paul Bové hoped Theory would lead literary studies 'intellectuals marginal to the dominant group and of subaltern groups to speak' (Bové 1992, 47), Denis Donoghue worried about the 'confusion of theories with principles and ideologies' along identitarian lines (Donoghue 1992, 48), Stanley Fish maintained that 'academic feminism, academic gay rights studies, and academic black studies do not cause anything' politically effective (Fish 1995, 86), Terry Eagleton complained that the turn to identity politics in literary studies had actually led to a depoliticization of Theory (Eagleton 2003), and so on. As with the Theory debate, so with the related canon debates: Paul Lauter (1991), John Guillory (1993) and Gregory S. Jay (1997) called for an opening up of the Anglo-American canon to the literature of marginalized identities, while Harold Bloom (1994) asserted the need to maintain the integrity of the Western canon.

If literary studies, in the process of institutionalizing Theory, became the ground for the performance of identity-based political aspirations and ended

up institutionalizing identity politics, sociology and anthropology and political theory had been devoted to unravelling the social processes underlying
identity from a somewhat earlier stage. The occurrences which characterized the period briefly outlined above were naturally immediately the *objects*
and *field* of sociological, anthropological and political analysis, and the
nuances of identity were theorized and retheorized for that purpose accordingly. Sociologists in particular had a long-drawn interest in identity as
something that is mediated between individuals and collectives and society
in general. Early sociological engagements with identity came from several
directions: Norbert Elias's attempts to structure the processes between 'I-
identity' and 'we-identity' since the 1930s were in this direction (Elias
1991); George Herbert Mead considered social processes that regulate
understanding of selves and the assuming of roles (Mead 1934); Marcel
Mauss attempted to delineate the social construction of the self in various
cultural contexts ([1950] 1979); Erving Goffman studied how individuals
perform themselves in everyday life (Goffman 1959) and how social identity is constructed and what role stigmatization plays in it (Goffman 1964);
and Erik Erikson put forward formulations of identity (Erikson 1968). The
problems of accommodating marginal group identities within liberal societies only really picked up in sociological study in the 1970s – in response
to some of the above-mentioned occurrences of the period. Henri Tajfel's
social psychological work based on inter-group discrimination experiments
conducted in the 1970s (Tajfel 1978, 1981) and John J. Gumperz's sociolinguistic research of collective identity construction (Gumperz 1982) were
significant interventions in this direction. Since then almost every influential political theorist and sociologist and anthropologist – John Rawls,
Jürgen Habermas, Ernesto Laclau, Chantal Mouffe, Thomas Nagel, Amy
Gutmann, Charles Taylor, Michael Walzer, Zygmunt Bauman, Ulrich
Beck, Anthony Giddens, Ralph Cohen, Seyla Benhabib and others – has
engaged with the question of collective and marginal identities in contemporary liberal democracies and in the contemporary international/global
social order. That literary studies from the 1980s onwards, and under the
institutional inculcation of Theory within the literary academy, was becoming the field wherein the ambitions and ambiguities of identity-based
political positions are centrally performed was something that sociologists
and political theorists could scarcely overlook. Some – such as Stuart Hall
and Arjun Appadurai (as mentioned already) – looked on this in a construc-
tive spirit and incorporated some of the cultural materialist positions that
were ensconced in literary studies. Others were more resistant to the
encroachments of Theory-driven literary studies on concepts of culture and
identity. Thus Habermas ([1985] 1987) took issue with the influence which
the philosophical godfather of Theory, Jacques Derrida, had wielded particularly on Anglo-American literary criticism. In Habermas's terms the
'philosophical text' (within which theories of culture and identity as the

sociologist or political scientist may approach it are located) should not be regarded a literary text, and literature cannot be regarded as a suitable ground for performing something relevant to everyday life and discourses:

If, following Derrida's recommendation, philosophical thinking were to be relieved of the duty of solving problems and shifted over to the function of literary criticism, it would be robbed not only of its seriousness, but of its productivity. Conversely, the literary-critical power of judgement loses its potency when, as is happening among Derrida's disciples in literature departments, it gets displaced from appropriating aesthetic experiential contents into the critique of metaphysics. The false assimilation of one enterprise to the other robs both of their substance (Habermas [1985] 1987, 210)

On the whole, however, in discussions of culture and identity in the context of globalization, sociologists have tended to be sympathetic to and incorporate where possible the perspectives of literary studies.

The debates on globalization and culture outlined earlier in this section have largely been devoted to understanding how cultural processes have been homogenized at a global level and yet worked with local variations. And, concurrently, they have engaged with the manner in which globalization processes have given rise to more emphatic localized claims and, more importantly, how these localised claims have accessed global visibility. Some consider these developments as globalization processes being countered by locally based fragmentations (e.g. Friedman 1994), while others see them as an interplay of elite globalization with localizations, alternative globalizations and sub-globalizations (e.g. Berger 2002), and yet others regard them as a process of globalization from above being countered by globalization from below (e.g. Brecher, Childs and Cutler 1993). The concept of identity has been central to each of these perspectives, at two levels. On the one hand, attention has been given to the manner in which globalization is raising the possibility of transcultural or cosmopolitan identities, which are in tune with globalization, which move across social and cultural boundaries easily, and which are ascribable to a global elite. On the other hand, a great deal of thinking has been devoted to the manner in which non-elite localized and marginal identities react to globalization processes, oppose these, or cohere into social movements that effectively become a globalization from below or alternative globalization. The literature is voluminous, and I have touched on some of this in chapter 1.

While literary studies becomes the *ground* on which the politics of identity plays out its aspirations, and while sociology (and, relatedly, anthropology, politics, etc.) addresses identity as both *field* and *object*, understanding globalization calls upon the resources of both kinds of approach. In fact, increasingly discussions of globalization and identity are informed conjointly by both. Sociologists are in conversation now with the claims of literary studies, just as literary scholars are increasingly in conversation with sociology. The next chapter, by focusing on discussions of postmodernism and postcolonialism, is devoted to tracing this convergence of literary and sociological/anthropological/political discourse in relation to culture and identity and globalization.

5 Postmodernism and Postcolonialism

POSTMODERNISM

The concept of postmodernism was hotly debated in the 1970s and 1980s, from a range of disciplinary perspectives. The history of the term and its connotative shifts over time have been ably discussed by Best and Kellner (1991, ch. 1) and Hans Bertens (1995), and needn't concern us here. Of interest to the present study is the manner in which formulations of post-modernism enabled literary studies to engage with apparently all dimensions of the contemporary social world, including increasing evidence of global integration. In a related fashion, also of interest here is the extent to which sociological approaches to questions of culture and identity – and therefore globalization processes – also reckoned with formulations of postmodernity. Arguably, it was primarily with regard to postmodernism that the literary and the sociological seemed to converge on discourses of globalization. But this convergence has been and remains, I observe below, a resistant one.

Thinking about postmodernism seems to consist in two strands. First, there is a registering of an experience of living in the contemporary world, or the experience of contemporary social existence, which is regarded as different from past experiences – a registering of the new, so to speak. That plays automatically and immediately with the registering of the new which, in a definitive way, has been associated with concepts of modernity. As Habermas points out, the presentation of the 'new age' as the 'modern age' was Hegel's mode of marking a historical break in the Europe of his time, with profound philosophical implications (Habermas [1985] 1987, 5). Mod-ernism's sense of engaging something unprecedented in the contemporary ethos has replicated itself before and since – as much, for instance, in Giambattista Vico's *Principi di una scienza nuova* ([1725] 2002) as in the early twentieth-century writings of T. E. Hulme, Ezra Pound and T. S. Eliot. Postmodernist newness is therefore in relation to modernist newness, pro-gressing from and yet disrupting manifestations of modernity. Second, there is an attempt to characterize postmodern newness in itself. Conceptualizing and formulating the postmodern, however, proves to be problematic and entails a constant questioning of the presumptions underlying concep-tual and formulating efforts themselves. In other words, understanding postmodernism involves a politically charged reflexiveness. Literary studies appears as a field – as it does for considerations of culture and identity, indeed through considerations of culture and identity – that is particularly amenable to postmodernist reflexiveness.

Registering the new in postmodernism in the 1970s and 1980s involved marking the global impact of information technologies and new media, the growing difficulty of grasping contemporary social and cultural existence in holistic ways, the perception that boundaries between high and low or dominant and marginal forms are becoming porous, and the prevailing feeling of fragmentation and disconnectedness. Thus philosopher and cultural theorist Jean Baudrillard felt that contemporary life is characterized by such a proliferation of informations, of signs and images, of ways of reporting and talking about and representing and branding things, that the experience of everyday life has been withdrawn from any possible perception of reality. Reality is not merely mediated any longer, it is mediated out of existence: 'So we live, sheltered by signs, in the denial of the real. [. . .] The image, the sign, the message – all these things we "consume" – represent our tranquillity consecrated by distance from the world, a distance more comforted by the allusion to the real (even where the allusion is violent) than compromised by it' (Baudrillard [1970] 1998, 34). Philosopher and critical theorist Jean-François Lyotard's engagement with the postmodern condition is, as he understands it, an engagement with the perception that the 'grand narratives' of science, philosophy, politics, religion, etc., which seemed to be able to give a unitary structure to all aspects of social life, have ceased to convince: 'The grand narrative has lost its credibility, regardless of what mode of unification it uses, regardless of whether it is a speculative narrative or a narrative of emancipation' (Lyotard [1979] 1984, 37). This has led to modernist anxieties about what sorts of political, social and cultural knowledge may be regarded as legitimate (noted in Habermas's *Legitimation Crisis* [1973] 1976); Lyotard finds that in the postmodern condition there is no longer a significant anxiety about this, and that legitimation continues to 'spring from [people's] own linguistic practice and communicative interaction' (Lyotard [1979] 1984, 41). In her attempt to clarify an aesthetics of postmodernism, literary theorist Linda Hutcheon understands postmodernism as 'fundamentally contradictory, resolutely historical, and inescapably political' (Hutcheon 1988, 4). Geographer David Harvey's study of postmodernism begins:

the most startling fact about postmodernism: its total acceptance of the ephemerality, fragmentation, discontinuity, and the chaotic that formed one half of Baudelaire's conception of modernity. But postmodernism responds to the fact of that in a very particular way. It does not try to transcend it, counteract it, or even to define the 'eternal and immutable' elements within it. Postmodernism swims, even wallows, in the fragmentary and the chaotic currents of change as if that is all there is. (Harvey 1990, 44)

Literary and cultural theorist Fredric Jameson to some extent takes his cue from Baudrillard and Lyotard in regarding the postmodernist sensibility as that of:

the subject [who] has lost its capacity to extend it pro-tensions and re-tensions across the temporal manifold and to organize its past and future into coherent experience. It becomes difficult enough to see how the cultural productions of such a subject could result in anything but 'heaps of fragments' and in a practice of the randomly heterogeneous and fragmentary and aleatory. (Jameson 1991, 25)

That selection of quotations conveys something of the manner in which postmodernist newness was registered in the 1970s and 1980s. Along with that came two kinds of agenda: first, there were attempts to explain, or find causes for, the prevalence of this condition; and, second, there were attempts to dispose the field of postmodern experience in a manner which – despite its nature – is structured after all (i.e. structured enough to be talked about and acted upon).

The dominant way of explaining the postmodernist condition has been by discerning a political and economic order which thrives on its fragmentations and ephemera and therefore sustains it: the advanced international capitalist order. In a paradoxical way, advanced capitalism therefore provides an underlying holistic structure for postmodernism, which is experienced and expressed in contemporary cultural forms and everyday life as comfortably fragmented and ephemeral. The most cogent treatment of this view is Fredric Jameson's – the title of his influential book *Postmodernism, or The Cultural Logic of Late Capitalism* (1991) speaks for itself. The phrase 'late capitalism', and the inspiration for Jameson's analysis, was taken from Ernest Mandel's Marxist economic analysis of post-Second World War capitalism in *Late Capitalism* ([1972] 1978). Jameson's ideological allegiance in engaging postmodernism was thus announced at the outset, and the study lucidly brings together perceptions of postmodernist fragmentation with a Marxist discernment of hegemonic capitalist practice:

If postmodernism, as an enlarged third stage of classical capitalism, is a purer and more homogeneous expression of classical capitalism, from which many of the hitherto surviving enclaves of socio-economic difference have been effaced (by way of their colonization and absorption by the commodity form), then it makes sense to suggest that the waning of our sense of history, and more particularly our resistance to globalizing or totalizing concepts like that of the mode of production itself, are a function of precisely that universalization of capitalism. [. . .]
But a mode of production is not a 'total system' in that forbidding sense; it includes a variety of countermoves and new tendencies within itself, of 'residual' as well as 'emergent' forces, which it must attempt to manage and control (Gramsci's conception of hegemony). Were those heterogeneous forces not endowed with an effectivity of their own, the hegemonic project would be unnecessary. (Jameson 1991, 406–7)

This kind of discernment of an advanced capitalist order underlying post-modernist experience and expression has influential forebears, notably Baudrillard and Harvey. Baudrillard's postmodernist subsuming of society within simulacra and away from apprehensions of reality is understood as the condition of a capitalist consumer society. For Harvey the capitalist process and postmodern fragmentation are held together by a clear proportional relation: 'Precisely because capitalism is expansionary and imperialistic, cultural life in more and more areas gets brought within the grasp of the cash nexus and the logic of capital circulation' (Harvey 1990, 344). That advanced capitalism is at the heart of the postmodern condition has been and continues to be widely accepted, often without the Marxist underpinnings of Jameson's approach. Lyotard's caution about undertaking explanations of or attributing causes for the postmodern condition, however, is worth keeping in mind:

The decline of [grand] narrative can be seen as an effect of the blossoming of techniques and technologies since the Second World War, which has shifted emphasis from the ends of action to its means; it can also be seen as an effect of the redeployment of advanced liberal capitalism after its retreat under the protection of Keynesianism during the period 1930–1960, a renewal that has eliminated the communist alternative and valorized the individual enjoyment of goods and services.

Anytime we go searching for causes in this way we are bound to be disappointed. Even if we adopted one or the other of these hypotheses, we would still have to detail the correlation between the tendencies mentioned above and the decline of the unifying and legitimating power of the grand narratives of speculation and emancipation. (Lyotard [1979] 1984, 37–8)

Lyotard's caution brings us to the other impetus in theorizing postmodernism: not so much to explain as to dispose the field so as to render it conceptually manageable. There are three main points to note here. First, in attempting to dispose the postmodern field, what could be thought of as a *taxonomical* approach is gradually abandoned. This field is not charted in terms of language groups or divisions, geopolitical zones such as nations and provinces, forms and genres, categories and typologies, chronologies and periods (these are only evoked to be interrogated); disciplines of knowledge seem gradually to dissolve into each other; even human and social stratifications gradually erode as notions of class erode, and the stabilities of identity (race, gender, sexuality, religion, etc.) are tested by hybridities, interfaces and interstices; boundaries are alluded to in increasingly relativized rather than static senses (such as margin and centre, dominant and minority, North and South). Instead of taxonomy, then, postmodern theory disposes its field of engagement in terms of what we may think of as *continua* in which complexities and interpenetrations and relativities can be reflected or manifested. Various kinds of continua-based approaches to postmodernism are available. Language is one such continuum which ripples and contains and absorbs postmodern discourse –

Lyotard's explanation of postmodernism as an end of grand narratives and a proliferation of 'language games' (Lyotard [1979] 1984, 9–11, drawing upon Wittgenstein's *Philosophical Investigations*, 1953) is a case in point. The centrality of Derrida's deconstructionist method in much postmodern theory comes with the conviction that close attention to the surface of language reveals slipperiness/fragmentariness/contradictions in all sorts of texts and discourses in a postmodern way. Texts and discourses go hand in hand with language in this continua-based approach of postmodernism. In a different vein, Harvey focuses on urban geography and architecture to describe postmodernism in terms of spatial and temporal dispositions of the field as, ultimately, a 'space–time compression'. In disposing the field thus he follows the methodology outlined in Henri Lefebvre's *The Production of Space* ([1974] 1991). Appadurai's '-scapes' neologisms for understanding globalized cultural flows are also in a continua mould.

The other two points are essentially a matter of emphasizing observations contained in the first. So, second, postmodern theory constantly seems to seep out of geopolitical boundaries, I observed, to spread across the boundaryless domain of continua which can extend to everything – tendentiously the contemporary world at large, the globe. Though Linda Hutcheon insisted that postmodernism 'does not really describe an international cultural phenomenon, for it is primarily European and American' (Hutcheon 1988, 4) – meaning that that's where it is talked about, observed, etc. – the methodology and reach of theorizing postmodernism is constitutionally expansionist and attends to a phenomenon it regards as expansionary. Postmodern theory, therefore, contains within itself at least an affinity, and probably a deep coincidence, with globalization theory. And, third, by disposing the postmodern field in terms of continua, the concept of culture assumes an extraordinary pre-eminence. Since continua such as language, text, discourse, space, '-scapes' and audiovisual fields are conventionally instantiated in cultural products and forms, the entire postmodernist perception of the world seems to become an extension of cultural discernment, an autonomous cultural production itself, or seems to contain all aspects of the world within a cultural gaze. Baudrillard's postmodern simulacra therefore characterize a pervasive consumer culture, and Jameson's late capitalist logic of postmodernism is entrenched in a constant reification of culture.

The institutionalization of postmodernist theory in literary studies departments was coeval with, indeed within the frame of, the institutionalization of Theory. And to some extent the reckonings of literature with social, economic, political and cultural processes that are now understood as globalization processes took place under the rubric of literary postmodernism. This is perfectly understandable given postmodernism's disposition of the field in continua – centred pre-eminently on language and texts – and reach to socially and politically contingent matters of tendentiously global import. That postmodernist literary theory and studies has seldom been identified with sociologically oriented globalization studies has more to do with disciplinary resistances than with the content of the project. I dwell on these disciplinary resistances below. Despite those resistances, the possible convergences of literary and sociological approaches to globalization are predicated on literature and literary studies' amenability to and institutionalization of (certainly by the 1990s) postmodernism within itself. At any rate, the literary reckoning with globalization, as that is understood in this study, is rooted in and arguably begins with literary postmodernism.

Literary postmodernism could be thought of as consisting both in the discernment of a postmodernist sensibility in literary texts and in the literary critical and theoretical practice of applying postmodernist methods of interpretation. Similarly literary modernism is also a matter of discerning a modernist sensibility and applying modernist interpretive methods. The shift from literary modernism to postmodernism is best demonstrated by charting modes of engaging literary texts which were received as modern and postmodern respectively – an exercise that is admirably fitted to the two texts I have been referring to intermittently: *Ulysses* and *Midnight's Children*.

Ulysses appeared amidst the peaking of high literary modernism, self-consciously cultivated as such in the circles that immediately received it, a year before that other iconic modernist text, T. S. Eliot's *The Wasteland* (1922). Its bewilderment effect was tempered by the discernment of a mythic structure that seemed to give the text's fragmentary and disparate dynamism a modernist unity, or, at least, an effort at unity. There are, of course, other unities to go with that – of time (set over one day) and of place (the Dublin focus) – but the mythic order juxtaposed on the anxiety of fragmentation in language and form seemed to have a larger import. This was gratefully hailed by T. S. Eliot, for instance, in 'Ulysses, Order and Myth' (1923): 'In using the myth, in manipulating a continuous parallel between contemporaneity and antiquity, Mr. Joyce is pursuing a method which others must pursue after him. [. . .] Instead of a narrative method, we may now use a mythical method. It is, I seriously believe, a step towards making the modern world possible for art' (Eliot [1923] 1970, 270–1). Joyce bolstered this sense of the modernist centrality of the mythic device (I have mentioned this already), the receptive/interpretive context absorbed it, and the category/period of modernity gained literary critical weight and obtained institutional sanction in academic production and curricula. In a not dissimilar fashion, *Midnight's Children* (1981) appeared in a critical context awash with a self-promulgated sense of being postmodern. It was immediately catapulted into public and critical attention by winning the Booker Prize. Its magical realist antecedents were clearly discernible within it, its play on the history of postcolonial India was self-evident, its multiple narrative layers and ploys could hardly be missed. That these were part and parcel of an apprehension not simply of a country but of a contemporary condition, a Zeitgeist, was suggested in interviews and essays by the author himself, which happily gelled with the critical reception. By the time the first book-length study of Rushdie's work and contexts appeared, Timothy Brennan's *Salman Rushdie and the Third World* (1989), there was little difficulty in recognizing *Midnight's Children* as a 'postmodern epic'.

So, at the intersection of author, text, reader, critic and their context the postmodern sensibility of *Midnight's Children* can be discerned. It uses fantastic dislocations from and therefore reconsiderations of reality typical of magic realism; according to Rushdie: 'It's a way of noticing certain kinds of reality which the traditional naturalistic novel can't notice because of its rules' (Rushdie [1983] 2001, 49). Interlaced with that are the narratorial ploys of Saleem telling Padma stories, inflected with the registers of class difference, and the rendering of Saleem's telepathic communicative abilities, drawing in and mixing up indiscriminately a plethora of registers. If all these are rendered with the ironic detachment of a Joyce-like 'arranger', that arranger is itself fissured, tellingly, along lines of unreliability. Rushdie offered his account of this too: it had to do with the mistakes that the author and Saleem made jointly, because: 'whenever a conflict arose between literal and remembered truth, I [Rushdie] would favour the remembered version. [. . .] His [Saleem's] truth is too important to him to allow it to be unseated by a mere weather report' (Rushdie 1991, 24–5). The unreliability of the narrator/author measures itself against recorded historical facts, but perhaps more importantly it registers itself against other perspectives on history. This is observed in the various meta-narratives that appear within Saleem's narratives in *Midnight's Children*. There is the measure of standard Indian history in the sequence of documented sociopolitically relevant events dated by the Gregorian calendar against the scale of mythic history:

Think of this: history, in my version, entered a new phase on August 15th, 1947 – but in another version, that inescapable date is no more than one fleeting instant in the Age of Darkness, Kali-Yuga, in which the cow of mortality has been reduced to standing, teeteringly, on a single leg! Kali-Yuga [. . .] . . . began on Friday, February 18th, 3012 B.C.; and will last a mere 432,000 years! (Rushdie 1981, 191)

And there is the measure of that standard history against the scale of Saleem's personal and family history:

Let me state this quite unequivocally: it is my firm conviction that the hidden purpose of the Indo-Pakistani war of 1965 was nothing more or less than the elimination of my benighted family from the face of the earth. In order to understand the recent history of our times, it is necessary to examine the bombing-pattern of that war with an analytical, unprejudiced eye.

Even ends have beginnings; everything must be told in sequence. [. . .] By August 8th, 1965, my family history had got itself into a condition from which what-was-achieved-by-bombing-patterns provided a merciful relief. (Rushdie 1981, 327)

This juxtaposing of perspectives of history is centred on the standard Indian history, but is also a mode of destabilizing the authority of that history by imaginary interventions. But no other dominant structure emerges – nothing as weighty as Joyce's mythical method surfaces. All that is there is the instability offered by micro-histories of persons and families and mega-histories of the mythic sort, sieved through unreliable and ironic narration. Nevertheless, this could be seen as fracturing not only the dominant version of standard Indian history but also official narratives of various sorts: Rushdie nudged his reader to contemplate the possibility that 'literature can, and perhaps must, give the lie to official facts' (Rushdie 1991, 14). Further, this view of Indian history, though often received as a particular prognosis (a somewhat pessimistic one) of postcolonial India, could be read as something larger, something that cannot be confined to the boundaries it seems to actualize and interrogate. The Indian focus here could itself be seen as encompassing the world at large, and the authorial consciousness that questions official and historical narratives thus could just be emphasizing a global consciousness – of the sort Rushdie succinctly expressed in a 1983 interview:

I think that, you see, the world is in a crisis right now. Not just India but everywhere. And what seems to be happening is a process, perhaps inevitable, by which the truth or reality itself is more and more being taken control of by certain groupings in society and put out of the hands of ordinary people. [. . .] I think there's a big struggle against that – the control of history by those who are powerful. It seems to me nowadays that it is very important for writers who can make alternative histories, who can put other pictures of the world to the ones the world would have you believe, to do that and to become adversaries of that process. (Rushdie [1983] 2001, 59)

By this extrapolation Rushdie featured himself as author and *thereby* political agent opposing a global process by another kind of global gesture. He opposed the 'grand narratives' of history by 'language games', to follow Lyotard's terms.

And the critics agreed very soon, within the decade in which the novel appeared. As Timothy Brennan observed: 'If neither Saleem nor Padma create "true" national images, it is because the truth of postwar nationalism is international' (Brennan 1989, 117). In concert with Rushdie's text and Rushdie's retrospective nudges for readers, interpretive readings of *Midnight's Children* accommodated it within the language of literary postmodernist theory and practice. In a way, the novel seemed to emerge as a realization of literary postmodernism as it had already been and was yet being formulated. Its narrative surface could be held against Ihab Hassan's formalistic schema of what are modernist traits and what postmodernist (Hassan 1987, particularly 91–2), and *Midnight's Children* comes up firmly on the postmodernist side. With reference to charges against *Midnight's Children* of distorting history in a politically dangerous fashion, Brian McHale has the following general observation to offer:

if only we could be sure that the historical record reliably captured the experience of the human beings who really suffered and enacted history. But that is the last thing we can be sure of, and one of the thrusts of postmodernist revisionist history is to call into question the reliability of official history. The postmodernists fictionalize history, but by doing so they imply that history may itself be a form of fiction. (McHale 1987, 96)

All the aspects of a postmodern poetics that Linda Hutcheon explored, 'historical knowledge, subjectivity, narrativity, reference, textuality, discursive content' (Hutcheon 1988, 231), to demonstrate the postmodernist spirit of being anti-totalizing, problematizing, interrogative, contradictory, and using devices such as parody, metafiction, narrative disruptions and intertextuality, could be exemplified in precisely those ways with *Midnight's Children*. A typical example of such exemplification appears in Hutcheon's book itself, in relation to her observations on feminist decentring (from their 'ex-centric' position) of ideologically dominant male discourse in an anti-totalizing postmodern vein:

Postmodernism does not move the marginal to the center. It does not invert the valuing of centers into that of peripheries and borders, as much as *use* that paradoxical doubled positioning to critique the outside from both the outside and the inside. Just as Padma, the listening, textualized female narratee of Rushdie's *Midnight's Children*, pushes the narration in directions its male narrator has no intention of taking, so the ex-centric have not only overlapped in some of their concerns with postmodernism, but also pushed it in new directions. (Hutcheon 1988, 231)

The play of the politics of identity in and with reference to *Midnight's Children* is a relevant issue in this context, and I return to it in the next section.

But, to pose the obvious question that appears at this juncture, do such concretizations of literary postmodernism as appear in and with reference to (for instance) *Midnight's Children* resonate at all with sociologically oriented approaches to globalization? It wouldn't be unreasonable to feel that there is a resonance. Insofar as the nation-state is apprehended as a socio-political construct, a politically contingent gesture of global or transnational import is arguably made, ideological margins and centres are negotiated, ideas of diversity and unity are troubled (at linguistic and formal levels) – all in an expansive postmodernist spirit – something akin to the sociological view of globalization has arguably occurred. If one carried out a sociological study of the place of India in the midst of globalization processes, the literary postmodernism of *Midnight's Children* would not be irrelevant to it. In a broader sense, leaving the singular literary example aside, the study of postmodernism (with its strong investment in literature and literary studies) and of globalization (with its strong investment in sociology and social studies) could be thought of in a conjoined direction. And, in fact, this has gradually been recognized, and there has taken place a convergence of terms and references, but only through the anxieties of disciplinary lenses. The determination of literary studies to stick to texts and discourses, to render these implacably resistant to any outside, happily coincided with the postmodernist perception of an all-embracing reification of culture – but remained largely resistant to the sociological objectivity that attaches to studying globalization processes. This was manifested not so much by its unawareness of the content of these processes as in a kind of perverse refusal to name them as globalization. In the matrix of terms and rhetoric with which literary studies has been identified since the rise of Theory – wherein 'postmodernism', 'identity', 'ideology', 'hegemony', 'Marxism', 'colonialism', etc., appear to acquire literary weight – 'globalization' has slipped through largely untouched (or extremely rarely touched) through the 1980s and 1990s. It is as if by silencing itself about the term, by not speaking it, the discipline would maintain its integrity.

On the other side, sociology has had no difficulty in registering the moves made by literary studies, its consonance with postmodernism, but has done so largely with irritation or as something other to sociology. Habermas's scepticism at the levelling of literature and philosophy has already been noted. More interesting perhaps are expressions of sociological caution and conditionality attached to taking heed of postmodernist theory. Zygmunt Bauman's 1988 essay 'Is There a Postmodern Sociology?' thus took it as a foregone conclusion that there isn't. Postmodernism is worth discussing, he observed, because it says something of sociological interest *about* those who talk about it, not because those who talk about it say anything that *is* sociologically interesting:

I propose that the concept of 'postmodernity' has a value entirely of its own in so far as it purports to capture and articulate the novel experience of just one, but crucial social category of contemporary society: the intellectuals. Their novel experience – that is, their reassessment of their own position within society, their representation of the collectively performed function, and their new strategies. (Bauman 1988, 217–18)

Bauman's was a strategy of confining postmodernism: according to him, it tells us not about society but about a stratum of society, a 'crucial' one perhaps but a 'novel' one really, ergo postmodernism has nothing to do with the rest of society. It is, so to speak, no more than ethnographic data about a professional tribe, and what is possible is 'a sociology of postmodernity, rather than a postmodern sociology' (ibid., 235). In a similar but slightly more generous vein, in Scott Lash's *Sociology of Postmodernism*, which appeared shortly afterwards in 1990, one also finds a containment strategy but a less restrictive and more predictable one: 'Postmodernism is, for me, not a condition, nor, as part of a fabric with post-industrialism, a type of society, in the sense that people speak of industrial society, or capitalist society, or modern society. Postmodernism is instead, I think, confined to the realm of *culture*' (Lash 1990, 3–4). The diligence with which the personal pronoun is repeated suggests that Lash was not wholly dismissing a broader view of postmodernism but was making a methodological decision. And in fact it is arguable that, in the careful study that follows, he endowed postmodernism and culture with a sociological weight and reach that seems to belie the need for this caution.

But in contemplating globalization, eventually, sociologists have found postmodernism, with its literary and cultural baggage, to be useful. A year before Appadurai's *Modernity at Large* appeared, Mike Featherstone's *Undoing Culture* (1995) endeavoured to 'draw lessons' from postmodernism and postcolonialism to inform his understanding of globalization. Like Lash, he regarded these terms as attached to the realm of culture and spoke of them as being outside sociology, but he was not insistent on containing postmodernism in culture or on thinking of culture as a contained field. In fact the substance of what he had to say about globalization *and* culture was contained in his succinct understanding of these terms, with their emphasis on text and discourse (note the appraising outsider air in his evocation of these terms):

From the point of view of postmodernism, modernism has been seen as entailing a quest to impose notions of unity and universality of thought and the world. In effect its mission is to impose order on disorder, to tame the frontier. Yet with the shifting global balance of power away from the West, with more voices talking back to the West, there is a strong sense that modernism will not be universalized. This is because modernism is seen as both a Western project and as the West's projection of its values on to the world. [. . .]

Instead of the confident sense that one is able to construct theory and map the world from the secure place of the centre, which is usually seen as higher and more advanced in symbolic and actual terms, postmodernism and postcolonialism present theory as mobile, or as constituted from an eccentric site, somewhere on the boundary. The movement of people from the global boundary to the centre is coupled with a displacement of theory to the boundary, with a weakening of authority. (Featherstone 1995, 10)

Through Featherstone's somewhat dry summative tone, the literary inflection of Theory and 'voices talking back to the West' comes through uninterrogated, indeed is accepted readily as constitutive of cultural flows that are significantly available both as and as countering globalization processes.

The quotation also brings us rather neatly to that other dominant frame of literary studies that is relevant here, postcolonialism.

POSTCOLONIALISM

In literary studies, attempts at coming to grips with sociologically oriented globalization studies and moves towards some incorporation of the discourse of globalization within literary studies have come primarily from those engaged with postcolonial literary theory and criticism. Though since the 1980s the concerns of the latter have overlapped substantially with those of globalization studies, often engaging with the contemporary world in aligned ways, the relationship between literary postcolonial studies and globalization studies has been an aloof and standoffish one. Such systematic attempts as are available towards a convergence on terms and ideas on the part of literary scholars have appeared mainly around and since 2000.

The reasons for both the attempt to find and the inertia about finding common ground have to do with the phases of the development of post-colonial theory and criticism in literary studies.

Literary theorists usually mark Edward Said's *Orientalism* (1978) as the pioneering work of postcolonial studies, deriving from it both the delineation of a field of investigation and a rich vein of politically nuanced and globally relevant strategies for engaging texts and discourses. The core of Said's argument was indicatively summarized by him:

[Orientalism is] a *distribution* of geopolitical awareness into aesthetic, scholarly, economic, sociological, historical and philological texts; it is an *elaboration* not only of a basic geographical distinction (the world is made up of two unequal halves, Orient and Occident) but also of a whole series of 'interests' which, by such means as scholarly discovery, philological reconstruction, psychological analysis, landscape and sociological description, it not only creates but also maintains; it *is*, rather than expresses, a certain *will* or *intention* to understand, in some cases to control, manipulate, even to incorporate, what is a manifestly different (or alternative and novel) world; it is, above all, a discourse that is by no means in direct, corresponding relationship with political power in the raw, but rather is produced and exists in an uneven exchange with various kinds of power, shaped to a degree by the exchange with power political (as with a colonial or imperial establishment), power intellectual (as with reigning sciences like comparative linguistics or anatomy, or any of the modern policy sciences), power cultural (as with orthodoxies and canons of taste, texts, values), power moral (as with ideas of what 'we' do and what 'they' cannot do or understand as 'we' do). (Said 1978, 12)

As a description of an area of study this has certain deliberate echoes of postmodernist theory: attention is given to fissures and contradictions in discourses in a way that is reminiscent of Jacques Derrida's work; power is conceived as dispersed across the body politic *à la* Michel Foucault and Louis Althusser; the connotations of 'othering' explored by Emmanuel Levinas in philosophy, Simone de Beauvoir in gender politics, Jacques Lacan in psychoanalysis, resonate with this; the underlying commitment against the totalizing mechanism of Orientalism is rather like Fredric Jameson's attitude towards late capitalist society; history is constructed within narratives, not unlike Hayden White's postmodernist view of history; disciplinary boundaries collide and blur into each other. And yet all this seemed at the time to present a *distinctive* perspective. Said had unexpectedly arranged the postmodernist echoes around an immediately persuasive, and in his terms immediately worldly, object and relational field which, so to speak, stands out – the object is the constructed Orient, the relational field is between the Orient and the Occident, which broadly aligns with other relations, such as West and East/North and South, First World and Third World, colonizer and colonized, colonial and postcolonial. Unlike postmodernist perceptions of a late capitalist or consumer society-driven coherence which can be discerned *hidden* behind comfortably disjunctive and fractured continua, here the object and relation in question are in the *foreground*, and provide a locus to analyse politically the already familiar dispositions of knowledge and power. The constructed object was Said's main occupation in the book. He examined the construction of the Orient and Orientalism through an extended history of cultural encounters and exploitations, he expounded on the pervasiveness of the strategies of that construction across different domains of knowledge, and he drew a line of continuity from historical past to happening present. The present is characterized by Orientalism *now*: manifested through popular images in a range of media and social science representations; through cultural relations policy (particularly in the United States); through professional academic research on Islam; through adsorption in scholarship and cultural forms in geopolitical locations that would be identified as within the Orient itself (Said 1978, 284–328). In Said's account the object of study, Orientalism, contained the relational field that was both actuated and instantiated through it.

Postcolonialism as it developed thereafter, however, shifted the emphasis to the relational field itself, with Orientalism as a particular knowledge–power arrangement among every other sort of knowledge–power arrangement in every sort of continua that describe both a historical and a contemporary world. It centred the relation of colonizer and colonized both as a historical process and as an accrual in the contemporary world, ostensibly providing a structure for understanding the politics of all sorts of texts and discourses. The term 'postcolonial' is expected to convey the relational emphasis. That has an obvious bearing on the history of empire-building in Asia, Africa, America, Australasia and within Europe, and the continuing effects of that global history – but that in itself is far from all the term connotes. In fact, that rather restrictive understanding of postcolonialism is constantly resisted by postcolonial theorists, who don't wish the term to suggest any optimistic break in power–knowledge relations (marked by a before and an after in colonial experience, by clearly colonial and postcolonial periods, or by colonial rule and independence and post-independence in specific countries). On the contrary, postcolonial theorists prefer to register continuities across the historical phases of colonization and de- or post-colonization (following Said's example in that), and hope that the term 'postcolonialism' would suggest a field of relationships wherein political inequities of various sorts can be examined and analysed and opposed in a coherent fashion. Various attempts have been made to reconfigure the term itself so as to discourage optimistic misapprehensions and widen its oppositional political remit, and sophisticated distinctions have been recommended between 'postcolonialism', 'postcoloniality', 'post-colonialism', and 'neocolonialism'. For the purposes of this study I stick to postcolonialism as a term that, in fact, rather like globalization, encapsulates manifold connotations in different phases and contexts of literary Theory's travels. At any rate, postcolonial theorists now expect postcolonial theory and studies not only to register and analyse colonialism and anti-colonialism and neocolonialism, but thereby also to rise above and beyond every specific experience of these and become that which, in Robert Young's words, 'focuses on forces of oppression and coercive domination that operate in the contemporary world [. . .] to develop new forms of engaged theoretical work that contributes to the development of dynamic ideological and social transformation' (Young 2001, 11). Similar views have appeared in numerous overviews of postcolonial theory and criticism, such as those by Bart Moore-Gilbert (1997), Ania Loomba (1998), Leela Gandhi (1998) and Elleke Boehmer (1995). Between Said's and Young's positions there are several important steps in the development of postcolonial theory and criticism which need to be registered in this context, and which I come to shortly.

The impetus that arises from Said's work in postcolonial theory and literary criticism establishes its assonances with the simultaneously developing sociologically oriented globalization studies. As I have outlined in chapter 1, 'globalization' has been the term around which, initially, applied economic and political modes of capitalizing on international markets/labour and conducting international regulation and, later, processes of social and cultural and ideological integration and disintegration of an international scale were formulated and registered. This sociological thrust of globalization studies has been on registering these developments in terms of available social, political, economic and cultural models. These could take account of (but, as Said observed, often didn't, and on the contrary played into) inequities arising out of constructions of Orientalism and the distortions of power–knowledge arising from colonial history. And obviously, as observed above, they eventually did – by attending to postcolonialism. Even if we leave aside a sociological commitment to empirical realities that are not necessarily understood as constituted in continua, it is evident that sociological models could not simply be predicated on an emphatic foregrounding of the colonizer–colonized, colonial–postcolonial relational field. From the sociological point of view, crucial as colonialism–postcolonialism might be for understanding contemporary developments, there is no reason to consider it to be pre-eminently and super-determinatively important. Postcolonial theory and criticism registered many facets of contemporary developments in the world along lines very similar to globalization studies, and often in a similar spirit. But, perhaps because of its commitment to discourses and texts as constitutive, it chose to make the relational field, and something of the object, hit upon by Said as the centred axis for understanding those developments. The colonizer–colonized relationship and the colonial–postcolonial relationship were emphatically *foregrounded*, following Said's inspiration. It was centred as the analytical, explanative, expandable, even metaphorical fulcrum around which *all* contemporary developments (that were also within the ken of globalization studies) could be located and understood (whereby it departed decidedly from globalization studies). Both globalization studies and post-colonial theory and criticism construct their historical approaches for grasp-ing the contemporary world. From the postcolonial point of view the sociological construction of history leading towards globalization processes often seems itself Eurocentric and imperialist. From the sociological glo-balization theorist's point of view the postcolonial construction of history might sometimes seem Euro-excluding (to coin an antonym) for the sake of maintaining a rhetorical oppositional stance. However, accommodations are undoubtedly possible and under way, as seen from the sociological globalization studies perspective above, and as shall be seen for the postco-lonial perspective later in this section.

Interestingly, *Midnight's Children* performs a literary centring of the colonial–postcolonial relationship in almost exactly the spirit of foreground-ing the postcolonial relational field that occurs with and after Said. Across the slippages between narratives of official national history, personal histo-ries, imagined histories, mythic or magical 'history', if there is a lowest common denominator of significance, it is in the moment of India's inde-pendence. The moment of India's birth as a postcolonial nation – marked by Nehru's famous 'tryst with destiny' speech – and the birth of Saleem Sinai are deliberately welded together in the novel:

The monster in the streets has begun to roar, while in Delhi a wiry man is saying, '. . . At the stroke of the midnight hour, while the world sleeps, India awakens to life and freedom . . .' And beneath the roar of the monster there are two more yells, cries, bellows, the howls of children arriving in the world, their unavailing protests mingling with the din of independence which hangs saffron-and-green in the night sky – 'A moment comes, which comes but rarely in history, when we step out from the old to the new; when an age ends; and when the soul of a nation long suppressed finds utterance . . .' while in a room with saffron-and-green carpet Ahmed Sinai is still clutching a chair when Dr Narlikar enters to inform him: 'On the stroke of midnight, Sinai brother, your Begum Sahiba gave birth to a large, healthy child: a son!' (Rushdie 1981, 115)

If Rushdie's intention had been to juxtapose alternative narratives with a view to questioning official historical narrative, to present a postmodernist sense of multiple histories, the description of this defining moment of the novel belies that. It presents a rather obvious in-your-face kind of symbolic conjunction: the accoutrements of official declarations subsume the narra-tive at every level – personal, national, symbolic, imaginary – as the colours of the Indian flag and the official announcement pervades and echoes across the passage. The colonial/postcolonial moment of official history is supersignified, attributed a superlative meaning, to become *more* than official history, to become both the assertion and the interrogation of that history in itself, and the defining structural centre of the novel. All postmodernist fissures and multiplicities are arraigned around that unitary slash between coloniality/postcoloniality described in this passage, and spiral out from it and with reference to it. All the bewilderingly diverse strands of the novel acquire their significance and narrative placement in relation to it. The novel's rebellious assessment of postcolonial development is thereafter driven home most trenchantly by direct reference to and reversal-repetition of the description of this moment – in the birth of Saleem's son:

Aadam Sinai arrived at a night-shadowed slum on June 25th, 1975. And the time? The time matters, too. As I said: at night. No, it's important to be more . . . On the stroke of midnight, as a matter of fact. Clock-hands joined palms. Oh, spell it out, spell it out: at the precise instant of India's arrival at Emergency, he emerged. There were gasps; and across the country, silence and fears. And owing to the occult tyrannies of that benighted hour, he was mysteriously handcuffed to history, his destinies indissolubly chained to those of his country. (Rushdie 1981, 405)

The politics of the novel is encapsulated in the structural significance of the relationship between these two moments, the latter's derivation from the former, and the former's superlative meaningfulness. In a paradoxical way, interrogating the dominance of official historical narrative in *Midnight's Children* involves reifying the highlighted point of that history itself. This is not meant as a political criticism of the novel, but as an observation on the novel's performance of a strategy which seems to pervade, in ever more complex and self-interrogative ways, the field of postcolonial theory and criticism itself.

To return to our theme, if postcolonialism's foregrounding of a relational field takes it away from sociologically oriented views of globalization, its political will to engage with the contemporary world keeps it tracing a parallel and overlapping track with globalization. To a great degree this derives from the alignment of postcolonial theory and identity politics/cultural studies that gradually took place over the 1980s and was institutionalized by the 1990s. The construction of literary studies as a field in which identity and culture can be performed (while globalization studies formulates the importance of identity in the cultural field) – as observed in the previous chapter – has now come largely under the aegis of postcolonial theory. Perhaps the most influential interventions in postcolonialism's incorporation of identity politics came in a series of papers written in the 1980s and early 1990s by Homi Bhabha and Gayatri Spivak. These enabled various identity-based political positions – based on gender, sexuality, race, ethnicity, religion, etc. – to find common ground in postcolonial theory, and to be able to locate and constitute their distinct oppositional and emancipative agendas in an interrelated fashion on that ground. This was partly down to postcolonial theory's disinvesting identity-based political positions from their essentialist proclivities (the notion that identity is somehow biogenetically prefigured in people, that gender, race, sexuality, ethnicity, etc., are ingrained in different groups), and thereby activating the notion that identities are socially constructed for ideological reasons. Thus, postcolonial theory produced a scholarly discourse in which notions of marginality, subalternity, hybridity, subjectivity, etc., were constantly reiterated and expanded, both to render the hardened categories of essential identities porous and malleable and to enable a coherence between different (marginalized) identities and their political claims. All this occurred nevertheless in terms of the foregrounded relation of colonizer–colonized. To take one of the various suggestive contributions in this direction from postcolonial theory, Bhabha's exploration of hybridity in his essay 'Signs Taken for Wonders' (first published in 1985) is worth pausing on. His argument is that colonial scholarship and administration sought constantly to fix identity (and cultural forms) in immovable hierarchical orders, according to race, for instance. The reality of the colonial experience, however, was that it enabled cross-cultural encounters and mixtures which produced hybrids (as much of persons as of cultures), which simply couldn't be absorbed into the colonial apparatus:

Hybridity is a problematic of colonial representation and individuation that reverses the effects of the colonialist disavowal, so that other 'denied' knowledges enter upon the dominant discourse and estrange the basis of its authority – its rules of recognition. [. . .] What is irremediably estranging in the presence of the hybrid – in the revaluation of the symbol of national authority as the sign of colonial difference – is that the difference of cultures can no longer be identified or evaluated as objects of epistemological or moral contemplation: cultural differences are not simply *there* to be seen or appropriated. (Bhabha 1994, 114)

The observation that colonial attributions of stable hierarchies of cultures and identities is opposed not so much by the assertion of those identities against oppression as by the very realization that identities are not stable and fixed has a bearing on the political self-perception of all identity-based alignments. This self-perception is informed by the colonial experience and its postcolonial interpretation. So, postcolonial theory's formulation of hybridity becomes both a mode of undermining essentialist identity politics and a meeting ground which invigorates a range of (marginalized) identity-based political claims.

Alongside such moves, postcolonial theory's incorporation of identity politics also succeeded partly because, paradoxically, it was able, at the same time, to allow different identity-based political positions to be *embodied* within its discourse. This is paradoxical because the destabilization of essentialist identities seems to go against the grain of identities being embodied. There is a subtle balancing act involved here, which can be illustrated through some of Spivak's writings – here I refer particularly to her essay

'Marginality in the Teaching Machine' (1993). This engages in a characteristic (for Spivak) interrogation of her presence in different academic
institutional forums, pondering the slippages between the various identities
that are attributed to/assumable for her: as an 'Asian' in Britain, an 'Indian'
in the United States, a 'Bengali' to herself, a woman, a 'well-placed
academic', and speaking 'as a teacher', 'as a feminist', 'as postcolonial', as
a 'radical academic'. The necessary enterprise that emerges for the postcolonial context through these reflections is of establishing a position of
postcolonial marginality within the literary academy, which can enunciate
itself without falling into universalizing claims:

> The radical academic, *when she is in the academy*, might reckon that names like
> 'Asian' or 'African' (or indeed 'American' or 'British') have histories that are not
> anchored in identities but rather secure them. We cannot exchange as 'truth', in
> the currency of the university, what might be immediate needs for identitarian
> collectivities. This seems particularly necessary in literary criticism today, with its
> vigorous investments in cultural critique. If academic and 'revolutionary' practices
> do not bring each other to productive crisis, the power of the script has clearly
> passed elsewhere. There can be no universalist claims in the human sciences. This
> is most-strikingly obvious in the case of establishing 'marginality' as a subject posi-
> tion in literary and cultural critique. (Spivak 1993, 53)

Intermeshed with caution about making strong universalist claims, and
keeping the provisionality and after-the-factness (the social constructionist
nature) of identity-based political claims in view, is the matter of 'establishing "marginality" as a subject position' for the 'radical academic, when she
is in the academy'. Insofar as Spivak may be seen in this quotation (this
paper as a whole) as doing the latter, insofar as she exemplifies how this
could be done by herself, an equivalence seems to be presented between
who speaks as the radical academic and *what* she says (and, for that matter,
between 'radicalism' and 'marginality'). Alongside explicit avowals of the
social constructionist apprehension of identity and its unstable nature stands
the self-evidence of marginality embodied by the postcolonial radical academic. It is useful, in brief, that Spivak can be and can appear to bear the
marginality that she speaks and questions – she can authorize what she says
because she embodies her identities while being cautious about their appro-
priations. This has been a constant and self-conscious strategy in postcolonial theory and criticism, and has generated heated debates therein. Often,
those postcolonial critics who find it difficult to embody their identities as
marginal accept the radical enunciations from embodied marginal subject
positions in a respectful fashion.

   These moves in postcolonial studies coincided with – or participated in
– the 1970s and 1980s turning of the left towards identity politics in a
social constructionist sense, particularly in Western Europe and the United
States. This turning towards identity politics was as much at the behest of
sociological as of humanities intellectuals, and was evidenced jointly or in
complementary ways in various debates and forums. The embracing of

identity politics as the heart of the left, after 1960s civil liberties and student movements, drew upon the gradual dissolution of the old left. That has to do with the crumbling of centralist communist governments and economics in the European Eastern bloc and the Soviet Union, which was attended with soul-searching both within the left and among liberals (evidenced also in a convergence of thinking between left and liberal ideologies). Post-Marxist Althusserians such as Barry Hindess and Paul Hirst (especially in *Pre-Capitalist Modes of Production*, 1975), and particularly liberals such as Ernesto Laclau and Chantal Mouffe (especially in *Hegemony and Socialist Strategy*, 1985), drew a line from critique of Marxist theory and practice towards the agency of identity-based collectives. Collapse of the Eastern bloc and the Soviet Union was complemented by the systematic undermining of trade unions, and the agency of the working class generally, in the West, leading to intellectual reassessments of the validity of 'class' – especially working class – as a contemporary concept. Sociologists were already exploring the replacement of working class as oppositional political agent by a structure of new social movements (notably in Alain Touraine's *The Voice and the Eye*, 1981, and Jürgen Habermas's 'New Social Movements', 1981). By the 1990s, whether social class was a redundant concept was under discussion by Jan Pakulski and others (*International Sociology* September 1993; Pakulski and Waters 1995; *Theory and Society* 1996). By this time, insofar as left-wing and liberal intellectuals went, there was little to differentiate the political resonance of identity for a sociologist interested in globalization and culture and a postcolonial theorist interested in discourses of power: Stuart Hall's 'new ethnicities' and Homi Bhabha's 'hybridizations', for instance, appear on the same political battleground.

And, of course, postcolonialism's complicity with identity politics reverberates with the literary texts attended to particularly by postcolonial critics – literary voices from postcolonial margins. *Midnight's Children* naturally offered the postcolonial critic plenty of food for thought in its negotiations with multiple levels of identity construction. At least three complex levels are immediately germane. First, there are the author's self-conscious retrospective pronouncements on the migrant perspective from which the novel was written:

writers in my position, exiles or emigrants or expatriates, are haunted by some sense of loss, some urge to reclaim, to look back, even at the risk of being mutated into pillars of salt. [. . . Our] physical alienation from India almost inevitably means that we will not be capable of reclaiming precisely the thing that was lost: that we will, in short, create fictions, not actual cities or villages, but invisible ones, imaginary homelands, Indias of the mind. (Rushdie 1991, 10)

The themes of migrancy and authorship have been constant refrains in Rushdie's subsequent fictional and critical writings and interviews – a matter I return to shortly. Second, imaginary as Rushdie's India is, it has an obvious reference to the nation-state and its demography. This in itself presents considerable challenges for such a novel, challenges which Rushdie embraced with open arms. So, through various devices the novel manages to scan the various communal (in India that generally means religious) sectors, multiple regional and ethnic and caste and class boundaries, and to suggest something of the linguistic plethora that India presents – all per-mutating and combining into bewilderingly prolific and fluid claims of identity and identity-based allegiances *within* India. Third, the novel delib-erately plays with the flickering nature of identity attributions and place-ments, and could be regarded as a prescient fictional enactment of the destabilizing possibilities in Bhabha's postcolonial hybridity. Parentage and bloodlines in the world of *Midnight's Children* – as in reality – have no categorical value whatever: the baby swap that Mary Pereira does with two midnight children emphasizes that. The confusion that ensues is not just a matter of racial and cultural hybridity, but also, as Padma immediately observes on hearing about it, a fracture in the identity-based assumptions of the novel's narrative:

'An Anglo?' Padma exclaims in horror. 'What are you telling me? You are an Anglo-Indian? Your name is not your own?'

'I am Saleem Sinai,' I told her, 'Snotnose, Stainface, Sniffer, Baldy, Piece-of-the-Moon. Whatever do you mean – not my own?'

'All the time,' Padma wails angrily, 'You tricked me. Your mother, you called her; your father, your grandfather, your aunts. [. . .] You are a monster or what?' (Rushdie 1981, 116–17)

In this discussion of the tandem trajectories of postcolonial theory and criticism and of globalization studies, there's another aspect of the former that needs to be registered. Along with, indeed deriving from, postcolo-nialism's incorporation of a new left identity politics, there also developed a kind of self-reflexive political economy of postcolonial studies. This is manifested in occasional, and sometimes vituperative, debates between the different margins of the postcolonial field. To a great extent such debates have revolved around the locations of postcolonial studies and their pro-ponents and the vested interests that come with these locations. The impetus for and the main proponents of postcolonial theory and criticism have appeared predominantly within the Western academy, especially in the United States, and have often been immigrant intellectuals. Postcolonial studies opened up (some would say, defined in a ghettoized fashion) a space for conventionally marginal intellectual and creative voices within the West. Postcolonialism has raised the visibility and influence of authors and intel-lectuals in marginalized locations outside the West too – particularly in former colonies – and has brought their ideas and products into global circulation. It has also invigorated creative and intellectual productivity, and the study of productions, of such marginalized locations *within* those locations, often with a sense of self-discovery and self-affirmation. The result is that postcolonialism often seems like a divided field, pursued with somewhat different perspectives in institutions located within globally dominant contexts and within globally marginalized contexts, within the West/ North and the East/South. The former often emphasize the migrant or diasporic point of view, as providing the link between margin and centre, as being – or at least being the voice of – the margin within the centre, as occupying a particular vantage point for analysing contemporary postcolonial inequities arising from its own displacement. The latter usually focalize the authenticity of the internal point of view, are endowed with the sense of understanding marginalized contexts and their histories from within, and occupy the vantage point of belonging to the post-colony, the East/ South – therefore are more in tune with its everyday life and aspirations. Despite this division, the postcolonial field stretches across both, and postcolonial theory and criticism have broadly similar ideological aspirations. This means that the division is mutually informed, indeed mutually constructed, and releases a careful questioning of the politics of location: i.e. of the economic and material advantages that derive from locations within the West/ North and within the East/South, of the migrant perspective or the internal perspective, of institutionalization within the Western academy or the postcolonial academy. In other words, there ensues a debate which is closely connected to the political economy of location and of located intellectual vested interests – in a way, on the nature of intellectual work itself – and disposes the field of postcolonial theory and criticism accordingly.

To turn intellectual attention on intellectuals as a social stratum or particular kind of class, and placing their expert and ideological discourses accordingly, has been an occasional sociological enterprise. It is exemplified in such focused studies of the sociology of the intellectual by Alvin Gouldner (1979), Regis Debray (1981) and Pierre Bourdieu (1988), and was recommended, as observed above, by Bauman as the way for sociology to come to grips with postmodernism. Debates about postcolonialism addressing the place of postcolonial intellectuals as an object of study have a similar sociological turn, and it is no surprise that the first serious critique of the then developing postcolonial theory and criticism was offered in precisely placing postcolonial intellectuals as a class. The much discussed debate between Fredric Jameson ('Third World literature in the Era of Multinational Capitalism', 1986) and Aijaz Ahmad ('Jameson's Rhetoric of Otherness and the "National Allegory"', 1987) in the journal *Social Text* was essentially a matter of discerning the political economy of location – of noting the slippages that occur between trying to take account of the marginalized (as Third World, as colonial, even as Indian) in an excessively generalized fashion from a metropolitan centre, and examining the particularities (Ahmad's example is drawn from Urdu literature) from within, as it were. By the time Ahmad put together *In Theory* (1992), which includes his critique of Jameson's essay, some of the thrust of his argument rested in a bringing to account (especially migrant) postcolonial intellectuals as a class stratum working towards their vested interests: 'They can now materially represent the undifferentiated colonized Other – more recently and more fashionably, the *post-colonial* Other – without much examining of their own presence in [the Western metropolitan] institution' (Ahmad 1992, 93–4). The debate on the location of intellectuals and claiming a postcolonial perspective has since been taken up continuously and variously, for and against, by, among others, Anne McClintock (1992), Rey Chow (1993), Arif Dirlik (1997), Ania Loomba (1998), Rajeshwari Sunder Rajan (1997), Gayatri Spivak (1999) and Timothy Brennan (2006). And this discussion has been repeatedly marked by debates between those assuming different physical/identitarian/ideological locations as intellectuals and questioning the vested interests that come with these placements. Almost everyone mentioned here, and others, debated the prerogatives of postcolonial identities and locations in the context of the Rushdie affair – following the *fatwa* issued by Ayatollah Khomeini on the publication of *The Satanic Verses* (1988). Gayatri Spivak's *A Critique of Postcolonial Reason* (1999) gave rise to a vociferous debate in the pages of the *London Review of Books*, when Terry Eagleton greeted it with a scathing review:

Gayatri Spivak remarks with some justification in this book that a good deal of US post-colonial theory is 'bogus', but this gesture is de rigueur when it comes to one post-colonial critic writing about the rest. Besides, for a 'Third World' theorist to break this news to her American colleagues is in one sense deeply unwelcome, and in another sense exactly what they want to hear. Nothing is more voguish in guilt-ridden US academia than to point to the inevitable bad faith of one's position. (Eagleton 1999)

Numerous letters were published in the couple of weeks following this review, and Eagleton retaliated by taking to task identity politics in literary studies, especially postcolonial theory and criticism, in *After Theory* (2003). This too involved a placing of intellectuals as a class stratum, reminiscent of Aijaz Ahmad's *In Theory*. When, marking fifty years of Indian independence, Salman Rushdie and Elizabeth West edited *The Vintage Book of Indian Writing, 1947–1997* (1997), all the pieces included, save one, were by expatriate Indian authors writing in English. In reply, Amit Chaudhuri edited *The Picador Book of Modern Indian Literature* (2001), where the majority of writers involved had lived or are living on the subcontinent, and which included in translation some works originally in Indian languages.

Sociologically oriented globalization studies has been less worried by questions of location, by this sort of self-reflexive political economy of location in postcolonialism. It is only occasionally that an objection is raised to the unabashed Eurocentrism of Jürgen Habermas (Ilan Kapoor 2002, is a case in point) or Ulrich Beck – whose universal-sounding pronouncements on 'deliberative democracy' or 'cosmopolitan democracy' seem ultimately to apply to a utopian and exclusive European Union. However, the somewhat tortured self-reflexiveness about location in postcolonialism –

especially where it gives rise to a kind of 'internal' self-questioning – leads to substantially similar realizations and endeavours as in globalization studies. The sensitiveness to location in postcolonialism seems ultimately to do with the perception of an increasingly one-dimensional (to echo Herbert Marcuse's [1964] sense of the grip of advanced capitalism) field which comfortably co-opts everything, outside of which the politically oppositional intellectual seeks to find a foothold and which the politically quiescent intellectual reifies. Just as postmodernists such as Baudrillard, Jameson, Harvey, Lefebvre and others, and globalization theorists such as Anthony Giddens, Ulrich Beck, David Held, Mike Featherstone, Arjun Appadurai, Samir Amin and others, try to characterize in different ways and with different *locus standi* a social field which is gripped ever more by a logic of global capitalism, of global cultural integration and fragmentation, of global information and communication flows, etc. – a knowledge–power field that can't be escaped, can't be stepped away from – so self-reflexiveness in postcolonialism is largely about trying to grasp the workings of an apparently uniformly disposed and all-embracing knowledge–power field. This was evidenced in Said's Orientalism, and in Bhabha's or Spivak's explorations of identity, and this has been clarified by postcolonialism's most querulous and interrogative theorists (critics).

To return to *In Theory*, Ahmad's point here was not so much that postcolonial intellectuals are buying into identity politics in a way that serves their material interests in Western/Northern universities, or so much that such well-heeled persons are in no position to engage what they ostensibly present themselves as – the marginalized. These are the suggestions that irked many at the time. Ahmad's point, however, was principally that this postcolonialism based on discourse analysis and identity politics increasingly symptomatized the entire humanistic field, seemed coeval with poststructuralism and postmodernism and Theory generally in literary studies (for instance), and actuates a comprehensive depoliticization of and misrepresentation within critical engagement while appearing to achieve the opposite. By removing attention from the manner in which global capitalism works and class contradictions operate, the apparently radical postcolonial gesture may well contribute towards the perpetuation of neo-imperialism and Third Worldism. For Ahmad, realistic and politically efficacious humanities call for a Marxist sense of economic materiality and class analysis in engaging a global reality. Much soul-searching about and within postcolonialism since has tried to come to terms with a sense of being caught within an ultimately monological field, of a desire for getting a perspective on and perhaps making a radical gesture *à propos* that field. Almost a decade later, when his *The Postcolonial Exotic* (2001) offered an analysis of the manner in which postcolonial theory and criticism had enabled a commodification of exoticism, Graham Huggan was engaged in a similar perception. Instead of a Marxist class and labour-value analysis, he drew upon a cultural sociological account of capitalism (from Bourdieu and

Harvey), to offer a crucial distinction between 'postcolonialism' and 'post-coloniality' as a mode of discerning the exotic:

Postcolonialism [. . . is] an anti-colonial intellectualism that reads and valorises the signs of social struggle in the faultlines of literary and cultural texts. Postcolonialism, in this sense, obviously shares some of *postmodernism's* relativistic preoccupations – with textual indeterminacy, the crisis of meaning, the questioning of the unitary subject, and so on. Yet it does not, or at least does not aim to, share postmodern-ism's somewhat irresponsible lack of commitment, its self-regarding obsession with play, or its Eurocentric frame of reference. Postcoloniality, on the other hand, is largely a function of *postmodernity*: its own regime of value pertains to a system of symbolic, as well as material, exchange in which even the language of resistance may be manipulated and consumed. Postcoloniality, in its function as a regime of cultural value, is compatible with a worldwide market whose power now 'extends over the whole range of cultural production' (Harvey 1989: 45). (Huggan 2001, 6)

The distinction made between 'postcolonialism' and 'postcoloniality' enables Huggan to maintain a somewhat resistant position within the former, and at the same time to discern in a resistant fashion the pervasiveness of global commodity capitalism and Eurocentrism. It is this small gestural fissure introduced between '-ism' and '-ity' which allows Huggan to perform his analysis of the postcolonial exotic as coincident with capitalism and Euro-centrism. The bringing together of the locational critique of Eurocentrism and the cultural sociological critique of global capitalism, in a way, reveals the similar strategies of postcolonial and globalization theorists.

The move towards a convergence of globalization studies and postcolo-nialism (in literary studies particularly, but also in the humanities at large) is available along various somewhat divergent tracks. In its simplest format, this is presented as the two fields converging along the lines of consequent historical explanations and concurrent but different emphasis with regard to the same concerns. Thus Bill Ashcroft (2001) asserts the following:

What, we may ask, is the place of post-colonial studies in the global phenomenon? [. . .] The answer to this question is twofold: firstly, we cannot understand global-ization without understanding the structure of global power relations which flour-ishes in the twenty-first century as an economic, cultural and political legacy of Western imperialism. Secondly, post-colonial theory, and particularly the example of post-colonial literatures, can provide very clear models for understanding how local communities achieve agency under the pressure of global hegemony. (Ashcroft 2001, 207–8)

This attempt to find accommodation between postcolonial studies (with its literary/humanities emphasis) and globalization studies (with its sociological orientation) accepts that these terms have different disciplinary locations. Ashcroft's position is so embedded *within* postcolonial studies that he would probably be surprised if a globalization theorist argued that the legacy of Western imperialism is not necessarily the only, or even the dominant, axis for understanding globalization processes, or that postcolonial literatures may exemplify a lack of agency as well as an exercise of agency under global hegemony. There might also be some quibbles about simplistically connoting 'globalization' as global hegemony, whereas, as observed in chapter 1, in the many shifts of the term it now also incorporates the opposite of that. But this reductive connotation is standard practice in postcolonial theory and criticism. Perhaps a more self-aware and cautious approach to the matter is involved in attempting to give a postcolonial perspective of globalization studies (roughly as Featherstone attempts to give a globalization studies perspective of postcolonialism). Simon Gikandi takes this path to suggest that: 'the postcolonial perspective on globalization has been the most salient attempt to question older forms of globalization based on the centrality of the nation and theories of modernization' (Gikandi 2001, 636). Gikandi thus announces his postcolonial scholar's position and tries to contain globalization within his perspective. The only problem is that what he understands as globalization – in new or older forms – has only a partial relation to what the term encapsulates now: the manifold processes top-down and bottom-up with which globalization studies concerns itself. Perhaps the most productive sort of convergence between postcolonialism and globalization studies is evidenced where the literary/ humanities scholar seeks to go beyond both. This usually occurs by understanding both as expressive of all-encapsulating and ideologically uneven power–knowledge fields, characterized by (locationally emphasized) Eurocentrism (and socio-politically understood) and neoliberal or cosmopolitan capitalism, which need to be radically opposed or somehow transcended. Such bringing together of postcolonialism and globalization as distinct yet coherent aspects of a common ground, in the grip of which intellectual work is caught, is effectively an aligned process. Their convergence lies in the aspiration of the literary/humanities scholar to go beyond while being informed of both. Revathi Krishnaswamy (2002) has made such a move in an even-handed manner:

while the culturalist turn in critical theory [in both globalization and postcolonial theory] opened up alternative conceptual frameworks for critiquing imperialism and Eurocentrism, the theoretical category of culture appears to have become far too overblown and overdetermined to be politically effective in the age of neoliberal globalization; indeed corporate globalization is thriving precisely by emptying out the subversive potential in culture by incorporating various oppositional to alternative forms of cultural expression across the globe. (Krishnaswamy 2002, 108)

Krishnaswamy is unable to recommend anything other than a need to rethink and repoliticize 'culture' in some way. Influentially, in a similar spirit of placing postcolonial and globalization studies as aspects of a conjoined and encompassing field, and of effectively converging these discourses in a bid to go beyond them, appear formulations from historians. Both Dipesh Chakrabarty and Arif Dirlik have made searching attempts at enunciating a historiography – a mode of narrativizing and practising history – which negotiates a path through globalization and postcolonialism to discover an effective stance against capitalist Eurocentric hegemony (uniting again the locational and socio-economic emphases of the two discourses). Both are concerned primarily with their postcolonial perception of the pervasiveness of Eurocentrism, and see it as coeval with globalization (viewed reductively as top-down). For Chakrabarty this is a matter of 'provincializing Europe', and moving beyond the conventionally practised oppositional analytical history of capitalism (such as Marxist history, which he calls History 1) towards a different sort of History 2, which:

> beckons us to more *affective* narratives of human belonging where life forms, although porous to one another, do not seem exchangeable through a third term of equivalence such as abstract labour. [. . .] Globalization does not mean that History 1, the universal and necessary logic of capital so central to Marx's critique, has been realized. What interrupts and defers capital's self-realization are the various History 2s that always modify History 1 and thus act as our grounds for claiming historical difference. (Chakrabarty 2000, 71)

In a similar vein, Arif Dirlik, who understands globalization as 'founded on the development of assumptions of capitalism' and postcolonialism as 'more of an accommodation with the current structure of power than an apology for it' (Dirlik 1999, 23), recommends a 'radical historiography' which is 'informed by a principled defense of autonomous political positions that question ever-shifting claims to reality, not by denying reality, but by critically evaluating its claims on the past and the present' (ibid., 27).

The latter are rhetorically plausible expressions of a desire to perform an oppositional history, or to delineate a politically effective oppositional historiography. But whether they suggest any practical method for or approach to doing history that is different from those produced as histories of postcolonialism or globalization is a moot point. It seems to me that they do not. The prevailing, and all too monological, consensus (even among such left-wing would-be radicals) on rejecting Marxist economics and class analysis wholesale, or accepting Marxism, against its grain, merely as a salutary discourse construction, oddly renders an Aijaz Ahmad-like or Fredric Jameson-like approach to postmodernism, postcolonialism, globalization more immediately effective. In the prevailing environment the unpopularity of Marxist analysis gives it an edge, which the rather ethereal 'radical' gestures through humanistic discourse in the academy fail to achieve. This 'radicalism' seems rather tame and fussy. But these are useful conceptual steps in the context of this study. Huggan, Krishnaswamy, Dirlik, Chakrabarty, etc., make moves towards a convergence of postcolonialism and globalization studies from *within* the humanities, from *within* literature, by perceiving an all-encompassing field which contains both and by trying to theorize a space outside and beyond both.

6 Academic Institutional Spaces

ENGLISH STUDIES

In the previous chapters I have occasionally mentioned the institutional imperatives which motivate and structure certain moves in the circulation of texts and ideas and critical practices. This chapter is devoted to a closer examination of the academic institutional processes which mediate the relationship between literature and globalization. This is presented in two broad sections focusing, respectively, on the institutional spaces of English studies and comparative literature in the increasingly globalized academy.

My approach to the academic space for English studies, including English literature, is determined by a number of obvious factors. To an extent this is the inevitable result of the language in which the present study is written and therefore the market for which it is primarily intended – an English-reading one, with an interest in literature available in English. That in turn has a relationship, both hopeful and problematic, with the processes under-lying the spread of English as a global language. The global spread of English is a much studied subject. It is widely recognized now that an unprecedented quarter of the world's population, widely dispersed, use the English language, which is acquiring the status of a global lingua franca. Useful models for approaching this spread are in place. Following Braj Kachru (1985), scholars often cite a model of dispersal in concentric circles, with the inner circle occupied by contexts where English is the traditional and primary language (the UK, the United States, Ireland, Canada, Australia, New Zealand), an outer circle – usually including contexts colonized by the inner circle (India, Nigeria, etc.) – where English has become part of key institutions, and an expanded circle where the importance of English is recognized and it is taught in a systematic fashion as a foreign language. Often levels of and norms in acquiring English are cited to model its dispersal in ways that are more fluid than the concentric circles model: native Englishes, British English and American English, Standard English, English as a Second Language (ESL), English as a Foreign Language (EFL) or English for Speakers of Other Languages (ESOL), and, for example, English for Academic Purposes (EAP) and Business English. Through and across these models there run numerous contentious and deeply politicized debates:

where and whether standards should be set, to what extent English is culturally owned or possessed in different locations, the dominations and hierarchies that operate with the spread of English and between different varieties of Englishes, the imperial history behind and commodification of English teaching and the ideological interests vested in that (these are succinctly covered in Pennycook 1994, 1998; Holborow 1999). These debates increasingly register a consonance between considerations attached to the global spread of the English language and the various nuances, contradictory and multilayered as they are, of globalization. These considerations come to grips with both the structural globalizing-embrace of unities, diversities and exclusions in the spread of English, and the geopolitics of globalization that is reflected in that spread. As David Crystal puts it: 'British political imperialism had sent English around the globe, during the nineteenth century, so that it was a language "on which the sun never sets". During the twentieth century, this world presence was maintained and promoted almost single-handedly through the economic supremacy of the new American superpower' (Crystal [1997] 2003, 10).

The status of English now, inflected though it is by the history of colonialism and the partisan geopolitics of globalization, is rather more complex than that selective quotation from Crystal might suggest. It could be argued, for instance, that the ever-growing interdependence of workers in certain specialist knowledge fields – especially the natural sciences and technology – brings an impetus of its own towards a worldwide convergence on English as a specialist language. The thrust of English might have originated in the disparities of colonial history and superpower politics, but the processes that sustain it now have something to do also, to stick to my example, with the internal rationale of how the disciplines of natural science work and how technological innovation and development are effected. It is simply the case that physicists around the world cannot work in isolation any longer, and therefore to a large extent the discipline is consensually and inter-communicatively constructed through the language that happens to have had a head start (say, by dint of concentrating resources in some Anglophone locations to begin with) in its history. Nor are the power relations that derive from colonial history and are arguably perpetuated in (North America-centred) globalization lacking in complexity in the current global uses and movements of English. This is captured well by Peter Hitchcock, who suggests that the spread of English paradoxically comes with a kind of dislocation from Englishness, with a decolonizing tendency, *within* and *as* globalization – and makes three related and relevant points in this regard:

First, what has defamiliarized the Englishness in English has been primarily Anglophone expression. Anglophone expression here means cultural practice that continues the work of decolonization by problematizing new conditions of inclusivity. It does not say that inclusivity is intrinsically wrong but reserves and preserves the right to refuse the terms in which it is being forwarded as long as they suppress the historical determinants that have made the brave new world of globalization possible. Second, the disjunction and difference in Anglophone expression has not only facilitated postcolonial agency of various kinds in a broad sense, but has challenged the institutional logic of English as a discipline by throwing into relief what facilitates its inclusiveness [. . .]. Third, since globalization is primarily economic, the point is not whether English will somehow headline world cultures but whether English as 'the living negative of power' can subtend what globalization wants to be. (Hitchcock 2001, 751)

What Hitchcock gestures towards, in brief, is the notion that English is not a passive linguistic/cultural formation that contains a persistent hegemonic character, and which can be instrumentalized to question and challenge that hegemonic character and thereby reconfigure the inequities in globalization through its global spread.

Literatures in English from different parts of the world have naturally reflected some of the anxieties and expectations found in debates about the spread of the language. However, whereas debates about the spread of English have necessarily reckoned with a global embrace and global geopolitics and political economy, insofar as that has attached to literatures in English the colonial–postcolonial axis and marginalized identities/cultures have inevitably focused attention. So, the politics of English language teaching (ELT) has been examined at all levels of the models mentioned above, whereas literature in English literary studies is held primarily at the politics of the tension between what Kachru thinks of as the inner and outer circles of English. This is a pragmatic focus, both since literary works in the English language have already been produced (and have formerly been neglected) in the outer circle for a considerable period and are relatively rare in the expanding circle, and since the influx of postcolonialism and marginalized writing into English literary studies has focalized, framed and revitalized that production. The rationale of these processes has been discussed already. Differences between the political self-positionings of authors in the outer circle or between the inner and outer circles vis-à-vis English are thus often cited in literary studies, and indeed in the study of the English language now. When Ngũgĩ wa Thiong'o said 'farewell to the English language as a vehicle of my writing, plays and short stories' (Ngũgĩ 1986, xiv) and declared that all his literary writings thereafter would be in Gĩkũyũ – 'I believe that my writing in Gĩkũyũ language, a Kenyan language, an African language, is part and parcel of the anti-imperialist struggles of Kenyan and African peoples' (Ngũgĩ 1986, 28) – it was immediately evident that he was voicing a political position that was widely held across the postcolonial and marginalized regions of the world. But so were the quite different, even contrary, positions taken by other postcolonial writers regarding English. Chinua Achebe, though not entirely unsympathetic to the Ngũgĩ-like position, was more circumspect about English:

Those of us who have inherited the English language may not be in a position to appreciate the value of the inheritance. Or we may go on resenting it because it came as part of a package deal which included many other items of doubtful value and the positive atrocity of racial arrogance and prejudice which may yet set the world on fire. But let us not in rejecting the evil throw out the good with it. (Achebe 1975, 219)

Salman Rushdie was more upbeat about the possibilities of English than Achebe:

As for myself, I don't think it is always necessary to take up the anti-colonial – or is it post-colonial? – cudgels against English. What seems to me to be happening is that those peoples who were once colonized by the language are now rapidly remaking it, domesticating it, becoming more and more relaxed about the way they use it – assisted by the English language's enormous flexibility and size, they are carving out large territories for themselves within its frontiers. (Rushdie 1991, 64)

On the whole, literary studies, within English departments in particularly the inner but also the outer circles of Kachru's model, and with the fissures and multiplicities of postcolonialism and identity politics in view, has tended to take Rushdie's view of the matter. There has been a substantial and hard-fought battle to render institutional practice in the study of English literature – in research, curriculum setting, teaching and learning – inclusive of marginal voices in English, different varieties and contexts of English, the different political anxieties surrounding English, and the exploitation of the reach of English to use it as a target language for translations (I return to the important issue of translations below). On the whole, this effort has been more in tune with a Rushdie-like optimism while being cognisant of the Ngũgĩ-like refusal, and largely in sympathy with the kind of complexity that the quotation from Hitchcock above gestures towards. But this effort has, to repeat, been structured largely around the axis of colonialism–postcolonialism and of marginalized identities/cultures.

The issue here is how the institutional space of English studies has responded to or been influenced by the theories and realities of globalization – in a context where the global spread of English can scarcely be denied even if not approved, and where postcolonialism is firmly ensconced in literary studies generally. Since this entails trying to gauge the discipline-defining space of English studies, we are concerned primarily with universities and research institutes, the tertiary/higher education sector. This focus takes us beyond existing work on the impact of postcolonialism and of the vested interests in ELT upon English studies. Towards the end of his book on the politics of ELT and the 'empire writing back' literatures in English that postcolonial literary studies have tried to embrace, Alastair Pennycook reflects on the possibility of adopting a 'teaching back' practice (Pennycook 1994, ch. 9). The consideration of literature and globalization in the institutional space of English studies in higher education has something to do with an idea of 'teaching back', but conceived beyond coloniality or postcoloniality and specific cultural marginalities – on a scale of global reconfiguration and political awareness.

To designate an institutional space in the academy as distinctively English literary studies is to be rather fussily particular. From its philological origins, English literary studies has more often been contained within a broader English studies or just 'English', incorporating English language, literary and cultural studies. University teaching and research is still disposed in all those terms in different contexts. There is a complicated history of the nomenclature for English/English studies/English literature and language, the ideological nuances of which were covered competently in Brian Doyle's *English and Englishness* (1989). Without going into that specific issue, some broad observations on modes of historicizing the development of the discipline of English studies (as a composite of English language/literature/culture, but with an emphasis on the literary) are of interest here, and lead to speculations about its current status and prospects *à propos* globalization.

D. J. Palmer made a relatively early postwar attempt to historicize the institutional development of the discipline of English. *The Rise of English Studies* (1965) came from what was then the left of the ideological spectrum. His exploration of the working-class affiliations of the discipline's origins in the nineteenth century were no doubt directed against the bourgeois establishment within which it had seemed to be ensconced since the Second World War. Looking back on its institutional history was effectively an act of retrieving an early investment in working-class interests:

However inadequately it was articulated, there was a widespread feeling [in the nineteenth century] that the spiritual and physical conditions of the industrial revolution impoverished the cultural lives of a large class of people, that they had been cut off from their traditional past, and that therefore they needed to be given new means of establishing connections with a national cultural heritage. Thus it was the historical attitude to literature which eventually emerged, and the missionaries of adult education were particularly concerned with the working classes. (Palmer 1965, 39–40)

For Palmer, therefore, English studies emerged as a utilitarian and evangelistic alternative from the elite education in classics and rhetoric, and was firmly associated with an early institutional space in mechanics' institutes and working men's colleges. The subsequent rise of English studies into academia was also a move away from those marginal origins, ending in the stronghold of the academic establishment with the founding of, as far as Palmer went, the Oxford English School. Palmer's sense of the marginal origins of the discipline and subsequent incorporation into the mainstream gave the enterprise of historicizing the institutional space of the discipline itself a certain contemporary political impetus. Talking about the history of the institution of English studies, in other words, could be a way of reconfiguring and reconsidering that institutional space and its practices in the present. In the UK, therefore, the conflict between margin and centre as shadowed in the history of the institution of English studies has been regularly reiterated, with further marginal factors being introduced and analytically located. Thus Chris Baldick's *The Social Mission of English Criticism, 1848–1932* (1983) noted the marginal factors that originally brought the discipline of English studies into institutional being – 'These are first, the specific needs of the British empire expressed in the regulations for admission to the India Civil Service; second, the various movements for adult education including Mechanic's Institutes and Working Men's Colleges, and extension lecturing; third, within this general movement, the special provisions made for women's education' (Baldick 1983, 61) – and then proceeded to examine closely English's institutional embracing of conservative values, through such canonized representatives of 'Englishness' as Arnold, Eliot, Richards and the Leavises. Brian Doyle's *English and Englishness* (1989) offered a more sustained examination of those marginal origins, emphasizing particularly the initial amateur feminine character of the area and the gradual masculinization of the discipline as it became professionalized. John Dixon's *A Schooling in 'English'* (1991) revisited the particularities of English's emergence through extension lectures. Robert Crawford's *Devolving English Literature* (1992) set out to 'force "English" to take account of other cultures which are in part responsible for the initial construction of "English literature" as a subject' (Crawford 1992, 11), and made the case for the Scottish and provincial English invention of English literature and then the Scottish invention of Scottish literature. This mode of accounting the development of the institutional space of English studies also proved particularly amenable to incorporation within postcolonialism and the political aspirations of worldly Theory. Where the context of English studies shifted to an accounting of its development in postcolonial institutional spaces, similar narratives were constituted. So, Gauri Vishwanathan's *Masks of Conquest* (1989) went back to the debate between Orientalist and Anglicist educationists in India to discern the placement of English literature as caught between the contrary logics of colonial assimilation and imperial cultural hegemony. This fed into influential reflections on the place of English in the contemporary Indian academy, notably in Svati Joshi's edited collection *Rethinking English* (1991), Rajeshwari Sunder Rajan's edited collection *The Lie of the Land* (1992), and Harish Trivedi's *Colonial Transactions* (1993). David Johnson's *Shakespeare and South Africa* (1996) charted the development of English studies in South Africa in the nineteenth and twentieth centuries, using the teaching and reception of Shakespeare there to exemplify different phases.

In the United States attempts at presenting the institutional history of English (not American) studies took off with the radical argument in Richard Ohmann's *English in America* (1976): 'The humanities are not an agent, but an instrument. [. . .] There is no sense in pondering the function of literature without relating it to the actual society that uses it, to the centers of power within that society, and to the institutions that mediate between literature and the people' (Ohmann 1976, 303). This involved a critique of the post-Second World War bourgeois culture within which the profession was then described, and which enabled a superficial discourse of freedom to contain the study of English within an elite and carefully depoliticized space. The humanism that was instrumentalized for this manoeuvre was beginning, Ohmann observed, to turn upon the profession itself to discern its politics. Taking some of this argument forward, but disinvesting it from radical outcomes, Gerald Graff's *Professing Literature* (1987) looked to the humanistic tradition in the academic discipline of English (and American) literature as a matter of continuities which are more replicated in the present than radically inverted or subverted. Somewhat belatedly by 1998, Robert Scholes's *The Rise and Fall of English* drew on that history to propose a return 'to the roots of our liberal arts tradition, and reinstate grammar, dialectics and rhetoric at the core of college educa-tion' (Scholes 1998, 120) – a conclusion reached through tortuous earlier considerations of the impact of Theory on English studies, and the need therefore to 'stop "teaching literature" and start "studying texts"' but without accepting political agency or responsibility (Scholes 1985, 16). If the path from Ohmann to Scholes seems to be one of retrogression from progressive to conservative politics, it was not because that was the domi-nant trend, but because each of these steps resists the dominant trends of their times. For Ohmann the radical argument was the oppositional position vis-à-vis the academy; for Graff, and more so for Scholes, the different degrees of conservative arguments were their oppositional positions to a Theory-imbued academia, especially in the parallel and diverging and broader (with area studies-like interdisciplinary aspirations) American studies.

Conservative arguments along the lines of Scholes's made their appear-ance in the UK too. Josephine Guy and Ian Small's *Politics and Value in English Studies* (1993) is a case in point, attempting a defence of the aca-demic discipline and institutional practice of English against Theory-inspired interdisciplinarity and politicization through a historical awareness of English in relation to other academic disciplines. More interestingly, something else apart from radical intending and conservative recuperating had emerged in that line of institutional historicizing of English from Palmer and Ohmann through Baldick, Graff, Doyle, Vishwanathan, Crawford, Scholes and others. What emerged was a sort of territorial imperative, which wasn't simply broadly located in ideological domains of left and right, radical and conservative, but increasingly sieved through narrower ideological domains of ethnicity, geopolitics, gender, race and migrancy. Whereas for Palmer and Ohmann the territorial placements of English were coeval with the expansive lines of class critique and analysis of bourgeois society, for most of the others the historicizing project became a ground of territorial investments and claims from more specific margins and centres. These were assessments of the discipline's history, and therefore its current institutional possibilities, conducted through the standpoints of Western liberalism and a Western humanist tradition, colonial and postcolonial environments, provincial and marginalized peripheries, gendered spaces and exclusions. That the historicizing project of English studies seemed completed in the 1990s doesn't mean that its ideological tendency has dissolved; it means that that project was absorbed into dominant institutional ideologies centred on identity politics and colonialism–postcolonialism. The demonstration of this would have to be a prolonged project, and unnecessary in this context. There are a host of books which chart the travels and travails of the profession of English studies which can be recruited to that project: Patrick Hogan's *The Politics of Interpretation* (1990), Carl Woodring's *Literature* (1990), Harold Fromm's *Academic Capitalism and Literary Value* (1991), Susan Gubar and Jonathan Kamholtz's edited volume *English Inside and Out* (1993), Robert Heilman's *The Professor and the Profession* (1999), Donald Hall's edited volume *Professions* (2001), Jeffrey Williams's edited volume *The Institution of Literature* (2002) and Philip W. Martin's edited *English* (2006) come to mind.

The result of these developments is that the institutional space of English studies is now a diverse and sprawling one. And yet, arguably, the above process has disposed that space in a way which is still unnecessarily limited. If the political reckonings possible through English studies, whether radical or conservative, are to go beyond the colonial–postcolonial divide and marginal identities towards some sort of confrontation with globalization, it is necessary to account for its development, to understand its institutional history, in an even more diverse and sprawling fashion. The institutional space of English studies is arguably already globalized in ways which are yet to be fully registered; it needs to be historicized and accounted accordingly and without self-imposed or politically predetermined limits.

To clarify what I mean by that, further delineation of current approaches to English studies is necessary. This can be done briefly with reference to one of the most ambitious attempts since the late 1990s to contain English studies in all its current aspects within two covers, Rob Pope's *The English Studies Book* ([1998] 2002). This is designed as a complete handbook (Pope's word) for the field, not meant to be read 'straight through from cover to cover', but to be used 'to move from one part to another, and from this text in one hand to another text in front of you, or in your mind's eye'. The 'you' (the reader is addressed thus throughout) is defined as:

primarily a student. You are somewhere between first and final years of a degree or similar programme [. . .]. Your programme probably involves a fair amount of English Literature (including Literature in English) and at least some work in English Language. There may also be some dimensions of Communication and

Composition of Cultural and Media Studies to what you do. You may be spending most or all your time in a department called 'English'. However, you may also
be studying English as part of a joint, combined, major-minor or modular programme. (Pope [1998] 2002, 1)

The 'you' also includes teachers or lecturers in English, Pope clarifies. In
other words, this volume is to be used mainly as a reference book which
covers all aspects of what a comprehensive institutional programme in
English studies may contain. It doesn't present a sustained argument or
point of view, but rather the sprawl of English studies in all its diversity.
What gives the book its coherence is not how it holds its many concerns
together but the institutional arrangements which have already brought
these concerns together: the manner in which an ideally inclusive institutional space of English studies may be disposed.

English studies is thus a diverse and multidirectional sprawl of a body,
but nevertheless it is already disposed as a disciplinary corpus, predefined
by its institutional status in higher education. One is not encouraged to
look around it, to wonder where the specific institution in question con-
cretely is, how it is particularly arranged in terms of programmes, what sort
of specific students are part of it, etc. The institutional body of English
studies thus presented, however, is not without its implicit locations and
geopolitically cognate predispositions – these have to be inferred from what
is presented. There are a couple of relevant observations possible here. First,
the discipline's content is understood predominantly in terms of sites of
production: where and when the different phases and varieties of the language originated and the authors/texts/other media products that represent
the literature/culture appeared. Thus, an account of Englishness underlying
English studies is centred, and interrogations and divergences are presented
accordingly. The centres (predominantly Britain, latterly the United States,
and even more recently certain post-colonies) and the margins within
(minorities) and without (mainly the post-colony) are all arraigned in that
order – in the chapters on language variation, literary and cultural production, theory and criticism – as the singular and obvious disposition. That
is how the order of the discipline will be received, it is clear here, wherever English studies is pursued. There is a central site of production which
is clearly accounted in history and in the history of the discipline and
maintained in a consensual fashion in the institutional practice of English
studies everywhere, and there is a constellation of departures from that into
other media, into language variation and their cultural productions, into
the productions of diasporas and postcolonial contexts. The axis of colonialism–postcolonialism provides the keystone of this structure. Second, English
studies is predominantly conceived within and presented as engaged within
an Anglophone institutional context. Students, teachers and their departments would, in other words, engage the discipline solely in English and
with an Anglophone-dominant socio-political consciousness. This might

seem to be an obvious and necessary assumption for a discipline that goes by the title of English studies. The 'Anthology of Sample Texts' – 'short texts and extracts for discussion, analysis and other activities' representing a 'wide variety of Englishes [. . .], past and present, "literary" and "non-literary", spoken, written and otherwise recorded' (Pope [1998] 2002, 281) – presents something like an expanded and of-our-time shadow canon for contemporary English studies. Interestingly, this consists of the following three translations from another language (among ninety-seven extracts): Native American Seminole chants (by way of exemplifying minority 'singing culture' in an Anglophone North American dominant culture), three versions of a *haiku* by Basho (exemplifying translation into English as a target language) and self-translation from the Hungarian by UK-based poet George Gömöri (exemplifying a minority phenomenon within the Anglophone dominant culture, and again into English as a target language). These, in a way, characterize the pervasiveness of the Anglophoneness amidst which institutional English studies is located, finding a small-scale reach to the limits of Anglophoneness in considering minority languages which exist within the Anglophone dominant or in the practice of translation into English as a target language.

Under conditions where the spread of English is not simply predominantly from Kachru's inner to outer circle, but also across the expanding circle (Crystal thinks it should be called the 'expanded circle' now; Crystal [1997] 2003, 60) – or where English is gradually acquiring the status of a global language and is central to processes of globalization – and moreover given the global ubiquity of the pursuit of English studies in tertiary or higher education, a reorientation of how English studies is thought about and practised is called for. The disposition of the discipline as exemplified in Pope's *The English Studies Book*, structured around the colonial–postcolonial axis and the Anglophone dominant, is arguably already incompatible with the global practice of the discipline. The conceptualizing, theorizing and reorienting of the discipline that is called for is, at present, a project of the imminent future – there is little at present (2009) in this direction. But the rationale and inevitability of this project, and the consequent accommodation of English studies with a globalized perspective, can already be outlined.

There are several factors which need to be foregrounded in this project. First, as an academic discipline English studies has considerable histories in ordinarily non-Anglophone contexts, often not much shorter than those in ordinarily Anglophone contexts such as Britain and the United States, or former British colonies such as India, South Africa, Nigeria, Singapore, etc. This history has been only sporadically charted. Balz Engler and Renate Haas's *European English Studies: Contributions towards the History of a Discipline* (2000), for instance, covers some of the ground with a European focus – in Portugal, Spain, Italy, France, the Netherlands, Norway, Denmark, Germany Austria, Poland, the Czech Republic, Slovakia, Slovenia, Serbia, Romania and Bulgaria. There are extended histories of the discipline of English studies in non-Anglophone contexts outside Europe – in Japan, China, Turkey, etc. – which are yet to be systematically explored (though moves in that direction have been initiated in some cases, e.g. for China in Bob Adamson's *China's English*, 2004). Such chartings as there are of this area, such as that of Engler and Haas, track the history of the discipline against the norm of its growth from philology pertaining to Britain and the United States, but also register within its institutional shifts local political and socio-cultural interests at work. And they chart an interlingual edge to the history of English studies in those contexts: a primary consideration in all contexts, for instance, is why certain English writers/texts were translated at particular times, or how certain contexts have been portrayed in English literature. Second, English studies is spreading as an academic discipline irrespective of institutional tradition. When David Crystal wrote *English as a Global Language* he was struck by the fact that: 'In 1996 [. . .] English replaced French as the chief foreign language in schools in Algeria (a former French colony)' (Crystal [1997] 2003, 5). Perhaps more striking is the development of English studies in higher education within a relatively short time in neighbouring Morocco, with a similar Maghrebi Islamic heritage and an educated ordinarily Arabophone/Francophone population. Though the discipline was introduced in universities recently (first in 1959–60 in Mohamed V University in Rabat), it is now one of the highest recruiting in the humanities (with 'Arabic' and 'Islamic studies/philosophy and society', and considerably higher than 'French') – with often more than a thousand students registered on English programmes, and departments with more staff than in most British universities. Morocco is by no means exceptional in this respect. Third, in most contexts outside the Anglophone inner circle and postcolonial institutions modelled accordingly, English studies is constructed through programmes which bring together language, literature and cultural studies as a composite discipline. Though applied English-language teaching courses are available (e.g. for translating and interpreting, for business purposes), by and large programmes deliver English language/linguistics and literature/culture in a composite fashion. It is relatively rare now for English-language teaching to be delivered without any grounding in English literary and cultural texts, and generally all are seen as aspects of a broad discipline of English studies. Fourth, in many contexts the adoption and growth of the discipline within higher education is connected – at the level of social perception and of policy – with processes of globalization that are expedient in the local context. For instance, it appeared that university English studies programmes in India were in crisis in the 1980s, with falling student recruitment, growing unpopularity and little injection of resources. It seems to be widely evidenced that more students are applying for English studies programmes towards the end of the first decade of the twenty-first century than can be accommodated, and that the discipline has hit upon an unprecedented growth phase in India. The usual explanation for this is positive social perceptions of the usefulness of English, its currently enhanced value as cultural capital, given the success of Indian ventures into business process outsourcing (BPO). The media coverage of the success of Indian call centres (as a focalized aspect of BPO) has been enormous. The quantities of foreign-exchange inflow, the affluence of English speakers who are able to use new technologies to provide everyday services in the United States and the UK and elsewhere, the technology transfers and innovations that have taken place, the manner in which they are trained and acclimatized to local cultures and everyday life within the UK and the United States despite living abroad, the economic and political mileage of the phenomenon, etc., have been prodigiously discussed in the media. That may account for a general higher estimate of the discipline of English studies in all its dimensions, and is perhaps a key factor in fuelling growth of the discipline in India. Similarly, in Morocco, English studies has come into the spotlight in the same period because of the higher education reforms that were proposed. The declared aim of the reform, launched in the academic year 2003–4, was to make higher education relevant to economic development and to bring Moroccan universities in line with Europe's university system in compliance with the EU–Morocco Association.

Most importantly, those observations on the current practice of English studies at a global level are best understood by *not* regarding the discipline as composed of a body of (however diverse and sprawling) knowledge that is centred on sites of linguistic/literary/cultural production, but contemplating it as centrally a site of receptions. How the *content* of English studies is characterized is far less important than how that content, whatever that may be at any point in time, is *received* and *modified* in various global contexts. The structure and disposition of the discipline is not inherent to or emanant from its content, such as it is, but derives from its receptive contexts. Theorizing this systematically would entail a dislocation both from the dominant notions of Englishness and coloniality–postcoloniality, and from the single-minded subsuming of the discipline within institutional Anglophoneness (from the English language itself, in a paradoxical way). This may well entail the most radical renovation that the discipline has encountered, and give it an impetus that will question institutional structures at the level of both local academies and global alignments. Such a reorientation in understanding the discipline would have to take into account several considerations beyond the factors foregrounded above. English studies, in teaching and learning as well as in scholarly productions, is likely to become primarily an interlingual site. A student of English studies in China, for instance, is often likely to have an initial sense of a canonical text in Chinese. The process of thinking about English language and literature for such a student, even when they are sufficiently competent in the language, is likely to be sieved through a constant process of translations. As it happens a great deal of English literature is delivered in

Chinese higher education, along with literatures in other foreign languages in Chinese translations. In the classroom where the course is delivered, the teacher is likely to be most effective if they are able to make the course seem relevant to immediate Chinese realities and everyday life, and refer to these. As for the student, the researcher working in an area of English studies would find their engagement constantly interpellated by the every-day life and environment in China where they work – if they don't resort to the pointless subterfuge of concealing this but self-consciously instru-mentalize it in their efforts. The archives and research resources that are available to them are grounded in the local, and they would find it expe-dient to bring those within the precincts of the professional space of English studies. Even if the canon of English literature in English studies pro-grammes in China is constructed according to norms prevalent in a British or North American context, the mechanics of the canon are likely to be read differently in the Chinese context. Much will depend on what seems relevant or might be extrapolated there, what has been or hasn't been translated and discussed there already, how the texts in question have been received in that context historically and why, how China and the Chinese have been depicted in those texts, if at all, what sorts of political and socio-cultural relations prevail within China and in the international realm, etc. It may be expected, further, that the acceptance of British or North American normativeness will come to be questioned as a more receptive view of the discipline is taken. English studies will become a site where the local perspective can be foregrounded by frames of reference provided by the discipline, and local perspectives will be structured and globalized as much by reference to as at the expense of those frames. It is already the case, for instance, that cultural studies courses in English studies pro-grammes in Morocco are sites which are used to examine immediate Moroccan realities and cultural trends. By the global spread of English and its growing ubiquity in higher education on a global scale, English studies could become that institutional academic space that is used as a stepping stone to engage local concerns and bring them to global forums at the expense of English studies itself, by the defeat of the discipline as constituted now.

What all that implies is that the current notion of English studies as a diverse body of knowledge structured and disposed out there, so to speak – as in Rob Pope's guidebook – is already increasingly becoming unten-able. English studies is now, and will only more emphatically come to be, *constructed* variously at various locations. Englishness is already not a unitary concept even within Britain; its constructions and ideological placements are constantly proliferating. And Americanness even more so. One way of thinking about this might be to regard Englishness and Americanness as a plethora of cultural imaginaries which have little to do with how English-ness or Americanness is imagined within Britain or the United States, but which make perfect sense in their particular contexts. Such cultural imaginaries may provide a grid that is ultimately dedicated to make Englishness or Americanness – and indeed the corollary axis of colonial–postcolonial – unimportant and irrelevant in English studies. In practice, the academic space of English studies could liberate itself entirely from any sense of possession by Anglophoneness or dominant geopolitical spaces or national histories; as receptive institutional spaces they are possessed and repossessed and dispossessed wherever they are found. Ultimately this would mean that an enterprise of writing a handbook for English studies with a view to embracing the discipline as a whole within two covers would become pointless: such an enterprise itself is a centralist claim that belies the spread of English and the growing global pervasiveness of the institutional space of English studies.

Whether such a globalized prospect for the discipline of English studies is matter for enthusiasm or dismay is not a question that I go into here. The potential for such a prospect is relevant for this study.

COMPARATIVE LITERATURE/WORLD LITERATURE

It may be justifiably felt that the English in English studies nevertheless inflects the possible global futures of literary studies in that institutional space in a partisan and ideologically weighted direction. In fact there is an interesting moment in Rob Pope's book where he considers the following:

One response to the globalization of English is to drop the 'English' altogether and substitute for it the adjective 'Literary'. This has the effect of at once broadening *and* narrowing the subject matter [. . .]. As usual, there are pluses and minuses all round. The international reach of the course can be attractive (there is an especial grandeur in courses billed as 'World literature'); but this may be at the expense of a firm grasp of any specific national or regional tradition. (Pope [1998] 2002, 43)

In a way, the kind of future envisaged above is somewhere in between the two poles Pope considers – between English studies as he describes it and literary (world literature) studies in general – and circumvents the anxiety about losing 'a firm grasp of any specific national or regional tradition' by envisaging a firm grasp of many 'specific national or regional traditions' working through and in English studies. Current contemplation of world literature in fact does not derive from English studies as Pope suggests, but is largely aligned with a somewhat different institutional space that is germane to literary studies – schools and departments of comparative literature. The manner in which notions of world literature have been reinvigorated in and since the 1990s, primarily in connection with the institutional space of comparative literature, has a necessarily close relation to the association between literature and globalization. This presents a somewhat distinctive institutional track or history when compared with English studies for the present study. In this track one finds negotiations on how literary traditions should be described and institutionally engaged, gradually moving away from conventional organization along national or regional lines towards a more joined-up international or global view.

René Wellek's well-known presentation at the Second Congress of the International Comparative Literature Association (ICLA) in 1958, 'The Crisis of Comparative Literature', was a reflection on the double-bind of the discipline at the time. On the one hand, it had found institutional form in the post–Second World War context 'as a reaction against narrow nationalism' (Wellek 1959, 153). On the other hand, Wellek felt its basis was and should remain comparison of 'national literatures'. The problem was, and this is why he perceived a crisis, that the basis of comparison in national terms allowed narrow nationalisms to reinsert themselves in insidious methodological ways. The method of constantly locating literary texts as subsidiary to (as the effects of) national contexts and social conditions was leading, in Wellek's view, to the emergence of 'a strange system of cultural book-keeping, a desire to accumulate credits for one's nation by proving as many influences as possible on other nations, or more subtly, by proving that my nation has assimilated and "understood" a foreign master more fully than any other' (ibid., 155). The remedy Wellek recommended for this crisis was not to throw the national basis of comparison out of the window, but to cultivate a distinctive understanding of literature as a medium which inevitably and necessarily enables a humanistic apprehension of 'ideal universality', so that: 'Man, Universal man, man everywhere and at any time, in all his variety, emerges and literary scholarship ceases to be an antiquarian pastime, a calculus of national credits and debts and even a mapping of networks of relationships' (ibid., 159). In brief, he recommended sticking with the national basis in the *comparative* of '*comparative* literature', and asserting an approach to the *literature* of 'comparative *literature*' that is predeterminedly universalist and doesn't allow the national basis to turn into nationalism. This was the position he consistently maintained in later reflections on the theme, in his responses to criticisms of this paper in 1965 at the meeting of the American Comparative Literature Association (ACLA) and in his essay 'The Name and Nature of Comparative Literature' (Wellek 1970). He didn't feel that the national basis of comparison should be meddled with by such distracting conceptualizations as that of world literature, or that the distinctive universalist vision of literature should be questioned.

Wellek's understanding of literature was akin to both the humanist liberal convictions and the New Critical methodological attention to close reading which were popular at the time in Anglo-American critical circles. The most significant shift in the understanding of literature that took place from the mid-1960s through the 1980s was, as discussed in chapter 4 above, the advent of Theory. The impact of Theory in the conceptualization of comparative literature as a discipline wasn't particularly profound in the 1970s. Robert Clements's survey of the academic field of comparative literature in 1978 essentially stuck with national literatures as the basis, but registered the impact of Wellek's warning and of the emerging Theory in the five substantive approaches that it identified for the discipline: 'the study of (1) themes/myths, (2) genre/forms, (3) movements/eras, (4) interrelations of literature with other arts and disciplines, and (5) the involvement of literature as illustrative of evolving literary theory and criticism. The reading of literature must be in the original language' (Clements 1978, 36). Not insignificantly, points (1) to (3) diverted attention away from territorial imperatives without undermining them, in line with the balance recommended by Wellek; and (5), perhaps to some extent (4), seemed to recognize that literary theory and criticism are now separate from critical engagement with literature in the conventional fashion. This was pretty much in line with the ACLA Greene report of 1975 (Bernheimer 1995a, 28–38) on the state of the discipline.

In the course of the 1980s, as also observed in chapter 4, several important developments took place: Theory became institutionalized in literary studies, and disposed literature as a field of political awareness and agency, especially along the lines of identity politics and cultural materialism. This reconfiguration of literary studies naturally had its effect on the discipline of comparative literature, which had to move away from some of the Wellek-like assumptions, away from the national basis of comparison in tandem with a universalist vision of literature. This effect was registered in various ways from the later 1980s to the mid-1990s. One kind of response was to emphasize the formalist or thematic basis of comparison in a more provisional and open fashion than theretofore, and without making it conditional on national or cultural bases. This was exemplified in Earl Miner's *Comparative Poetics* (1990), which assumed a suitably tentative 'practical principle' of comparison as follows:

> The practical principle holds that comparison is feasible when presumptively or formally identical topics, conditions, or elements are identified. Of course what is presumptively but not actually identical soon betrays difference. With tact and luck, however, we may find the difference just great enough to provide interest, and the presumed identity just strong enough to keep the comparison just. (Miner 1990, 22)

This formed the basis of the study of particular Western and Eastern (primarily Japanese in this instance) texts, implicitly presented as a particularly revealing exercise of this method because of the perceived extent of cultural difference. An East–West comparison had since the 1960s occasionally been seen as a sticky patch in comparative literature, which puts particular pressures on Eurocentric comparative practices and works above the conventional national basis of the discipline. With 1980s literary and political preoccupations in mind, it was ploughed as particularly fertile ground in Euro-American comparative literature, but the harvest was limited. This was because of practical reasons: the kind of linguistic competence required limited the field, especially given the emphasis on working with original languages rather than translations to which the discipline had traditionally adhered. But the possibilities of East–West as a comparative basis was attractive, not least because this seemed a suitable field in view of the worldly Theory-informed political aspirations that literary studies now had, and especially with the growing importance of identity politics and postcolonialism. This led to some rethinking about the status of translations in the discipline. A. Owen Aldridge, for instance, put up a spirited defence for the use of translations in the field of East–West comparative literature in *The Reemergence of World Literature* (1986). Aldridge's book is of interest in other ways too – it recommended a move away from comparative literature to 'universal literature' or world literature, which would thereafter increasingly be regarded with favour. The need to respond to the political impetus of Theory took other directions too in thinking about the discipline in the early to mid-1990s. Wlad Godzich's essay 'Emergent Literature and Comparative Literature' put in a clear call to align comparative literature with larger political and literary critical conceptual directions: 'I would like to put forward the following claim: the "field" of Comparative Literature is field. In other words, I take it that, within the prevalent organization of knowledge, it is incumbent upon comparatists to inquire into the relationship of culture to givenness, to its other' (Godzich 1994, 284). For Godzich this meant greater attention to what he called 'emergent literature', defined fairly neutrally as 'literatures that cannot be readily comprehended within the hegemonic view of literature that has been dominant within the discipline' (ibid., 291). More circumspectly, but with not dissimilar intentions, came Charles Bernheimer's 1993 report to the ACLA, with disciplinary recommendations to expand comparative literature curricula to include 'ideological, cultural and institutional contexts as well as close analysis of rhetorical, prosodic and other formal features'; to mitigate 'old hostilities to translation' while accepting that 'knowledge of foreign languages remains fundamental'; and to play an 'active role in multicultural recontextualization of Anglo-American and European perspectives' (Bernheimer 1993, 42–6). Bernheimer's own misgivings, and those of other notable comparatists (such as Peter Brooks), about this direction are documented in the discussion of this report that he edited shortly afterwards (Bernheimer 1995a) – as was the anxiety about comparative literature remaining institutionally valid and discrete as a discipline.

The anxiety about institutional validity came with good reason. The institutional adjustments arising from the political thrust of Theory led to the creation of sub-disciplinary spaces akin to literary studies and absorbing some of the energies of literary studies which took over and reoriented some of the key markers of comparative literature. In the course of the 1980s and 1990s cultural studies began working across ethnic, linguistic and geopolitical boundaries not only with sociological methodologies, but also with close attention to texts (particularly mass media and new media texts) and with a particular awareness of the impact of Theory on literary studies. One of the responses to the Bernheimer report was Rey Chow's paper 'In the Name of Comparative Literature', which found little to distinguish the ambitions of comparative literature as set out in the report from cultural studies as it was already being conducted, and suggested that: 'Instead of simply resisting or discrediting cultural studies [. . .] comparative literature could borrow from cultural studies by way of opening itself to the study of media other than word-based literature' (Chow 1995, 115). Steven Tötösy de Zepetnek's edited volume *Comparative Literature and Comparative Cultural Studies* (2003a) presented several papers trying to give content to a rapprochement between cultural studies and comparative literature, notably in the editor's own contribution, which recommended a merged field of 'comparative cultural studies' and laid out the substantive principles for it (Zepetnek 2003b, 259–62). Perhaps more than cultural studies however, the prerogatives of comparative literature began slipping into sub-disciplinary spaces *within* the literary studies that were previously devoted to the study of canonical literatures, particularly English and American literature. These were, in keeping with the politics of Theory, now primarily identity-centred spaces, aligned with postcolonial studies, black studies, women's studies, gay studies, and so on. It was difficult to see how accepting Bernheimer's recommendations could alleviate the anxieties of disciplinary recognizability or distinctiveness for comparative literature. It was rightly observed that the political possibilities of comparing literatures had shifted from nation bases (the need to interrogate national politics while at some level accepting national boundaries) to identity bases (the need to interrogate identity politics while at some level accepting identity-based differences), and that somehow this shift has taken place outside the disciplinary ken of comparative literature. Identity politics was regarded as the threat and challenge to the integrity of comparative literature for comparatists. Bernheimer himself expressed this anxiety most succinctly:

Identity politics are particularly anxiogenic for the comparatist who ventures beyond the European arena or gets involved with ethnic cultures at home. No matter how many years you may have given to the study of a culture, if it is not yours 'in the blood', it will always be possible for you to be found lacking in some quality of authenticity. The more literatures you try to compare, the more like a colonizing imperialist you may seem. If you stress what these literatures have in common – thematically, morally, politically – you may be accused of imposing a universalist model that suppresses particular differences so as to foster the old humanistic dream of man's worldwide similarity to man. If, on the other hand, you stress differences, then the basis of comparison becomes problematic, and your respect for the uniqueness of particular cultural formations may suggest the impossibility of any meaningful relationship between cultures. (Bernheimer 1995b, 9)

Bernheimer expressed a paradox of which all were aware.

A response to these anxieties about the disciplinary place of comparative literature began emerging from within the discipline in the late 1990s. This consists primarily in rethinking and reworking the idea of world literature, drawing upon and away from the *Weltliteratur* of Goethe (in a letter to Johann Peter Eckermann in January 1827) and Erich Auerbach (for a discussion of these, see Hoesel-Uhlig 2004 and Birus 2003) or Tagore's understanding of world literature (see Tagore 2001, ch. 17). Aldridge, in *The Reemergence of World literature* (1986), had already revived the idea in the context of East–West comparative literature. Actually the potential of the idea had been gestured towards and along similar lines in R. K. Dasgupta's presentation in 1967 at the Fifth Congress of the ICLA, comparing Goethe and Tagore, and giving world literature a threefold definition: '(1) the sum total of all literatures of the world, or (2) works in the different literatures of the world which have attained world recognition, or (3) the different literatures of the world conceived as one literature' (Dasgupta 1969, 399). But in European and American academia the promise of that gesture was quickly lost in a Wellek-like dismissal of the concept. Aldridge's reiteration of world literature or, rather, 'universal literature', defined as 'the sum total of all texts and works throughout the world', was given as separate from comparative literature, which was understood as 'the study of any literary phenomenon from the perspective of more than one national literature or in conjunction with another intellectual discipline or even several' (Aldridge 1986, 56). Aldridge expected the practice of the latter to be enhanced by the conceptual possibilities in the former, especially insofar as remote, and therefore pressured, comparison is at stake – as in an East–West embrace. By and large, up to this point world literature had been regarded as more an idealistic than a functional concept, useful for considering literature in an abstract way rather than for the institutional practice of literary studies.

The idealistic thrust of world literature, from Goethe to Aldridge, has, however, been pushed towards a more pragmatic and real-world turn, and the consequent process of reconceptualization is still underway. Inevitably this entails, as the phrase 'world literature' suggests, a cautious calling up of universalist political thinking to offset and question the emphasis on differences and fissures in postmodernism and postcolonialism. The impetus of a conditional universalism is expressed thoughtfully in Gayatri Spivak's consideration of comparative literature in *Death of a Discipline* (2003). This tries to mediate the 'radical' political agenda of Theory in comparative literature both by maintaining the particular importance of taking 'the languages of the Southern Hemisphere as active cultural media rather than as objects of study by the sanctioned ignorance of the metropolitan migrant' against the hegemony of 'global English' (Spivak 2003, 9), and by maintaining a presumptive conceptual horizon that recognizes collectivity: 'the collectivity that is presumed to be the condition and effect of humanism is the human family itself' (ibid., 27). However, Spivak's cautious gesture towards the universal horizon of the 'human family' is left as the idealistic anterior of the discipline, an idea that is always *before* the critic, a question rather than an answer that makes the comparative enterprise provisional itself, a formulation that always 'begs the question'. Spivak's idea for a new comparative literature therefore doesn't have much to do with world literature as a distinctive mode of institutional practice, and recommends instead some sort of mutually beneficial alignment with the disciplinary spaces of area studies. She sees this as akin in an abstract way to what she calls a 'planetary' perspective (by way of eschewing such ideologically loaded terms as 'universal' or 'global' or 'worldly'), where 'planetary [is regarded as an] undivided "natural" space rather than differentiated political space' (ibid., 72).

Rather more institutionally friendly thought, in the sense of making it amenable to curriculum-building and pedagogy and scholarship, is given to the idea of world literature by Pascale Casanova in *The World Republic of Letters* ([1999] 2004), in essays by Franco Moretti in the *New Left Review* in 2000 and 2003, and by David Damrosch in *What is World Literature?* (2003). Casanova produces a theory of international literature based on competition between different national literatures, with each fighting for control over 'literary time'. This involves a curious doubletake. On the one hand, it suggestively outlines a theory of world literature as a sort of autonomous 'republic' in itself, following a literary logic and sense of time and space irrespective of geopolitical boundaries and conflicts:

> What is apt to seem most foreign to a work of literature, to its construction, its form, and its aesthetic singularity, is in reality what generates the text itself, what permits its individual character to stand out. It is the global configuration, or composition, of the carpet – that is, the domain of letters, the totality of what I call world literary space – that alone is capable of giving meaning and coherence to the very form of individual texts. [. . .] In this broader perspective, then, literary frontiers come into view that are independent of political boundaries, dividing up a world that is secret and yet perceptible by all (especially its most dispossessed members); territories whose sole value and sole source is literature, ordered by power relations that nevertheless govern the form of the texts that are written in and that circulate throughout these lands; a world that has its own capital, its own provinces and borders, in which languages become instruments of power. (Casanova [1999] 2004, 3)

On the other hand, however, it later turns out that this space is mapped out by Casanova according to the emergence and politics of nation-states in Europe after the sixteenth century, through the medium of national languages. This is a move that defeats the suggestive assertion quoted above, and moreover in practice takes the whole concept in a peculiarly Eurocentric direction. Casanova's appears retrospectively as precisely the kind of conservative position that Spivak struggles to oppose with her abstract 'planetary' perspective in *Death of a Discipline*. Nevertheless, the conceptual suggestiveness of Casanova's global 'Republic of Letters', of world literature in those terms, does lead into more politically nuanced and methodologically plausible and institutionally realizable ideas of world literature.

Franco Moretti's provocative essay 'Conjectures on World Literature' (2000) makes several proposals of a practical sort that are of interest here. Assuming a world-systems perspective of literature, Moretti contemplates the scholarly pursuit of world literature as occurring at a meta-theoretical level of 'distant reading' – where the conventions of close reading and attention to particular literary texts are dispensed with in favour of discerning patterns and regularities/irregularities in scholarship which has read, interpreted and assimilated literary texts in different languages and traditions already. According to Moretti, to understand literary history in terms of a world-system rather than a national or linguistic tradition means that:

it will become 'second hand': a patchwork of other people's research, *without a single direct textual reading*. Still ambitious, and actually even more so than before (world literature!); but the ambition is now directly proportional *to the distance from the text*: the more ambitious the project, the greater must the distance be. (Moretti 2000, 57)

After pondering the somewhat sanctified status that close reading and the integrity of the literary text has held and continues to hold in literary studies, Moretti goes on to clarify what the relation of literary texts to such distanced reading in world literature might be:

Distant reading: where distance, let me repeat it, *is the condition of knowledge*: it allows you to focus on units that are much smaller or much larger than the text: devices, themes, tropes – or genres and systems. And if, between the very small and the very large, the text itself disappears, well, it is one of those cases when one can justifiably say, Less is more. If we want to understand the system in its entirety, we must accept to lose something. (Moretti 2000, 57)

This is a pre-eminently practical suggestion, even if somewhat shocking given the conventions of a literary education that prevail everywhere. It is possible to envisage its adoption within the institutional practice of a world literature course, perhaps at a third-year undergraduate or a postgraduate level, where students will already have experience of both analytical literary reading and engagement with literary scholarship. Similarly practical suggestions, but from a quite different direction, appear in David Damrosch's *What is World Literature?* (2003). Here, instead of, like Moretti, beginning with an adjustment to the modes of critically engaging a problematic and broad-ranging concept such as world literature (the totality of all literature), Damrosch begins by defining the concept so as to delimit it and render it manageable (but without losing its global scope):

I take world literature to encompass all literary works that circulate beyond their culture of origin, either in translation or in their original language. [. . .] a work only has an *effective* life as world literature whenever, and wherever, it is actively present within a literary system beyond that of the original culture. (Damrosch 2003, 4)

Or, as he puts it otherwise: 'My claim is that world literature is not an infinite, ungraspable canon of works but rather a mode of circulation and of reading' (ibid., 5). This mode of defining and delimiting the field of world literature has implications for the manner in which literary studies would be practised or engaged, but those are consequent on the definition. These implications for practice may be inferred from Damrosch's threefold definition of world literature, focused in his conclusion on 'the world, the text, and the reader':

1.   World literature is an elliptical refraction of national literatures.
2.   World literature is writing that gains in translation.
3.   World literature is not a set canon of texts but a mode of reading: a form of detached engagements with worlds beyond our own time and place. (Damrosch 2003, 281)

The pragmatic edge of Damrosch's approach, and its possible usefulness for institutional purposes, is self-evident. Damrosch has himself made moves towards the institutional entrenchment of his version of world literature by taking the first necessary steps – setting the parameters of a course by putting together an anthology, and delineating pedagogic practices for the field. He edited the *Longman Anthology of World Literature* (2004) and wrote a companion volume for it, *Teaching World Literature* (2005).

These moves towards harnessing world literature within institutional practice, as an offshoot from or reorientation of the institutional space of comparative literature, and perhaps even as a component of English studies, are not without their problems. The contradictions within Casanova's views I have noted already. It remains unclear whether Moretti's world literature through distanced reading is, in practice, realizable in a meaningful way given the unevenness of available primary scholarship in terms of close reading and different national/linguistic traditions, or whether such removed reading wouldn't be at such a remove from literary texts and their specific contexts that various distortions will be introduced in studies of world literature. Damrosch's 'culture of origin' which texts of world literature cross out of or from is conceivably open to doubt. Where and how a text originates may be thought of as neither determinate nor attributable (cultural influences that feed into a text's productions and receptions are seldom homologous). Nevertheless, what seems to be emerging is an idea of the institutional practice of literary studies which is increasingly described not by linguistic or national norms but in terms of an extensive field of literature which is, at least conceptually, all-encompassing. The point of the emerging institutional practice is not to try to contain everything that such a field might consist in, but to engage with literature and literary criticism and theory in such a way that the normativeness of linguistic and national traditions is undermined and the horizons of the extensive field of literature in the world are within view. In effect this is a matter of grasping the processes of this field of literature in the world, rather than focusing simply on the content and the categories thereof. Texts and contexts are, in this view, not given in fixed relationships of locations, chronologies and categories. Rather texts move, and the world of and around texts is composed of a multiplicity (both as numbers in each level and as variety of levels) of boundaries which are constantly traversed, and which shift into and overlap and differentiate themselves from each other in a dynamic processive and contingent fashion. Literature thus traverses environmental/physical geographical boundaries; political and administrative boundaries, including nation-state boundaries; demographically defined boundaries; economic boundaries; cultural and social boundaries of various sorts, including linguistic, class, religious, ethnic, etc., boundaries; historically recognized boundaries – and all those also in a constant flux. Even if this flux and extent is conveyed by symptomatic practice within an institutional space of world literature, if it can be brought to consciousness and consistently held on to in literary engagement and criticism, the literary academy would be substantially transformed. Arguably such an institutional space would bring globalization firmly *within* literature and literary studies. Conceiving and dealing with the extensive field of world literature disposed according to the multiplicity and flux of boundaries is, in fact, precisely the exercise which occupies engagement with globalization from various disciplinary standpoints. Globalization, with its many connotations and nuances – from above and below, pro- and anti-, as homogenizing or fracturing, as mediating or subsuming the local, as working through difference and hybridities and commonalities across culture and identity, etc. – is manifested precisely in terms of the multiplicity and flux of boundaries around which world literature may be organized for institutional delivery and consumption.

The potential globalization of literary studies in the form of world literature in the academy is not merely a matter of the responsiveness of literature and literary studies to the world at large, but also of the manner in which globalization processes impinge upon all institutions, including the academic. In an essay entitled 'The Impact of Globalization and the New Media on the Notion of World Literature' (2004), Ernest Grabovsky noted several such extrinsic factors impinging upon institutional academic activity. These included international regulation of copyright and intellectual property, the international markets that academic institutions tap into and buy from, the manner in which socio-political and economic structures everywhere are becoming globally linked, the consolidation of publishing and media, the digitization of knowledge and the democratization of cyberspace. Some of these factors I have touched on above, and some are outside the remit of the present study. But the broad observation is worth keeping in view: if there are gestures and motions towards a globalization of literary studies in its institutional formations, that is as much because of pressures from within the discipline as due to pressures on the academy itself. The latter will be picked up to some extent in the next and final chapter.

A NOTE ON TRANSLATION

The two prospects for an institutional development of literary studies discussed in this chapter – through English studies and through comparative/world literature – approach and contend with globalization from distinct directions. For English studies this is a matter of orienting itself as a receptive field which has already expanded through the global spread of the English language to become a global institutional space, in a manner which may come to defeat its still subsuming placement within Anglophone exchange and centred Englishness and Americanness and coloniality/postcoloniality (mutually comprehended, of course). For the move from comparative to world literature, this entails adopting institutionally viable and pragmatic (pedagogic and scholarly) practices which would enable a global field, with a fluid and dynamic mode of negotiating it and conceiving the boundaries within it, to be brought to and retained consistently in literary critical engagement. Perhaps a globalization of literature and literary studies in institutional practice would lie somewhere in a conjunction of these directions. The scope for combining notions from both directions is considerable.

In these two prospects the single most important issue is undoubtedly the role that translation will play, not only transparently within the interstices of conveying texts across boundaries and in the academy in different parts of the world but also opaquely as an issue in itself. Translation is not just to do with transmitting texts and communicating across languages, but is a constitutive part of social, political and economic existence. In both prospects this is the issue that is likely to cause (indeed, has already caused) the greatest unease and instantiate the most vehement debates. The prospect of conceiving a globalized English studies that decentres and even leads towards the defeat of its location within Anglophoneness is one of shifting institutional prerogatives and vested interests in ways which will be resisted. That English studies is already an institutional area which absorbs literary works in other languages with the assumption of itself as a normative target language has been variously observed. Lawrence Venuti remarks, for instance, that in pedagogy in English and American studies there is often perceived: 'on the one hand, an utter dependence on translated texts in curriculum and research; on the other hand, a general tendency, both in teaching and publications, to elide the status of translated texts as translated, to treat them as texts originally written in the translating language' (Venuti 1998, 89). The prospect is of having that situation reversed within the institutional practice of English studies. The institutional practice of comparative literature, especially in the European and American models, has worked with the pragmatics of comparing literary works of different national traditions in their *original* languages. Attempts to foreground translation as a constitutive element in comparative analysis are often viewed with scepticism. Corngold, for instance, asserts with some determination that:

Doing comparative literature means studying works written in different languages without the benefit of translation. It means not reading to translate, on the claimed strength of being able to translate. So what we project as the specific competence of the comparatist is his or her ability to put in immediate relation things conjured by the words in different languages. (Corngold 2005, 141)

In moving towards a reorientation of comparative literature – in the direction of world literature – it is urged that, under conditions of global inequity and concentration of resources and ideological influence in Europe and America, Corngold's kind of principles have made the discipline narrowly Eurocentric. That is precisely where Spivak's call to make 'the languages of the Southern Hemisphere as active cultural media rather than as objects of study by the sanctioned ignorance of the metropolitan migrant' (Spivak 2003, 9) hits home. It is also plausibly argued against the Corngold-like view that comparing literary works in different languages, even with native competence in those languages, involves translation. Translation is not merely the practical activity of rewriting, but that which mediates the relationship between different languages and impinges upon social and political relations between those language constituencies. In fact, outside the Eurocentric fold, comparative literature has for a considerable period been institutionally and professionally practised already without a strong original-language requirement – in China and Japan, for instance. It allows for a broader reach towards literature at large, arguably in the direction of world literature.

In contemplating the two prospects, therefore, the issue of translation will appear at the forefront, and will constantly need to be addressed. The question that arises is: with what methodological emphasis will that be done? As literary studies becomes globalized within the academy alongside the pressures of globalization impinging upon the academy (in the ways envisaged above and in the next chapter), in what ways could translation be negotiated and understood?

Translation has been fairly prodigiously discussed, particularly within the fold of literary studies, since the 1980s. Susan Bassnett's and André Lefevere's works have to a large measure been instrumental in bringing it within the institutional space of literary studies – through textbooks such as Bassnett's *Translation Studies* (1980) and Lefevere's *Translating Literature* (1992). These were written with a sense of breaking new ground in literary studies and rescuing translators from ill-deserved negligence. Apart from widening the contexts of translation beyond the simplistic notion of transmission between languages, these also led to a considerable production of academic scholarship demonstrating that translation studies cohere closely with the worldly desires of Theory. In particular, the manner in which the inequities of colonial/postcolonial and identity-based power and domination are exercised through translation, emphatically through literary translation, has received considerable attention (e.g. Venuti 1995; Sherry 1996; Venuti 1998; Bassnett and Trivedi 1999; Tymoczko 1999;

Tymoczko and Gentzler 2002). Insofar as the relationship between translation and globalization goes, it has been recognized variously that there is a close complicity. Following the colonial–postcolonial axis and identity politics that configures so much of the institutional practice of literary studies, Venuti reads globalization as a term denoting the uneven political and economic relations between what he calls 'hegemonic countries' (such as the United States and Britain) and 'developing countries' (Asian, African, South American), and considers that 'translation is uniquely revealing of the asymmetries that have structured international affairs for centuries', and especially now (Venuti 1998, 158). However, in his view translation also opens up an anti-hegemonic and anti-globalization direction, and turns attention to the manner in which the colonial–postcolonial situation uses translation to release hybridities, transgress hegemonic values, and redirect indigenous traditions and refashion identities (ibid., 178). But this rather reductive understanding of globalization, which serves to centre coloniality–postcoloniality as the organizing principle of the political thrust of literary studies, is not quite consistent with the connotations that the term has acquired. To repeat, in chapter 1 and in this study generally, I have suggested that globalization has accrued within itself both top-down and bottom-up moves, both pro- and anti- nuances, both cohesive and fragmentary possibilities. In this broader sense, and without losing sight of the hegemony that is clearly evident in prevailing global geopolitical arrangements, perhaps Michael Cronin's understanding of *globalization as translation* is more to the point – especially the observation that 'there is no single model of globalization which is adopted willy-nilly by different nation-states but that each country or community *translates* elements of the global and informational economy into local circumstances' (Cronin 2003, 34; my emphasis). This mode of viewing the matter contains both sides of the political agency of translation as Venuti presents them, and is more consistent with the variegated connotations that globalization now evokes.

There is another related point to consider before drawing this chapter to a close. As the matter stands now, translation studies within the institutional practice of literary studies is heavily grounded on the political ideas and structuring principles which govern the latter. If the kinds of prospects for literary studies envisaged above begin to be realized, it is worth pondering whether translation would or could continue to be conceptualized as at present. That is, as the globalization in literary studies and the relationship between globalization and literature grow closer, and as the convergence between sociological and literary perceptions of globalization observed in the previous chapter unfolds, would the recently acquired place of translation in the literary academy have to be renegotiated? I suspect this might be a matter of broadening the scope of translation within the literary academy as being more than a literary matter. In fact some mutterings about the wisdom of sticking to *literary* translation as a discrete field (that is, as separate from other areas of translation, such as commercial translation, translation is everyday communication, interpreting in political forums, translations on the media, scientific and technical translation, etc.) have already been aired. Consider the two following quotations, for instance, taking apparently contrary views on the issue and giving reasons for doing so. The first is from Maria Tymoczko's *Translation in a Postcolonial Context*:

Within translation studies voices have sometimes been raised calling for the field to move beyond literary translation [. . .] But descriptive studies of translations of literary texts will still often offer the best, most comprehensive evidence about cultural interface, for a number of reasons. First, the record of translating literary texts frequently preserves the best evidence for an analysis of the cultural relations between two groups, based on the methods of translation studies: most types of non-literary texts are translated more sporadically and more locally than are impor tant literary texts. Second, literary texts typically have greater cultural complexity and cultural involvement than other types of texts, reflecting not just poetics but values, cultural patterns, and cultural structures as well; frequently the cultural picture is also a dialogic one, so that a literary text holds a record of cultural tensions and difference. (Tymoczko, 1999, 30)

The second quotation is from Cronin's *Translation and Globalization*:

any attempt to discuss translation and its role in human society and culture must take into account the essential relation between *technē* and cultural development. For this reason, conventional moves to separate literary from non-literary (predominantly scientific, technical and commercial) translation have a number of unfortunate consequences. First, the exosomatic dimension to human development is ignored and there is a tendency to privilege more idealist accounts of human engagement with language and culture. Second, the role of tools in the practice of literary and religious translation down through the centuries is either marginalized or wholly disregarded. Third, the tendency to view tools almost exclusively in the domain of new technology leads to predominantly descriptive readings of their use (what they do) and a subsequent neglect of the wider implications of their presence in the world of translation (what they represent). (Cronin 2003, 28)

Despite appearances, these appear to me to be not so much contrary views as a progressive opening up of the contemplation of translation in a similar direction. The reasons Tymoczko gives for sticking with a focus on literary translation are not invalidated by Cronin's reason for a broader view, or *vice versa*. Cronin's points are additional to Tymoczko's, and could well enrich what she points to as advantages in focusing on the literary while retaining the distinctiveness of literary from other kinds of translation. In other words, what looking at these arguments side by side suggests is that literary translation needs to be placed in relation to other kinds of translation, both to extend its scope and depth of analysis and to maintain its distinctiveness as addressed to the literary. Insofar as Cronin's points are indeed particularly relevant to globalization processes, the globalized prospects envisaged above for institutional literary studies would probably necessarily have to attend to a larger and more synthetic understanding of literary translation.

7 The Globalization of Literature

DYING AUTHORS

Roland Barthes's famous declaration in 1968 of the 'death of the author' was effectively a postmodernist apprehension of texts as sites of writing, or rather of 'multiple writings, drawn from many cultures and entering into mutual relations of dialogue, parody, contestation' (Barthes 1977, 148). In dismissing the notion of the author as originator of texts, whose intentions can be discerned and who can guide interpretations, he was effectively asserting the centrality of writing (a process of instrumentalizing language to a functional end) and the importance of reading (in his view, that which gives texts coherence). Despite the resonance of this declaration with developments in late twentieth-century literary theory, and Barthes's own sense of having hit upon a 'modern' realization, the idea has a generally applicable and acontextual air about it. Though Barthes framed the 'death of the author' as a declaration that had only recently become possible, the idea of writing and reading that he foregrounded instead could be understood as implicit in all texts of all times and everywhere – implicit in the nature of textuality itself. Barthes's 'death of the author' was therefore an indicative critical moment, but didn't have a significant impact on the continuing production and reception of literary texts as products of authors, as authored. As a functional or explanatory construct, as a subject in whom intellectual property is vested, as an implicit biographical subject or historical reference point, the author remains critically salient for literary texts – as Sean Burke (1992) and Karl Miller (1989), for instance, have observed.

There is a somewhat different kind of 'death of the author' pondered in the late twentieth and early twenty-first century which is of more importance in this study of literature and globalization. This is not so much a critical gesture as a kind of literary self-awareness which is squarely grounded in its millennial context. It appears most potently in the delineation of literary authorship *within* literary texts, in the portrayal of fictional authors *within* fiction.

Let's consider a few more or less random but indicative instances – some passages, some plots – where such fictional authors figure. To begin with, a passage from Don DeLillo's *Mao II* (1991), in which the reclusive novel-ist Bill Gray is the main protagonist. In the passage of interest here, Bill is persuaded by a photographer, Brita, who specializes in capturing images of authors, to make himself available for a photography session. As Brita pro-ceeds with her craft they engage in conversation, and Bill offers the fol-lowing bitter observations on the contemporary situation of novelists:

'There's a curious knot that binds novelists and terrorists. In the West we become famous effigies as our books lose the power to shape and influence. Do you ask your writers how they feel about this? Years ago I used to think it was possible for a novelist to alter the inner life of the culture. Now bomb-makers and gunmen have taken that territory. They make raids on human consciousness. What writers used to do before we were all incorporated.'
    'Keep going. I like your anger.'
    'But you know all this. This is why you travel a million miles photographing writers. Because we're giving way to terror, to news of terror, to tape recorders and cameras, to radios, to bombs stashed in radios. News of disaster is the only narrative people need. The darker the news, the grander the narrative. News is the last addiction before – what? I don't know. But you're smart to trap us in your camera before we disappear.' (DeLillo 1991, 41–2)

The bitterness of these observations could be explained in terms of Bill's frustration with his current efforts, the novel he has been working on for a prolonged period but without success. When he expresses this frustration to Brita he also expresses an ideal of authorship, a unity of author and writing and language, which is noteworthy:

Every sentence has a truth waiting at the end of it and the writer learns how to know it when he finally gets there. On one level this truth is the swing of the sentence, the beat and poise, but down deeper it's the integrity of the writer as he matches with the language. I've always seen myself in sentences. [. . .] I've worked the sentences of this book long and hard but not long and hard enough because I no longer see myself in the language. (DeLillo 1991, 48)

Interestingly, Bill doesn't think of his current failure to achieve the autho-rial unity he seeks as a personal one, but as arising from the contemporary condition of authors, as consequent on their impotent place in the world. Eventually, he abandons his work in progress and goes to Lebanon in a bid to join a publicity effort to rescue an abducted Swiss poet from ter-rorists, and quietly dies there. Without pausing on this passage at the moment, but also without losing sight of it, other fictional authors come to mind in this context. Gilbert Adair's novels in the early 1990s inter-rogated ideas of authorship through the portrayal of fictional authors in suggestive ways. His *Love and Death on Long Island* (1990) is about a London-based novelist, Giles, who mistakenly walks into a showing of a film entitled *Hotpants College II* and finds himself curiously attracted to a young actor in it, Ronnie Benstock. This attraction quickly develops into an obsession which Giles pursues by voraciously consuming teenybopper magazines featuring Benstock, and eventually leads to his travelling to Long Island to meet the unwary Benstock in the flesh, with predictably tragic consequences. This plot obviously alludes to an earlier fictional author, Gustave von Aschenbach, in Thomas Mann's *Death in Venice* ([1912] 1932), and comparison is invited in the unfolding of Adair's novel. Whereas Aschenbach represented an earlier *fin de siècle* intellectual Zeitgeist in his austere pursuit of his vocation, and is a literary icon of his times, Giles – though as austere in his way – is a rather marginalized figure, recognized as an unfashionably and rather preciously classical writer of the more recent *fin de siècle*. Aschenbach finds the object of his desire in a decaying cholera-ridden old world Venice, as an aesthetic-erotic personification of his desires, within touching distance. Adair's protagonist finds the object of his desires first within his conservative London life, not in the flesh but improbably shadowed in media images from the 'new world', in what is for him the tasteless products of teenage consumer culture. Where Aschenbach's high-minded intellectualism is overtaken by repressed desires in a way that is visibly reflected in the environs of Venice, Giles finds that the defeat of his classical pose by his secret desires is all too readily catered for in images but is entirely out of character with the reality of Benstock in the middle-class suburban Long Island. Death is the meeting ground between Aschenbach and Giles. Again moving on to another instance without losing sight of the above, Orhan Pamuk's *Snow* ([2002] 2004) presents the adventures of the minor poet Ka when he visits the Turkish town of Kars to write a journalistic report on cases of young women who had committed suicide in protest against a ban by the secular Ataturkian state on wearing head-scarves. In the politically charged atmosphere of Kars, Ka witnesses an Islamist assassination, finds himself snowbound and cut off from the rest of the world, becomes involved in a short-lived coup by a revolutionary socialist theatre troupe, falls in love, and later escapes from Turkey to settle in Germany, where he is himself eventually assassinated. Somehow, during his hectic stay in Kars, Ka unexpectedly discovers his poetic faculty, and writes a series of poems with the kind of inspired authorial unity that DeLillo described through Bill Gray. Ka's first attempt at poetry in Kars appears as follows:

Because he'd never before written a poem like this – in one flash of inspiration, without a single pause – there was a corner of his mind that doubted its worth. But as line followed line, it seemed to him that the poem was perfect in every way, and this made his joyful heart beat faster still. So he carried on writing, hardly even pausing, leaving spaces only here and there for the words he had not quite heard, until he had written thirty-four lines.
    [. . .]
    Much later, when he thought about how he'd written this poem, he had a vision of a snowflake. This snowflake, he decided, was his life writ small; the poem that had unlocked the meaning of his life he now saw sitting at its centre. (Pamuk [2002] 2004, 89)

The irony is that Ka's inspired poems never see the light of day. They are lost. They are described in prosaic detail in the novel but cannot be reproduced. The missing poems thus convey a yearning for texts of perfect self-expression, and render the narrator's desire actually to read poems expressive of such authorial unity seem natural. The loss of the poems, however, is not simply an unfortunate accident. It is presented as symbolic of a social apathy towards poetry and a widespread absorption in the superficial and sensational. When the narrator approaches the audiences of some of Ka's poetry readings in the hope of recovering some of the lost lines, he finds:

> Most of those who attended these literary evenings had been present for Ka's poetry reading, but it was clear that most had come to see him for political reasons or simply by chance. They could tell me little about his poems, in marked contrast to their detailed recollections of the charcoal-coloured coat he had never taken off, his pale complexion, his unkempt hair and his nervous mannerisms. However, though they were uninterested in Ka's life and work, they were quick to take an interest in his death. I heard quite a few conspiracy theories: he'd been assassinated by the Islamists, MIT, the Armenians, German skinheads, the Kurds, Turkish nationalists. (Pamuk [2002] 2004, 386)

As final as the death of the man is his death as an author here, despite his own perception of having achieved poetic self-realization.

Different as these portrayals of fictional authors are, they all seem to subscribe to a similar anxiety about authorship and sense of the impotence or irrelevance of the author. In these (and there are other similar accounts) it is not so much that the idea of the author is in doubt or is being undermined, as it is in Barthes's 'death of the author'; on the contrary, the notion of authorship as a process of self-realization, as a unity of authorial intention and language, as a quest for an ideal of literary expression, is consistently maintained. The possibility of authorial achievement forms a palpable horizon against which the defeat of the author, another sort of death of the author, is discerned. This sort of death of the author has to do with a social condition where authors and their texts and audiences are dissociated from each other, where authors find themselves dissociated from their works, where authors are misrecognized or simply not recognized in their works, where authorial aspirations simply cannot be realized through their works because literature is itself dissociated from the world. The slippages between authors and literature and world, from this perspective, derive from the contemporary Zeitgeist – the late twentieth- and early twenty-first-century socio-cultural ethos. In all three cited instances the relationship between author and work and reader is interfered with by the pervasiveness of audiovisually-centred media, and the immediacy with which global realities circulate through these. Each fictional author, in a way, fails in his ability to come to grips with the contemporary world and to communicate with it because his vocation is in competition with other kinds of producers and products which are more successful. Those other kinds of producers and products, media producers and their primarily audio-visual products, simply reconstitute the social sense of the world, and mould consumer expectations, in a way that authors and their literary products are unable to work against or alongside – which defeats and ultimately co-opts these authors and their works, and effectively kills them. So Bill finds that the very quest of the author for literary expression is interfered with by the immediacy of audiovisual media and the sensationalism of news – 'we're giving way to terror, to news of terror, to tape recorders and cameras, to radios, to bombs stashed in radios' – so that not only is literature itself rendered ineffective, disenchantment grips writing itself. If the surge of Aschenbach's forbidden desires in Venice was a sort of culmination of his literary aesthetic sensibility, a concretization of a desired object that renders his art redundant, Giles's forbidden desires are actually never really concretized, and his literary vocation loses out not to a real object of desire but to a simulation thereof. In other words, Giles's literary sensibility, out of synch with the contemporary world to begin with, is really defeated by a trite and adolescent media-driven sensibility. The reality of Benstock in Long Island is not, Giles discovers, in tune with the object of desire that Giles finds in teenage flicks and teenybopper magazines. Ka is able to hit a pitch of perfect poetic self-expression only when he is cut off in Kars from the wider world and immersed in a discrete microcosm where ideologies and personalities meld into each other and the newsworthy political world becomes immediate and tangible. Once that temporary condition ceases to obtain, Ka's poems simply miss their mark and fail to make any impression on audiences who are absorbed by the visual surfaces and sensational conspiracies that they have grown accustomed to consuming.

All three fictional authors in question here end up dead. They die *as* authors as much as persons. The classicist Giles in Adair's novel was a marginal reclusive presence even in the world of letters; by the end of the novel he is wiped clean away. Bill Gray's and Ka's fates are similar in DeLillo's and Pamuk's novels respectively. Bill Gray is, however, aware of being a 'famous effigy in the West', someone whose image has a price in the media world. And Ka leaves behind a hint of himself as an actor in a sensational story, an image of a person faintly etched in the minds of those who saw him. What's left of them is what can be co-opted into the news and media world, the audiovisually-centred consuming consciousness, which defeats and erases them as authors. The anxiety of authorship that these fictional authors express, or that is expressed through these fictional authors, and the kind of literary 'death of the author' that is performed in these fictions, has something to do with the place of literature in the late twentieth- and early twenty-first-century socio-cultural *marketplace*. I choose the word 'marketplace' here advisedly. The defeat of the author described above is redolent with the oppression of a particular historically contingent consuming culture, with modes of production and selling and buying of culture, with the kind of consciousness that is both moulded and catered for by cultural industries, in late twentieth-century global capitalism. Fictionally here the ideals of literature and authorship give way to the thrust of cultural technologies and commodifications that marks the theory and practice of late twentieth-century globalization. Not irrelevantly, the death of authors in the above occurs literally across boundaries, away from the confines and comforts of 'home' – the American Bill dies in Lebanon, the British Giles in the United States, and the Turkish Ka in Germany.

It might appear that the pessimistic prognosis for literature and authorship under late twentieth- and early twenty-first-century conditions in the above novels is conditional on their own market locations. These are all novels that are likely to be found in a particular slot of publishers' catalogues and bookshop shelves, and are likely to be reviewed and purchased and placed on curricula accordingly: they are all books that would be regarded as 'serious fiction', 'literary fiction' or 'quality fiction'. As such, they belong to that category of literature which may have the most currency in terms of cultural capital – in terms of cultural reputation and status – but are usually relatively modestly placed by other significant measures of literary markets (the most significant measures for markets in general): the breadth of their reach in the market and the profits they generate for corporations marketing them. Within the literary field the fiction with a wider market reach and ability to generate larger profits is usually denoted as 'mass-market fiction', 'popular fiction' or 'trade fiction', and is often categorized variously in a somewhat derogatory manner as inexpensive and disposable ('mass-market paperbacks', 'dime novels', 'pulp fiction'), in terms of their sensationalism and easy readability ('potboilers', 'page-turners', 'railway/airport novels'), or in terms of popular genres with specific target readers ('thrillers', 'detective stories', 'romance novels', 'comics' and 'graphic novels', 'chick lit', 'science fiction' and 'fantasy', 'children's fiction', etc.). As Feather succinctly puts it in his survey of publishing in the twenty-first century:

Literary fiction is understood to be more complex and have a more serious purpose. It may even be a commercial success, but the author and the publisher are also seeking critical acclaim, through reviews (especially in certain newspapers) and through the enhancement of the author's reputation. Popular fiction, sometimes called *trade fiction*, on the other hand, is aimed at a mass market, and seeks no such acclaim. It aspires to amuse and to entertain, and to make a profit. (Feather 2003, 61)

Though some of the latter fiction genres have attained a degree of academic respectability with the advent of Theory and the cultural turn in literary studies, there is still often a certain stuffiness attached to perceptions of the more popular and easily marketable end of literary production. Behind that lies the fairly recent notion – not much in advance of the twentieth century – that literary and artistic pursuits should be indifferent to commercial prospects and adhere to aesthetic and normative values which are disinterested and self-contained, and should be subjected to literary critical attention accordingly. That in turn has a relation to the professionalization of literary criticism, since the academic professions traditionally justified themselves as developing knowledge for social benefit and in terms of the integrity of its internal rationale. Perhaps more pertinently, this is rooted in the class biases of literacy, pedagogy and cultural production, so that literature has conventionally been constructed as an elite field which eschews 'low culture', the 'popular' or the 'common' and the 'lowbrow' and literary criticism as the stronghold of the elite who define the 'canon', 'high culture', what is worthy of being 'literature' itself. Both the professional critic's claim and the elitist undertone in disparaging mass-market literature is clearly discernible in such early literary critical approaches to them as those of Q. D. Leavis (1932) and F. R. Leavis (1930). Arguably the kind of fictional deaths of authors picked up above, subtly expressive as they are of anxiety about the defeat of literature in the late twentieth-century cultural marketplace, derive from the tacit elitism and the ingrained conservatism which coincides with the place of 'serious' or 'quality' or 'literary' fiction.

Plausible as this argument sounds, the dissociations and slippages observed through the fictional authors above are occasionally available in definitively mass-market fiction too. No literary work has more mass-market credibility, at a global level, in the first decade of the twenty-first century than the seven 'children's fantasy' novels in J. K. Rowling's Harry Potter series (1997–2007). At the time of writing (December 2007), books in the series have reportedly sold over 400 million copies worldwide, have been translated into over sixty languages, have been turned into films which have each been extraordinary box office hits, have been used successfully for the benefit of the toy and computer game industries, have been subjected to the most sustained and congratulatory mass-media exposure ever, have turned the fortunes of several firms associated with Harry Potter products (starting with the publisher Bloomsbury), and have helped make its author one of the richest and most celebrated in the world. So prodigious has the commercial success and popular reception of the Harry Potter series been that it seems scarcely explicable through the texts – where literary criticism is still most comfortable – and appears more as a kind of socio-politico-economic *phenomenon*. In fact serious analytical attention to the series began with attention to the 'Harry Potter phenomenon' as well as to the Harry Potter texts (Zipes 2000; Blake 2002; Whited 2002; Gupta 2003; Heilman 2003). Arguably, literary studies may overcome its ingrained elitism (as it increasingly aspires to do) by approaching literature as consisting both of texts in the world and of commodified material objects – as commercial phenomena – in the world. Or, in other words, the democratization of literary studies may happen by bringing the market aspects of literature within the analytical equations of literary studies. This is still the preserve of a minority within relatively marginalized fields such as book and publishing history and bibliography.

But I am straying from the point, which was that in such exemplary mass-market fiction as the Harry Potter books a sort of fictional 'death of the author', a sense of dissociations and slippages between authors and texts and readers, is also available. This appears, for instance, in the second book in the series, *Harry Potter and the Chamber of Secrets* (1998). Here the character Gilderoy Lockhart is introduced – a celebrated wizard author, hero of his own books, firmly in the public eye and widely adored and revered. The twist is that this *author* Gilderoy Lockhart who is in the public eye is a carefully constructed and unreal author-hero, and bears no relation to the *person* and *writer* Gilderoy Lockhart, who is neither an author, it turns out, nor a hero, because his stories are stolen and the deeds his books describe are enacted by others. And there is a kind of inevitability in this mismatch. When it comes to the final confrontation and he is forced to face up to his fraudulent practices, he shifts the blame from himself. 'Books can be misleading', he points out to Harry and Ron; and explains:

My books won't have sold half as well if people didn't think *I'd* done all those things. No one wants to read about some ugly Armenian warlock, even if he did save a village from werewolves. He'd look dreadful on the front cover. No dress sense at all. And the witch who banished the Bandon Banshee had a hare lip. I mean, come on . . . (Rowling 1998, 220)

The author that is marketable, in other words, is a pure surface, an image, a fictional construct to fulfil existing market demands and consumer tastes, which the book industry could capitalize on and the mass media could play to.

Rowling's is an exaggerated representation of the perception that the contemporary idea of the author, insofar as it is available in the public consciousness, is a kind of industrial construct brought together through publicity and mass-media frames, and bears little relation to either the real writer or the texts that that writer produces. The dissociation of the public perception of the producer – that which gives celebrity or makes a celebrity – from the real producer and the content of products, the manufacture of celebrity in the marketplace for marketing reasons, is a familiar observation about late twentieth-century culture (e.g. Marshall 1997). That this holds for literary celebrity is argued in Loren Glass's study of celebrity American writers in the late nineteenth and twentieth century. This maintains that modernist literary celebrity was cultivated through much of the twentieth century by authors themselves, by a self-presentation of their subjective (and often resistant) location in the world, usually mediated by a carefully constructed 'hypermasculinity', but that this mode of achieving literary celebrity ceased to obtain in the late twentieth century: 'Celebrity obviously persists, and certainly some authors are famous, but the specific articulation of the private authorial genius versus the mass marketplace is no longer possible in a society no longer based on the opposition between art and commerce' (Glass 2004, 27).

Rowling's fictionalized 'death of the author' has obvious affinities with those of DeLillo and Adair and Pamuk, but is more squarely focused on the mechanics of the market. It does share with the latter authors' fictions, however, a more abstract sense of the dissociation of authors and texts and readers, a sense of a mendacious instability and slipperiness in the processes that link these. In *The Chamber of Secrets* also appears T. M. Riddle's diary – a book, too, and the site of the ultimate violation of innocence, where authors become readers and readers authors, where authors and readers meet and change places while the text shifts ceaselessly. Through it the unscrupulous author and reader Tom Marvolo Riddle (incarnation of the evil Voldemort) exploits both the integrity of the author ('It took a very long time for stupid little Ginny to stop trusting her diary' [Rowling 1998, 229]) and the credulity of the reader ('I wrote back, I was sympathetic, I was kind. Ginny simply *loved* me' [ibid., 228]) for nefarious self-serving ends. The commercial consciousness which underlies the Harry Potter phenomenon, and is arguably available too within the Harry Potter books in various ways (for a more complete treatment, see Gupta 2003, especially ch. 18; Brown 2002a and 2002b), is evidently not incommensurate with the kind of fictional 'death of the author' in question here. What these together draw attention to is the growing importance of literary markets in the literary sensibility, in the pursuit of literature, and increasingly in the pursuit of literary studies in the late twentieth century. In fact, the most significant aspect of the relationship between literature and globalization probably rests in the marketplace – in that intersection of consumption and production where globalization most immediately finds meaning and impetus. A few brief observations on this draw this study to a close.

LITERARY INDUSTRIES

A discussion of the globalization of the publishing industry and exploitation of global markets in relation to literature and literary studies is obviously an enormous subject, regarding which only a few symptomatic observations are possible here. The following points are presented in a spirit of gesturing towards a field that is still in the process of opening up as far as literary studies is concerned.

The most prolifically discussed development in the publishing industry in the late twentieth century has been the process of its globalization, that is, from being a stronghold of a large number of independent and largely nationally based firms to becoming dominated by a limited number of multinational corporations. The process is summarized by John Feather as follows:

Since about 1950, there has been an almost continuous process of takeovers and mergers in the American publishing industry. Where historic names survived, they often did so only as parts of larger organizations. This was the driver of significant cultural change within the industry in the United States itself, but was also a significant factor in the growing internationalization of publishing throughout the world. [. . .] The creation of conglomerate publishing industries, however, was only one aspect of a multi-faceted process. These companies were competing with each other on a global scale. A traditional understanding that British and American publishers divided the world market in English language books between them collapsed in 1976 under the threat of legal action in the United States. [. . .] Since the early 1980s, therefore, the vast global market for books in English has seen intensive competition between British and American publishers. [. . .] From the late 1980s onwards, the publishing conglomerates became transnational and then multinational corporations. There are now key players in English language publishing whose holding companies are based in Germany, France and Australia as well as in Britain and America. The publication of books, like their distribution and sale, has become a truly international business. (Feather 2003, 21–2)

The economic logic of these developments coincides with trends that are discerned in almost all productive industries and has evoked polarized discussions and divisions between approbatory and denunciatory perspectives, much as globalization in general has. The implications for literature, insofar as those have been considered, have tended – and rightly – to be viewed with misgivings. The profit-driven rationale to which multinational corporations subscribe has meant that the consolidation of all publishing – including literary publishing – has resulted in a corresponding narrowing down of the kinds of literature that are made widely accessible and of the kinds of literary innovation and experimentation that are now likely to reach the reading public. André Schiffrin, who was managing director of the publishing house Pantheon for thirty years and quit in 1990 to establish the non-profit New Books to publish serious books which are unlikely to be taken on by market-driven publishers, gave a somewhat personal account of the globalization of the publishing industry in *The Business of Books* (2000). Some of the points he made here are germane to the prospects of literature and therefore significant for literary studies – for instance:

For much of the twentieth century, trade publishing as a whole was seen as a break-even operation. Profit would come when books reached a broader audience through book clubs or paperback sales. If this was true of nonfiction, it was doubly true of literature. Most first novels were expected to lose money (and many authors have been described as writing a lot of first novels). Nonetheless, there have always been publishers who regard publishing new novelists as an important part of their overall output.

New ideas and new authors take time to catch on. It might be years before a writer finds an audience large enough to justify the costs of publishing her book. Even in the long run the market cannot be an appropriate judge of an idea's value, as is obvious from hundreds, indeed thousands, of great books that have never made money. Thus, the new approach – deciding to publish only those books that can be counted on for an immediate profit – automatically eliminates a vast number of important works from catalogs. (Schiffrin 2000, 104)

Schiffrin goes on to demonstrate how this drive for profits has changed practices across the book industry – in the manner in which editors and agents work, retailing is structured, public libraries operate, etc. As far as literature goes, these observations give a somewhat different twist to the 'death of the author' tracked through fictional representation above. What we have here is evidently a matter not so much of decongesting the conventional class elitism of literature and literary culture as of registering the centrality of an advanced corporate capitalist elite which works not so much *through* literary expression as by a manipulation of literary products from, so to speak, *outside* literature. Another way of putting this is that literary canons are arguably no longer being determined as much by dominant class interests embedded in cultural institutions and academia as by processes of controlling the production, marketing and circulation of books at a well-orchestrated global level. It seems plausible that this orchestration incorporates cultural institutions and academia themselves, with profound effects on concepts of literary value and public perceptions of literary status, and simply in the very constitution of reading habits. And, of course, these developments are reformulating access to and apprehension of literary texts themselves, through a form of tacit market censorship. Certain sorts of texts simply do not have the opportunity to surface for the gauging of informed readerships; certain sorts of texts are pre-framed in a manner that makes them unavoidably visible before they are read in any meaningful fashion; and certain sorts are pushed on readers in so concerted and predetermined a fashion (by their pricing, design, publicity) that their readerships are circumscribed in advance. These factors in turn structure literary studies, which are dependent on markets too and which therefore have to attend to what is made visible and available for literary pedagogy and research. The dispersal of elite interests that conventionally worked through literature is being replaced by the assertion of dominant interests that work by instrumentalizing literary products. To emphasize this point differently: the relation between globalization and literature that has occupied the previous chapters appears at the level of the *content* of literary texts and literary studies. Underlying those, however, there is a concrete relation between globalization and literature, which works around and manipulates literature from outside by the globalization of the book industry. Within the content of literature one gets only the most tangential hints of this in such moments as those fictional 'death of authors'; and in literary studies it consequently remains a marginal sociological outpost of the institutional space.

One of the implications of the global consolidation of the book industry with a bearing on an issue discussed in chapter 6 is picked up by Feather:

Publishing and language are symbiotically connected. [. . .] The more readers there are, the larger the total market, and the greater likelihood of a viable number of potential readers even for the most specialized literature. This in turn makes such languages attractive to those who, while not being native speakers themselves, seek an audience among those who read the language. Since the middle of the twentieth century this has increasingly meant, in practice, one thing only: that more and more authors, especially of academic and professional books, write in English regardless of where they are in the world, or what language they use in their daily lives. [. . .] British and American companies are not the only publishers who benefit from the dominance of English. There is a significant trade in the publication of English books in India, for example, where it is the largest of more than a dozen publishing languages, and there are publishing industries in all the major English-speaking countries such as Australia, South Africa and Canada. But the world's largest book market, defined by language, is very largely supplied by the two countries which have the largest number of native English speakers, the United Kingdom and the United States. (Feather 2003, 18)

The role of publishing in the global spread of English in the late twentieth century can hardly be underestimated. In numerous ways this contributes to the prospects for English studies outlined in the previous chapter, including the possibility of dispensing with Englishness from English studies and Americanness from American studies. Equally, though, the centring of the global publishing industry in English in the United States and the United Kingdom may well undermine that envisaged possibility, and perpetuate and extend the cultural imperialism of Englishness and Americanness in new guises. Despite Venuti's dark prognosis of the unevenness of and absences within what is translated for Western readers (mentioned in the previous chapter too), the global cultural capital that English is acquiring and the global reach of publishing in English suggests that translations into English from all languages will pick up further. Anxieties may very reasonably attach to the modes of selection and emphasis that will mediate such increased scope of translations into English. Whether the dominance of English will continue to the detriment of various minority languages that are still used for literary production and consumption, and the industries that serve them, remains to be seen – it seems likely that would happen. These are the predictable paths that seem to lie before us. However, it is worth unpicking some of the complexities and contradictions which lie within these very generalized expectations too – for which the specific context of Indian publishing in English at the beginnings of the twenty-first century is worth pausing on.

A traditionally small English-language publishing industry in India, focused primarily on academic books and textbooks and only in a minuscule way on literary works, has expanded in a significant fashion since about 1990. In a visible way this expansion has taken place with regard to both Indian literary writing in English and translations into English from literature in Indian languages. Various explanations are offered for this. The success of some Indian authors writing in English in international Anglophone markets – such as Salman Rushdie, Vikram Seth, Amatav Ghosh, Arundhati Roy – has drawn attention to the possibilities for literary production that exist in India. Publishers had always been aware that the potential market of English-language readers in India, though confined to a relatively small proportion of the population, is still a large number in absolute terms and growing – in the early twenty-first century this number has been ambitiously estimated to be as large as 200 million. However, the relatively low consumer power of Indians had meant that English-language publishing in India was seldom regarded as a profitable business. With economic growth and increasing affluence in the relevant section of the Indian population at the turn of the century this perception has changed. Towards the end of the twentieth century and early in the twenty-first, therefore, the number of publishers within India who were publishing literary books in English for the Indian market (especially original fiction and translations) had increased many times – in terms both of independent firms (such as Ravi Dayal, Zubaan, Rupa, Katha, Roli, IndiaInk, Stree, Srishti) and of international publishing conglomerates and, later, multinational corporations with bases in India (notably Penguin, HarperCollins, Random House, Hachette Livre). This happy coexistence of growing numbers of independents and multinational corporations hasn't yet turned into the spree of takeovers and mergers seen in the United States and the UK in the 1980s and 1990s, but that could be expected to happen in due course. At this nascent stage of the Indian book industry's expansion, at any rate, international business interest has been evidenced by the drawing up of market profiles, such as that by Rob Francis for the UK Publishers' Association (2003, updated 2008) and Khullar Management's for American businesses (1999). Despite the underdevelopment of the retailing and library sectors and poor regulation of piracy and black markets, it is clearly felt now (in the early twenty-first century) that the Indian book publishing market – especially in English, and including the literary – presents extraordinary promise and opportunities (for a gauging of pros and cons, see the 'documents page' of the *Contemporary Indian Literature in English and the Indian Market* project [2007] at http://www.open.ac.uk/Arts/ferguson-centre/Indian-lit/documents/).

All this might appear to make the Indian scene in publishing consistent with global developments, but in terms of on-the-ground realities in literary production and consumption this phenomenon presents certain interestingly complex and contradictory characteristics. For one thing, insofar as this trend focuses on the publication of literature in English, this growth has instigated a drive for producing original literary works of a sufficient diversity – from 'serious literature' to all categories of 'mass market literature' – from *within* India and targeting consumers primarily *within* India. Thus, a spate of popular fictional works by Indian writers have appeared – especially Chetan Bhagat's *Five Point Someone* (2004) and *One Night @ the Call Centre* (2005) and Anurag Mathur's *The Inscrutable Americans* (1991) – which are enormously popular bestsellers in India, but unusually without going through the usual circuit of prior testing in Western markets and without even being made available in the latter. Publishers in India focusing on literary production in English seem at present bent on diversifying popular literary production by Indian authors for Indian readers, in keeping with the profit-driven moulding of the book market seen in the UK and the United States. A 2007 report in the national daily the *Hindustan Times* observed:

Over the last year or so, V. Karthika, editor in chief at HarperCollins India, has actively sought writers to write the kind of books that Indian writers haven't written in English so far – or at least not in volumes.

 She's looked for writers who'll do chick lit, who'll do thrillers, who'll do contemporary urban stories, who'll write for young adults . . . In short, writers who write the kind of books that the majority of us like to read. Books that are not highbrow, that tell a good story without necessarily probing the murky depths of human experience, that entertain and are simply a damn good read. She's succeeded at least to the extent that, in the space of one year, HarperCollins India has 50 new books to offer the reading public on a wide variety of subjects. A greater variety than Indian writing in English has ever had at one time before. (Gulab 2007)

In a curious way, therefore, it appears that the extension of the global book industry into India is functioning now by *containing* the Indian market – by developing book circulation in all its facets (authoring, editing, designing, distributing, marketing, retailing) *within* India. Customizing Indian literary products for Indian readers seems to be the motto underlying these developments. This is noteworthy because it demonstrates the paradoxical fashion in which globalization of the publishing industry can result in the containment of a certain variety of literary production and consumption (a 'certain variety', of course, because international mass-market books such as the Harry Potter series or Dan Brown's *The Da Vinci Code* [2003] were marketed and consumed in India as successfully as anywhere else) or in the indigenization of Indian English writing and Indian literature in translations as a brand. It may be surmised that these developments, especially insofar as Indian English literature is implicated, are likely to initiate reconsideration of postcolonial literary theory and criticism as currently conducted in the academy. That, however, is too complex an exercise to be undertaken here – the point here is to register the possibility.

 There are other ways too in which the globalization of the book industry as it embraces India seems to open up unexpected possibilities. One of the consistent fears about globalization processes has been that they lead to a homogenization of culture – evidenced, for instance, in misgivings about the survival of vernaculars and minority indigenous linguistic cultures before the relentless expansion of global languages such as English. This is a particularly sensitive issue in a markedly multilingual context such as India. The gradual incorporation of Indian literature markets within the global publishing industry, however – though instigated by the status of English therein – seems to promise some revitalization of publishing in Indian languages too. Thus Sarah Brouillette, in an article published in 2007, observes:

Transnational firms now commit to publishing the same vernacular languages they were once engaged in marginalising, as they recognise that English is not the only globalisable South Asian language. The structures of production and circulation that exist within the dominant Western publishing market, having so readily incorporated South Asian writing in English, may well treat vernacular works in much the same fashion. Such texts serve a myriad of functions: they can be exported to or locally produced for communities of South Asians living either in the region or abroad, or sold to those who are more competent or comfortable in the vernacular as well as those who want to maintain the alternative cultural cache that comes with continued support for one's 'mother tongue'. A celebrated and romanticised localism is just as marketable as an ostensibly delocalised cosmopolitan English-language writing. This is something that the transnational companies operating in South Asia are now beginning to realise, and there is little doubt that they will quickly absorb and expand the existing markets of vernacular literatures, establishing those new rules for the game, from lower price points to more lavish marketing, that will make it hard for the many existing smaller firms to compete. (Brouillette 2007, 37)

She notes the intention of several multinational publishing corporations operating in India to start publishing in Indian languages other than English.

Leaving this digression on the Indian publishing industry behind and returning to general observations on the globalization of the publishing industry and its impact on literature: what appears to be called for is an approach to the relationship between globalization and literature not from *within* literature and literary studies but, so to speak, on the surface of both from *outside*. Of course, that is a rhetorical way of stating the matter. Even approaching it thus would effectively mean bringing the surface of literature and literary studies and the agents working upon them inside literature. This may sound like a rhetorical conundrum but is, in the present context, very much worth engaging more energetically than is customary. Literary studies has so far intervened in the mediations between authors/texts/readers and broad historical/ideological/cultural contexts to only a limited extent, and with little attention to the exigencies of markets and circulations. Book and publishing history and studies of reading practices and attention to textual media (e.g. arising from the implications of digitization and hypertext) are areas affiliated to literature and literary studies that come closest at present to apprehending the impetus of markets and circulations. Useful as those are, for what I have in mind these are still rather limited approaches to the matter and are in themselves yet incompletely excavated fields. When Bryant programmatically called for a consistent understanding of 'fluid texts', he listed the agents he saw as contributing to the production of textual fluidity – 'writers, editors, publishers, translators, digesters, and adapters' (Bryant 2002, 4); interestingly, some of these agents still remain invisible in literary studies, even in the field of book history and text editing. But, beyond that, even the processes working on the surface of literature that book historians have registered (if not explored) are limited by a kind of fetishization of texts. The overdetermined attention to the concretizations of texts (in notebooks, typescripts, proofs, codices, specific editions, cassettes, audio CDs, digitized surfaces, etc., of author versions, editor versions, editions, translations, adaptations, screenplays, hypertexts, etc.), and to the industries that are implicated in the literary product as product, effectively downplays the depth and range of the industries surrounding literature and acting upon literary circulation. A fuller apprehension of the latter would involve coming to grips with the fluidity not only of texts but also of authors and readers, and with the notion that it is not only texts that are concretized and produced by industrial processes but also authors and readers. Literary texts, literary authors and literary readers are all industrial products, all commodities in the circulatory matrix of literature and literary studies, and the industrial sectors involved are not one and the same. To a great extent the industrial sectors overlap – the book publishing industry, the media industry and the academic sector (which increasingly works along advanced capitalist industrial lines) have crucial roles in the production of fluid authors, texts and readers – but other sectors which do not overlap are also involved, working with distinct economic rationales and prerogatives.

Stanley Fish's argument, that literary interpretation is conducted not in terms of encounters between critics and texts but in terms of 'interpretive strategies' which exist already in 'interpretive communities' (Fish 1980), had an immediate plausibility – despite objections raised by reader-response theorists (such as Iser 1989; equally Fish [1989] also objected to Iser's formulations). Within that formulation could be recognized something of the practical experience of most academic literary critics, who really do acquire and share and employ in an institutional fashion a critical discourse which instantiates a sense of disciplinary communal belonging. Fish's idea obviously also extends to an apprehension of readerly fluidity: not just literary criticism but all kinds of reading employ 'reading strategies' which are in some sense pre-given and which operate through 'reading communities'. Readers, like academics, really do form communities, and come together with different senses of akinness or communal belonging – in, for instance, virtual or real fan-sites, book clubs, coffee-table discussions, poetry or literature festivals, informal or formal public readings and bookshops, or, more individualistically (and yet with a kind of shared sensibility), by following certain genres. And equally, corporations of various sorts – certainly in the book and media and academic industries, but also in those connected to public relations and advertisement and celebrity, in those for cultural products (films, images, art, music, etc.) connected to literature, and sometimes in those producing consumer products that can be branded through literary association – seep into and begin to produce such reader communities. They operate by shaping reading spaces, by categorizing readers as niche markets, by turning reading into lifestyle indicators. These operations have something to do with the manner in which publishers' catalogues and shelves in bookshops categorize books for the attention of target audiences. They have something to do with the manner in which various coffee-vending chains provide spaces in bookshops or spaces for readers. They have something to do with media celebrities endorsing literary books for their followings (for instance, through the 'book clubs' of UK television breakfast-show hosts Richard and Judy and US chat-show host Oprah Winfrey). The associations unwind in an enormously complex web of readerly fluidity that does not just happen spontaneously but is manufactured by a range of industries.

Similarly, authors are also constantly and explicitly manufactured. This argument has come up already in connection with the depiction above of fictional authors, especially in Rowling's characterization of Gilderoy Lockhart. The dissociative quality of late twentieth-century literary celebrity that was remarked above is very much part of this authorial fluidity, of authors being manufactured. The degrees to which authors' public images and appearances and statements are now engineered by corporate entities and their agents (literary agents, publishers, media persons, advertisers, product designers and commodity pushers of various sorts working in collaboration) to appeal to certain readers and their expectations is an as yet underexplored area. This process of manufacturing authors according to market contexts is, obviously, coeval with manufacturing readers. The production of one is in some sense the production of the other, and both unravel in ways that are unregistered *within* literature and literary studies and yet surely influence the pursuit of both not just in material ways but at textual and interpretive levels too. An aspect of this process, with obvious effects on literature and literary studies, which has received some critical attention has to do with literary prizes. Literary prizes are sometimes rather obvious brand investments by corporations with little stake in literature or literary studies: the Man Booker, Costa, and Orange literary prizes come immediately to the minds of English-language readers as modes of selling brands through literary association. But, besides that, it has been observed consistently that literary prizes, whether through corporate sponsorship or otherwise, increasingly make literary reputations and market value through means that have less to do with literary content than with surrounding rituals and controversies. In 1986 Adair had observed that, while the Booker Prize increases sales for shortlisted books, its mode of doing so was at the expense of literary evaluation:

Since it was essential for the success of the Booker Prize that the world of books as a whole be implicated in its prestige, it became necessary, paradoxically, almost to underplay the importance of individual novels and their authors and concentrate instead on the *year*: in other words, to invest books with the concept of *vintage* (an idea cribbed, aptly enough, from the French: the Booker might reasonably be regarded as the British Goncourt). For if a book is the intellect's loaf of bread, why should it not also be its wine, that inevitable 'poetic' complement of bread? The rest is, as they say, history; now, every October, during the run-up to the prizegiving itself, the classic connoisseurial anxieties can be heard expressed: Is it a good year? A disappointing year? A vintage year? (Adair 1986, 146)

In a paper in 2002 on literary (and other culture) prizes, James English observes a kind of spreading of Booker Prize-like tactics, focusing on the effect of controversies or 'scandals' (such as authors refusing to accept prizes):

While the Booker is possibly the most talked-about of high-cultural prizes, the relationships to criticism, scandal, and the field of journalism are largely unexceptional. [. . .] Indeed, we find other prizes more and more often being compared to the Booker, usually in order to suggest the 'Bookerization' of the whole cultural-prize phenomenon. So that when a 'scandal' or 'row' breaks out in connection with some literary or arts prize these days, those who attack and denigrate or . . . embarrass the prize are less likely to be perceived as acting within the long tradition of sincere animosity between artists and bourgeois consecrations – artistic freedom fighters on the old model of art versus money – and more likely to be seen as players in a newer cultural game whose 'rules' and 'sides' are more obscure and of which the Booker happens to be the best known, and hence the most generic, instance. (English 2002, 118–19)

In English's account, then, no gesture is possible in the early twenty-first century by an artist or author which isn't incorporated into the market logic of prizes, and that logic operates irrespective of the content of the literature which or stance of the author whom it seems to promote. Both are *produced*, so to speak, by the market logic of literary prizes and their mediations or mediatizations. English extends this argument, with a great deal of useful information and further analysis of the industrial processes underlying and cutting into literary prizes, in his book *The Economy of Prestige* (2005).

Another area which registers the fluidity of authors and texts with global effects on literature and literary studies, and has received a modicum of scholarly attention, is that of international property regulation. It is well known that, from the Berne Convention of 1886, the first multilateral copyright agreement between sovereign nation-states, to the Agreement on Trade-Related Aspects of Intellectual Property Rights (TRIPS) of the World Trade Organization of 1994, the regulation of the rights of authors (among other kinds of 'creators') and publishers (among other kind of cultural industries) at a global level has come to be increasingly uniformly regulated and policed. The manner in which copyright law has attempted variously to 'fix' (reduce) authorship, in a rational and purposive legal discourse which is indifferent to literary analysis or estimation, is redolent with illustrations of the fluidity of both literary texts and literary authors. In fact the attribution of authorial rights could be seen as a mode of producing authors and texts (including literary) – or of stabilizing authors and texts against the grain of their fluidity – through means which have little to do with the prerogatives of literature and literary studies. Along with the purely juridical rationale of this process, under conditions where culture industries (such as literary publishing) are becoming increasingly globalized and consolidated, the international regulation of intellectual property rights coheres with such globalization and consolidation. Indeed, the effects of such intellectual property regulation is often seen as having substantially the same effects on cultural production as those Schiffrin had observed on literature in the context of global market-driven publishing. Ronald Bettig, for instance, in a wide-ranging study of the effect of international property rights regulation on cultural production, *Copyrighting Culture* (1996), foresees:

new rules governing intellectual property [that] will greatly facilitate the process of global commodification of human intellectual and artistic creativity. Cultural activities, in particular, will continue to be incorporated into the global market system, produced and sold primarily for their exchange value. This commodification will lead to an even greater concentration of copyright ownership in the hands of the global cultural industries. The profit orientation of these industries leads them to produce and distribute homogeneous cultural products. Their market power, in turn, fosters the erosion of national, regional, ethnic and group autonomy, undermines democratic participation in cultural expression, and increases inequalities between people and nations. (Bettig 1996, 226–7)

Again, it is mainly in book and publishing history vis-à-vis literature and literary studies where the working of copyright law on conceptualizing texts, authors, readers – on the very constitution of literature – is occasionally discussed at present.

A systematic examination of market processes which work *upon*, as I have put it, literature and literary studies, without being evident *within* these is an enormous project which is just beginning to be undertaken. This project needs to engage with textual, readerly and authorial fluidities, and the points of concretization in these, through a complex network of corporate and market agents and interests. The foothold into this area that has already been enabled in book and publishing history is a fruitful one, but should be expanded to develop a more nuanced and less predeterminedly text-centred sense of the industries and markets that incorporate literature. Though the influence of new digital media on cultural processes has been profound – and has so to speak been manifested *within* literature and literary studies – the area of printed book publishing in the global market still provides, and will continue in the foreseeable future to provide, a broader understanding of the markets and industries underlying literature. The situation may increasingly become otherwise for the academic pursuit of literary studies, but the circulation of literary texts appears to be embedded in the form of the printed book – which devolves into textual and readerly and authorial fluidities – in still dominant ways. Taking stock of the impact of digitization and the development of the internet on publishing, John B. Thompson, in *Books in the Digital Age* (2005), discerns three phases. The first phase was one of the 'inflated expectations of the mid-1990s', when the demise of the printed book was foreseen in favour of cheaper production and circulation of texts through electronic means, and enormous investments were made accordingly. The second phase, around late 2000, was one of disappointed expectations and scepticism, with only limited growth of the electronic book market and the bursting of the dot com bubbles. The third and current phase, according to Thompson, is of cautious experimentation:

The areas where electronic delivery of book content has failed to live up to expectations (such as general trade books) have been sidelined and attention focused increasingly on those areas (reference, professional and scholarly publishing) where the prospects for electronic delivery seem more promising. [. . .] The phase of cautious experimentation is generally premised on the assumption that printed books will remain the principal source of revenue for most book publishers for the foreseeable future. (Thompson 2005, 311)

It may therefore be expected that, while the printed book will continue to be the principal mode of concretizing literary texts, the digital form may become the dominant medium of the literary studies text. The globalization of the industries that impinge *upon*, rather than immediately *within*, literature and literary studies needs to be examined accordingly.

But all that remains within the realms of possibility. The note on which I wish to conclude this study is clear already: ultimately the relationship between globalization and literature is arguably most immediately to be discerned not in terms of what is available *inside* literature and *within* literary studies but in terms of the manner in which globalized markets and industries act *upon* and from *outside* literature and literary studies. This requires a great deal more attention than it has yet received *within* literature and literary studies.

References

Achebe, Chinua (1975). 'English and the African Writer', in Ali Al'Amin Mazrui, *The Political Sociology of the English Language: An African Perspective*. The Hague: Mouton, pp. 216–23, Appendix B.

Adair, Gilbert (1986). 'Le Booker nouveau est arrivé', in *Myths and Memories*. London: Fontana, pp. 144–7.

Adair, Gilbert (1990). *Love and Death on Long Island*. London: Heinemann.

Adamson, Bob (2004). *China's English: A History of English in Chinese Education*. Hong Kong: Hong Kong University Press.

Ahmad, Aijaz (1987). 'Jameson's Rhetoric of Otherness and the "National Allegory"', *Social Text*, 17, autumn: 3–25.

Ahmad, Aijaz (1992). *In Theory: Classes, Nations, Literatures*. London: Verso.

Albrow, Martin (1990). 'Introduction', in Albrow and Elizabeth King (eds), *Globalization, Knowledge and Society: Readings from International Sociology*. London: Sage and International Sociology Association.

Albrow, Martin (1996). *The Global Age: State and Society beyond Modernity*. Cambridge: Polity.

Aldridge, A. Owen (1986). *The Reemergence of World Literature: A Study of Asia and the West*. Newark: University of Delaware Press.

Alexander, Jeffrey C. (2003). *The Meanings of Social Life: A Cultural Sociology*. New York: Oxford University Press.

Annesley, James (2006). *Fictions of Globalization: Consumption, the Market and the Contemporary Novel*. London: Continuum.

Appadurai, Arjun (1990). 'Disjuncture and Difference in the Global Cultural Economy', in Mike Featherstone (ed.), *Global Culture: Nationalism, Globalization and Modernity*. London: Sage with *Theory, Culture & Society*, pp. 295–310.

Appadurai, Arjun (1996). *Modernity at Large: Cultural Dimensions of Globalization*. Minneapolis: University of Minnesota Press.

Archibugi, Daniele, and David Held (eds) (1995). *Cosmopolitan Democracy: An Agenda for a New World Order*. Cambridge: Polity, 1995.

Armand, Louis (2004a). 'Introduction: Literary Engines', in Armand (ed.), *Joycemedia: James Joyce, Hypermedia and Textual Genetics*. Prague: Litteraria Pragensia, pp. 1–28.

Armand, Louis (ed.) (2004b). *Joycemedia: James Joyce, Hypermedia and Textual Genetics*. Prague: Litteraria Pragensia.

Armstrong, Paul (1987). *The Challenge of Bewilderment: Understanding and Representation in James, Conrad and Ford*. Ithaca, NY: Cornell University Press.

Ashcroft, Bill (2001). *Post-Colonial Transformations*. London: Routledge.

Attenberry, Wendy, and Sarah Hatter (eds) (2006). *The Very Best Weblog Writing Ever.* Lulu.com.

Augé, Marc (1995). *Non-Places: Introduction to an Anthropology of Supermodernity*, trans. John Howe. London: Verso.

Baker, Nicholson (2004). *Checkpoint*. London: Chatto & Windus.

Baldick, Chris (1983). *The Social Mission of English Criticism, 1848–1932*. Oxford: Clarendon Press.

Barthes, Roland (1977). 'The Death of the Author', in *Image, Music, Text*, selected and trans. Stephen Heath. London: Fontana.

Bassnett, Susan (1980). *Translation Studies*. London: Routledge.

Bassnett, Susan, and Harish Trivedi (eds) (1999). *Post-Colonial Translation: Theory and Practice*. London: Routledge.

Baudrillard, Jean ([1970] 1998). *The Consumer Society: Myths and Structures*, trans. George Ritzler. London: Sage.

Bauman, Zygmunt (1988). 'Is There a Postmodern Sociology?', in Mike Featherstone (ed.), *Postmodernism*, special issue of *Theory, Culture, Society*, 5/2–3: 217–35.

Bauman, Zygmunt (1998). *Globalization: The Human Consequences*. Cambridge: Polity.

Beck, Ulrich ([2002] 2005). *Power in the Global Age*, trans. Kathleen Cross. Cambridge: Polity.

Beck, Ulrich ([2004] 2006). *The Cosmopolitan Vision*, trans. Ciaran Cronin. Cambridge: Polity.

Belsey, Catherine (1980). *Critical Practice*. London: Methuen.

Benhabib, Seyla, with Jeremy Waldron, Bonnie Honig and Will Kymlicka (2006). *Another Cosmopolitanism*, ed. Robert Post. Oxford: Oxford University Press.

Berger, Peter L. (2002). 'Introduction: The Cultural Dynamics of Globalization', in Berger and Samuel Huntington (eds), *Many Globalizations: Cultural Diversity in the Contemporary World*. Oxford: Oxford University Press, pp. 1–16.

Berman, Art (1988). *From the New Criticism to Deconstruction: The Reception of Structuralism and Post-Structuralism*. Urbana: University of Illinois Press.

Bernheimer, Charles (1993). 'Comparative Literature at the Turn of the Century' [Bernheimer Report to the ACLA], in Bernheimer (ed.), *Comparative Literature in the Age of Multiculturalism*. Baltimore: Johns Hopkins University Press, pp. 39–48.

Bernheimer, Charles (1995a). 'Introduction: The Anxieties of Comparison', in Bernheimer (ed.), *Comparative Literature in the Age of Multiculturalism*. Baltimore: Johns Hopkins University Press, 1–17.

Bernheimer, Charles (ed.) (1995b). *Comparative Literature in the Age of Multiculturalism*. Baltimore: Johns Hopkins University Press.

Bertens, Hans (1995). *The Idea of the Postmodern: A History*. London: Routledge.

Best, Steven, and Douglas Kellner (1991). *Postmodern Theory: Critical Interrogations*. Basingstoke: Macmillan.

Bettig, Ronald V. (1996). *Copyrighting Culture: The Political Economy of Intellectual Property*. Boulder, CO: Westview Press.

Bhabha, Homi (1994). *The Location of Culture*. London: Routledge.

Bhagat, Chetan (2004). *Five Point Someone*. New Delhi: Rupa.

Bhagat, Chetan (2005). *One Night @ the Call Centre*. New Delhi: Rupa.

Bhagwati, Jagdish (2004). *In Defense of Globalization*. New York: Oxford University Press.

Birus, Hendrik (2003). 'The Goethean Concept of World Literature and Comparative Literature', in Steven Tötösy de Zepetnek (ed.), *Comparative Literature and Comparative Cultural Studies*. West Lafayette, IN: Purdue University Press, pp. 11–22.

Blake, Andrew (2002). *The Irresistible Rise of Harry Potter: Kid-Lit in a Globalised World*. London: Verso.

Bloom, Harold (1994). *The Western Canon: The Books and School of the Ages*. New York: Harcourt Brace.

Boehmer, Elleke (1995). *Colonial and Postcolonial Literature: Migrant Metaphors*. Oxford: Oxford University Press.

Bolter, Jay David (1991). *Writing Space: The Computer, Hypertext, and the History of Writing*. Hillsdale, NJ: Lawrence Erlbaum.

Bourdieu, Pierre (1988). *Homo Academicus*, trans. Peter Collier. Cambridge: Polity.

Bové, Paul A. (1992). *In the Wake of Theory*. Hanover, NH: Wesleyan University Press.

Brecher, Jeremy, John Brown Childs and Jill Cutler (eds) (1993). *Global Visions: Beyond the New World Order*. Boston: South End Press.

Brennan, Timothy (1989). *Salman Rushdie and the Third World: Myths of the Nation*. London: Macmillan.

Brennan, Timothy (2001). 'Cosmo-Theory', *South Atlantic Quarterly*, 100/3: 659–91.

Brennan, Timothy (2006). *Wars of Position: The Cultural Politics of Left and Right*. New York: Columbia University Press.

Brooker, Joseph (2004). *Joyce's Critics: Transitions in Reading and Culture*. Madison: University of Wisconsin Press.

Brouillette, Sarah (2007). 'South Asian Literature and Global Publishing', *Wasafiri*, 22/3: 34–8.

Brown, Stephen (2002a). 'Harry Potter and the Marketing Mystery', *Journal of Marketing*, 66/1: 126–30.

Brown, Stephen (2002b). 'Marketing for Muggles', *Business Horizons*, 45/1, 6–14.

Browner, Stephanie, Stephen Pulsford and Richard Sears (2000). *Literature and the Internet: A Guide for Students, Teachers and Scholars*. New York: Garland.

Bryant, John (2002). *The Fluid Text: A Theory of Revision and Editing for Book and Screen*. Ann Arbor: University of Michigan Press.

Budgen, Frank (1934). *James Joyce and the Making of Ulysses*. London: Grayson & Grayson.

Burgess, Anthony (1962). *Clockwork Orange*. London: Penguin.

Burke, Sean (1992). *Death and Return of the Author: Criticism and Subjectivity in Barthes, Foucault and Derrida*. Edinburgh: Edinburgh University Press.

Butler, Judith, John Guillory and Kendall Thomas (eds) (2000). *What's Left of Theory? New Work on the Politics of Literary Theory*. London and New York: Routledge.

Cain, William E. (1984). *The Crisis in Criticism: Theory, Literature and Reform in English Studies*. Baltimore: Johns Hopkins University Press.

Callinicos, Alex (2003). *An Anti-Capitalist Manifesto*. Cambridge: Polity.

Callus, Ivan, and Stefan Herbrechter (2004). *Post-Theory, Culture, Criticism*. Amsterdam: Rodopi.

Casanova, Pascale ([1999] 2004). *The World Republic of Letters*, trans. M. B. DeBevoise. Cambridge, MA: Harvard University Press.

Castells, Manuel ([1972] 1977). *The Urban Question: A Marxist Approach*, trans. Alan Sheridan. London: Edward Arnold.

Castells, Manuel (2001). *The Internet Galaxy: Reflections on the Internet, Business and Society*. Oxford: Oxford University Press.

Chakrabarty, Dipesh (2000). *Provincializing Europe: Postcolonial Thought and Historical Difference*. Princeton, NJ: Princeton University Press.

Chaudhuri, Amit (ed.) (2001). *The Picador Book of Modern Indian Literature*. London: Picador.

Chow, Rey (1993). *Writing Diaspora: Tactics of Intervention in Contemporary Cultural Studies*. Bloomington: Indiana University Press.

Chow, Rey (1995). 'In the Name of Comparative Literature', in Charles Bernheimer (ed.), *Comparative Literature in the Age of Multiculturalism*. Baltimore: Johns Hopkins University Press, pp. 107–16.

Chow, Rey (2001). 'How (the) Inscrutable Chinese Led to Globalized Theory', Special Topic: Globalizing Literary Studies, *PMLA*, 116/1: 69–74.

Chrisafis, Angelique et al. (2003). 'Millions Worldwide Rally for Peace: Huge Turnout at 600 Marches from Berlin to Baghdad', *The Guardian*, 17 February.

Chua, Amy (2003). *World on Fire: How Exporting Free Market Democracy Breeds Ethnic Hatred and Global Instability*. London: Heinemann.

Clements, Robert (1978). *Comparative Literature as Academic Discipline: A Statement of Principles, Praxis, Standards*. New York: Modern Languages Association of America.

Clemetson, Lynette (2003). 'Protest Groups Using Updated Tactics to Spread Antiwar Message', *New York Times*, 15 January.

Conradi, Peter (2003). 'Demos Follow Sun around the Globe', *The Times*, 16 February, p. 2.

Contemporary Indian Literature in English and the Indian Market (2007), Open University, Ferguson Centre for African and Asian Studies: http://www.open.ac.uk/Arts/ferguson-centre/indian-lit/documents/index.html.

Cooper, Dennis (ed.) (2007). *The Userlands: New Fiction from the Blogging Underground*. New York: Akashic Books.

Corngold, Stanley (2005). 'Comparative Literature: The Delay in Translation', in Sandra Berman and Michael Wood (eds), *Nation, Language and the Ethics of Translation*. Princeton, NJ: Princeton University Press, pp. 139–45.

Coupland, Douglas (1991). *Generation X: Tales for an Accelerated Culture*. London: Abacus.

Crawford, Robert (1992). *Devolving English Literature*. Oxford: Clarendon Press.

Cronin, Michael (2003). *Translation and Globalization*. London: Routledge.

Crystal, David ([1997] 2003). *English as a Global Language*. 2nd edn, Cambridge: Cambridge University Press.

Damrosch, David (2003). *What is World Literature?* Princeton, NJ: Princeton University Press.

Damrosch, David (ed.) (2004–). *Longman Anthology of World Literature*. New York: Longman.

Damrosch, David (2005). *Teaching World Literature: A Companion to the Longman Anthology of World Literature*. New York: Pearson Education.

Dasgupta, R. K. (1969). 'The Concept of World Literature: A Comparative Study of the Views of Goethe and Tagore', in Nikola Banaševic (ed.), *Proceedings of the Fifth Congress of the International Comparative Literature Association*. Amsterdam: Swets & Zeitlinger, pp. 399–404.

Debray, Régis (1981). *Teachers, Writers, Celebrities: The Intellectuals of Modern France*, trans. David Macey. London: New Left Books.

De Jour, Belle (2005). *The Intimate Adventures of a London Call Girl*. London: Weidenfeld & Nicolson.

DeLillo, Don (1991). *Mao II*. London: Jonathan Cape.

DeLillo, Don (2003). *Cosmopolis*. London: Picador.

Deming, Robert H. (ed.) (1970). *James Joyce: The Critical Heritage*. London: Routledge & Kegan Paul.

Derrida, Jacques (1984). 'Two Words for Joyce: He War', in Derek Attridge and Daniel Ferrer (eds), *Post-Structuralist Joyce: Essays from the French*. Cambridge: Cambridge University Press.

Dirlik, Arif (1997). *Third World Criticism in the Age of Global Capitalism*. New York: Westview Press.

Dirlik, Arif (1999). 'Is There History after Eurocentrism? Globalism, Postcolonialism, and the Disavowal of History', *Cultural Critique*, 42, spring: 2–27.

Dixon, John (1991). *A Schooling in 'English'*. Buckingham: Open University Press.

Donoghue, Denis (1992). *The Pure Good of Theory*. Oxford: Blackwell.

Doyle, Brian (1989). *English and Englishness*. London: Routledge.

Eagleton, Terry (1983). *Literary Theory: An Introduction*. Oxford: Blackwell.

Eagleton, Terry (1990). *The Significance of Theory*. Oxford: Blackwell.

Eagleton, Terry (1999). 'In the Gaudy Supermarket', *London Review of Books*, 13, May.

Eagleton, Terry (2003). *After Theory*. London: Allen Lane.

Easthope, Anthony (1991). *Literary into Cultural Studies*. London: Routledge.

Eco, Umberto (1979). *The Role of the Reader*. London: Hutchinson.

Elias, Norbert (1991). *The Society of Individuals*, trans. Edmund Jephcott. Oxford: Blackwell.

Eliot, T. S. (1923). 'Ulysses, Order and Myth', in Robert H. Deming (ed.), *James Joyce: The Critical Heritage*. London: Routledge & Kegan Paul.

Ellis, Brett Easton (1991). *American Psycho*. London: Picador.

Engler, Balz, and Renate Haas (eds) (2000). *European English Studies: Contributions towards the History of a Discipline*. Leicester: English Association.

English, James F. (2002). 'Winning the Culture Game: Prizes, Awards, and the Rules of Art', *New Literary History*, 33/1: 109–35.

English, James F. (2005). *The Economy of Prestige: Prizes, Awards, and the Circulation of Cultural Value*. Cambridge, MA: Harvard University Press.

Ensler, Eve (2001). *The Vagina Monologues*. 2nd edn, New York: Villard.

Erikson, Erik (1968). *Identity: Youth and Culture*. New York: Norton.

Fairclough, Norman (2006). *Language and Globalization*. London: Routledge.

Feather, John (2003). *Communicating Knowledge: Publishing in the 21st Century*. Munich: K.G. Saur.

Featherstone, Mike (ed.) (1990). *Global Culture: Nationalism, Globalization and Modernity*. London: Sage with *Theory, Culture & Society*.

Featherstone, Mike (1995). *Undoing Culture: Globalization, Postmodernism, and Identity*. London: Sage.

Felperin, Howard (1985). *Beyond Deconstruction: The Uses and Abuses of Literary Theory*. Oxford: Clarendon Press.

Fish, Stanley (1980). *Is There a Text in this Class? The Authority of Interpretive Communities*. Cambridge, MA: Harvard University Press.

Fish, Stanley (1989). 'Why No One's Afraid of Wolfgang Iser', in *Doing What Comes Naturally: Change, Rhetoric and the Practice of Theory in Literary and Legal Studies.* Oxford: Clarendon Press.

Fish, Stanley (1995). *Professional Correctness: Literary Studies and Political Change.* Oxford: Clarendon Press.

Francis, Rob ([2003] 2008). *Publishing Market Profile: India.* Rev. edn, UK Publishers Association.

Friedman, Jonathan (1994). *Cultural Identity and Global Process.* London: Sage.

Fromm, Harold (1991). *Academic Capitalism and Literary Value.* Athens, GA: University of Georgia Press.

Fukuyama, Francis (1992). *The End of History and the Last Man.* London: Penguin.

Gabler, Hans Walter, with Wolfhard Steppe and Claus Melchior (eds) (1984). *Ulysses/James Joyce: A Critical and Synoptic Edition.* New York: Garland.

Gaggi, Silvio (1997). *From Text to Hypertext: Decentring the Subject in Fiction, Film, the Visual Arts.* Philadelphia: University of Pennsylvania Press.

Gandhi, Leela (1998). *Postcolonial Theory: A Critical Introduction.* Edinburgh: Edinburgh University Press.

García-Berrio, Antonio ([1989] 1992). *A Theory of the Literary Text.* Berlin: Walter de Gruyter.

Giddens, Anthony (1990). *The Consequences of Modernity.* Cambridge: Polity.

Gikandi, Simon (2001). 'Globalization and the Claims of Postcoloniality', *South Atlantic Quarterly*, 100/3: 627–58.

Gilbert, Stuart (1930). *James Joyce's Ulysses: A Study.* London: Faber & Faber.

Gillespie, Michael Patrick, and A. Nicholas Fargnoli (eds) (2006). *Ulysses in Critical Perspective.* Gainsville: University Press of Florida.

Gillespie, Michael Patrick, and Paula F. Gillespie (2000). *Recent Criticism of James Joyce's Ulysses: An Analytical Review.* Rochester, NY: Camden House.

Gills, Barry, and William R. Thompson (eds) (2006). *Globalization and Global History.* London: Routledge.

Glass, Loren (2004). *Authors Inc.: Literary Celebrity in the Modern United States 1880–1980.* New York: New York University Press.

Godzich, Wlad (1994). *The Culture of Literacy.* Cambridge, MA: Harvard University Press.

Goffman, Erving (1959). *The Presentation of Self in Everyday Life.* Harmondsworth: Penguin.

Goffman, Erving (1964). *Stigma: Notes on the Management of Spoiled Identity.* Harmondsworth: Penguin.

Goodheart, Eugene (1984). *The Skeptic Disposition in Contemporary Criticism.* Princeton, NJ: Princeton University Press.

Goreau, Fredrick H. (1983). 'The Multinational Version of Social Sciences', *International Social Science Journal*, 35/2: 379–90.

Gorman, Herbert (1941). *James Joyce: A Definitive Biography.* London: John Lane.

Gouldner, Alvin (1979). *The Future of Intellectuals and the Rise of the New Class.* London: Macmillan.

Grabovsky, Ernest (2004). 'The Impact of Globalization and the New Media on the Notion of World Literature', in Steven Tötösy de Zepetnek (ed.), *Comparative Literature and Comparative Cultural Studies.* West Lafayette, IN: Purdue University Press, pp. 45–57.

Graff, Gerald (1979). *Literature against Itself: Literary Ideas in Modern Society*. Chicago: University of Chicago Press.

Graff, Gerald (1987). *Professing Literature: An Institutional History*. Chicago: University of Chicago Press.

Greenblatt, Stephen (2001). 'Racial Memory and Literary Studies, Special Topic: Globalizing Literary Studies, *PMLA*, 116/1: 48–63.

Groden, Michael (1977). *'Ulysses' in Progress*. Princeton, NJ: Princeton University Press.

Groden, Michael (2004). 'Problems of Annotation in a Digital *Ulysses*', in Louis Armand (ed.), *Joycemedia: James Joyce, Hypermedia and Textual Genetics*. Prague: Litteraria Pragensia, pp. 118–34.

Gubar, Susan, and Jonathan Kamholtz (eds) (1993). *English Inside and Out: The Places of Literary Criticism*. New York: Routledge.

Guillory, John (1993). *Cultural Capital: The Problem of Literary Canon Formation*. Chicago: University of Chicago Press.

Gulab, Kushal (2007). 'Desperately Seeking Authors', *Hindustan Times*, 23 September; also at: http://www.open.ac.uk/Arts/ferguson-centre/indian-lit/documents/pub-doc-kushal-gulab-sept07.htm.

Gumperz, John J. (ed.) (1982). *Language and Social Identity*. Cambridge: Cambridge University Press.

Gunn, Giles (2001). 'Introduction', Special Topic: Globalizing Literary Studies, *PMLA*, 116/1: 16–31.

Gupta, Suman (2003). *Re-Reading Harry Potter*. Basingstoke: Palgrave.

Gupta, Suman (2006). *The Theory and Reality of Democracy: A Case Study in Iraq*. London: Continuum.

Gupta, Suman (2007). *Social Constructionist Identity Politics and Literary Studies*. Basingstoke: Palgrave.

Guy, Josephine, and Ian Small (1993). *Politics and Value in English Studies: A Discipline in Crisis?* Cambridge: Cambridge University Press.

Habermas, Jürgen ([1973] 1976). *Legitimation Crisis*. London: Heinemann Educational.

Habermas, Jürgen (1981). 'New Social Movements', *Telos*, 49, fall: 33–7.

Habermas, Jürgen ([1985] 1987). *The Philosophical Discourse of Modernity: Twelve Lectures*, trans. Fredrick Lawrence. Cambridge: Polity.

Hall, Donald (ed.) (2001). *Professions: Conversations on the Future of Literary and Cultural Studies*. Urbana: University of Illinois Press.

Hall, Peter (1966). *The World Cities*. London: Weidenfeld & Nicolson.

Hall, Stuart (1991). 'The Local and the Global: Globalization and Ethnicity', in Anthony King (ed.) *Culture, Globalization and the World System*. Basingstoke: Macmillan, pp. 19–39.

Hartman, Geoffrey H. (1980). *Criticism in the Wilderness: The Study of Literature Today*. New Haven, CT: Yale University Press.

Harvey, David (1973). *Social Justice and the City*. London: Edward Arnold.

Harvey, David (1989). *The Condition of Postmodernity: An Enquiry into the Origins of Cultural Change*. Oxford: Blackwell.

Hassan, Ihab (1987). *The Postmodern Turn: Essays in Postmodern Theory and Culture*. Columbus: Ohio State University Press.

Hegel, G. W. F. ([1837] 1956). *Philosophy of History*, trans. J. Sibree. New York: Dover.

Hegel, G. W. F. ([1807] 1977). *Phenomenology of Spirit*, trans. A. V. Miller. Oxford: Clarendon Press.

Heilman, Elizabeth (ed.) (2003). *Harry Potter's World: Multidisciplinary Critical Perspectives.* New York: RoutledgeFalmer.

Heilman, Robert (1999). *The Professor and the Profession.* Columbia: University of Missouri Press.

Held, David (2004). *Global Covenant: The Social Democratic Consensus to the Washington Consensus.* Cambridge: Polity.

Held, David, and Anthony McGrew (2002). *Globalization/Anti-Globalization.* Cambridge: Polity.

Held, David, Anthony McGrew, David Goldblatt and Jonathan Perraton (1999). *Global Transformations: Politics, Economics and Culture.* Cambridge: Polity.

Himes, Chester (1990). *The End of a Primitive.* London: Allison & Busby.

Hindess, Barry, and Paul Hirst (1975). *Pre-Capitalist Modes of Production.* London: Routledge & Kegan Paul.

Hitchcock, Peter (2001). 'Decolonizing (the) English', *South Atlantic Quarterly*, 100/3: 749–70.

Hobsbawm, Eric (1975). *The Age of Capital 1848–1875.* London: Weidenfeld & Nicolson.

Hoesel-Uhlig, Stefan (2004). 'Changing Fields: The Directions of Goethe's *Weltliteratur*', in Christopher Prendergast (ed.), *Debating World Literature.* London: Verso, pp. 26–54.

Hogan, Patrick Cohn (1990). *The Politics of Interpretation: Ideology, Professionalism, and the Study of Literature.* New York: Oxford University Press.

Holborow, Marnie (1999). *The Politics of English: A Marxist View of Language.* London: Sage.

Hopkins, Raymond F. (1978). 'Global Management Networks: The Internationalization of Domestic Bureaucracies', *International Social Science Journal* 30/1: 31–46.

Huggan, Graham (2001). *The Postcolonial Exotic: Marketing the Margins.* London: Routledge.

Hutcheon, Linda (1988). *A Poetics of Postmodernism: History, Theory, Fiction.* New York: Routledge.

Independent Commission on International Development Issues (1980). *North–South: A Programme for Survival.* London: Pan.

International Sociology (1993). 'Debate: Are Social Classes Dying?' *International Sociology*, 8/3.

Iser, Wolfgang (1978). *The Act of Reading: A Theory of Aesthetic Response.* London: Routledge & Kegan Paul.

Iser, Wolfgang (1989). 'Interview 42', in *Prospecting: From Reader Response to Literary Anthropology.* Baltimore: Johns Hopkins University Press.

Jakubowski, Maxim (ed.) (2005). *The Mammoth Book of Sex Diaries.* New York: Carrol & Graf.

Jameson, Fredric (1986). 'Third World Literature in the Era of Multinational Capitalism', *Social Text*, 15, fall: 65–88.

Jameson, Fredric (1991). *Postmodernism, or The Cultural Logic of Late Capitalism.* London: Verso.

Jay, Gregory S. (1997). *Taking Multiculturalism Seriously: Ethnos and Ethos in the Classroom.* New York: Cornell University Press.

Jay, Paul (2001). 'Beyond Discipline? Globalization and the Future of English', Special Topic: Globalizing Literary Studies, *PMLA*, 116/1: 32–47.

Johnson, B. S. (1969). *The Unfortunates.* London: Panther.

Johnson, David (1996). *Shakespeare and South Africa*. Oxford: Clarendon Press.

Joshi, Svati (ed.) (1991). *Rethinking English: Essays in Literature, Language, History*. New Delhi: Trianka.

Joyce, James (1939). *Finnegans Wake*. London: Faber & Faber.

Joyce, James ([1922] 1993). *Ulysses*, ed. Jeri Johnson. Oxford: Oxford University Press.

Kachru, Braj (1985). 'Standards, Codification and Sociolinguistic Realism: The English Language in the Outer Circle', in Randolph Quirk and H. G. Widdowson (eds), *English in the World: Teaching and Learning the Languages and Literatures*. Cambridge: Cambridge University Press, pp. 11–16.

Kapoor, Ilan (2002). 'Deliberative Democracy or Agonistic Pluralism? The Relevance of the Habermas–Mouffe Debate for Third World Politics', *Alternatives: Global, Local, Political*, 27/4: 459–87.

Khullar Management and Financial Investment (1999). *India: Book Publishing*. Washington, DC: US Department of State.

Kilminster, Richard (1997). 'Globalization as an Emergent Concept', in Alan Scott (ed.), *The Limits of Globalization: Cases and Arguments*. London: Routledge.

King, Anthony (ed.) (1991a). *Culture, Globalization and the World-System: Contemporary Conditions for the Representation of Identity*. Basingstoke: Macmillan.

King, Anthony (1991b). *Global Cities: Postimperialism and the Internationalisation of London*. London: Routledge.

Klein, Naomi (2001). 'Reclaiming the Commons', *New Left Review*, 9, May/June: 81–9.

Krishnaswamy, Revathi (2002). 'The Criticism of Culture and the Culture of Criticism: At the Intersection of Postcolonialism and Globalization Theory', *Diacritics*, 32/2: 106–26.

Kuhns, Peter, and Adrienne Crew (2006). *Blogsphere: Best of Blogs*. Indianapolis, IN: Que.

Laclau, Ernesto, and Chantal Mouffe (1985). *Hegemony and Socialist Strategy: Toward a Radical Democratic Politics*. London: Verso.

Lamy, Paul (1976). 'The Globalization of American Sociology: Excellence or Imperialism?', *American Sociologist*, 11/2: 104–13.

Landow, George P. (1992). *Hypertext: The Convergence of Contemporary Critical Theory and Technology*. Baltimore: Johns Hopkins University Press.

Lash, Scott (1990). *Sociology of Postmodernism*. London: Routledge.

Lauter, Paul (1991). *Canons and Contexts*. New York: Oxford University Press.

Leavis, F. R. (1930). *Mass Civilisation and Minority Culture*. Cambridge: Gordon Fraser.

Leavis, Q. D. (1932). *Fiction and the Reading Public*. London: Chatto & Windus.

Lee, Abby (2007). *Diary of a Sex Fiend*. New York: Skyhorse.

Lefebvre, Henri ([1974] 1991). *The Production of Space*, trans. Donald Nicholson-Smith. Oxford: Blackwell.

Lefevere, André (1992). *Translating Literature: Practice and Theory in a Comparative Literature Context*. New York: Modern Languages Association of America.

Leitch, Vincent, and Jeffrey Williams (2005). *After Theory*. London: Routledge.

Lentriccia, Frank (1983). *Criticism and Social Change*. Chicago: University of Chicago Press.

Levitt, Theodore (1983). 'The Globalization of Markets', *Harvard Business Review*, 61/3: 92–102.

Loomba, Ania (1998). *Colonialism/Postcolonialism*. London: Routledge.

Lyotard, Jean-François ([1979] 1984). *The Postmodern Condition: A Report on Knowledge*, trans. Geoff Bennington and Brian Masumi. Manchester: Manchester University Press.

McClintock, Anne (1992). '"The Angel of Progress": Pitfalls of the Term Post-Colonialism', *Social Text*, 31/32: 84–97.

McEwan, Ian (2006). *Saturday*. London: Vintage.

McGann, Jerome (1983). *A Critique of Modern Textual Criticism*. Chicago: University of Chicago Press.

McGann, Jerome (2001). *Radiant Textuality: Literature after the World Wide Web*. Basingstoke: Palgrave.

McGrath, Patrick (2006). *Ghost Town: Tales of Manhattan Then and Now*. London: Bloomsbury.

McHale, Brian (1987). *Postmodernist Fiction*. London: Routledge.

McLuhan, Marshall (1962). *The Gutenberg Galaxy: The Making of Typographic Man*. London: Routledge & Kegan Paul.

McLuhan, Marshall (1964). *Understanding Media: The Extensions of Man*. London: Routledge & Kegan Paul.

McQuillan, Martin (1999). *Post-Theory*. Edinburgh: Edinburgh University Press.

Malkani, Gautam (2006). *Londonstani*. London: Fourth Estate.

Man, Paul de (1986). *The Resistance to Theory*. Manchester: Manchester University Press.

Mandel, Ernest ([1972] 1978). *Late Capitalism*, trans. Joris De Bres. London: Verso.

Mann, Thomas ([1912] 1932). *Death in Venice*, trans. H. T. Lowe-Porter. London: Secker.

Marcuse, Herbert (1964). *One-Dimensional Man*. London: Sphere.

Marshall, David (1997). *Celebrity and Power· Fame in Contemporary Culture*. Minneapolis: University of Minnesota Press.

Martin, Philip W. (ed.) (2006). *English: The Condition of the Subject*. Basingstoke: Palgrave.

Mathur, Anurag (1991). *The Inscrutable Americans*. New Delhi: Rupa.

Mauss, Marcel ([1950] 1979). *Sociology and Psychology*, trans. Ben Brewster. London: Routledge & Kegan Paul.

Mead, George Herbert (1934). *Mind, Self and Society*. Chicago: University of Chicago Press.

Miller, J. Hillis (2002). *On Literature*. London: Routledge.

Miller, Karl (1989). *Authors*. Oxford: Clarendon Press.

Miner, Earl (1990). *Comparative Poetics: An Intercultural Essay on Theories of Literature*. Princeton, NJ: Princeton University Press.

Moore-Gilbert, Bart (1997). *Postcolonial Theory: Contexts, Practices, Politics*. London: Verso.

Moretti, Franco (2000). 'Conjectures on World Literature', *New Left Review*, 2nd ser., 1: 54–68.

Moretti, Franco (2003). 'More Conjectures', *New Left Review*, 2nd ser., 20: 73–82.

Moses, Michael Valdez (1995). *The Novel and the Globalization of Culture*. New York: Oxford University Press.

Nederveen Pieterse, Jan (2003). *Globalization and Culture*. Lanham, MD: Rowman & Littlefield.

Newman, Robert (2003). *The Fountain at the Centre of the World*. London: Verso.

Ngũgĩ wa Thiong'o (1986). *Decolonising the Mind: The Politics of Language in African Literature*. London: Currey.

Obel, Karen (2001). 'The Story of V-Day and the College Initiative', in Eve Ensler, *The Vagina Monologues*. 2nd edn, New York: Villard.

O'Brien, Susie, and Imre Szeman (2001). 'Introduction: The Globalization of Fiction/ The Fiction of Globalization', *South Atlantic Quarterly*, 100/3: 603–26.

Ohmann, Richard (1976). *English in America: A Radical View of the Profession*. New York: Oxford University Press.

O'Rourke, Kevin H., and Jeffrey G. Williamson (1999). *Globalization and History: The Evolution of a Nineteenth-Century Atlantic Economy*. Cambridge, MA: MIT Press.

Pakulsi, Jan, and Malcolm Waters (1995). *The Death of Class*. London: Sage.

Palmer, D. J. (1965). *The Rise of English Studies*. London: Oxford University Press.

Pamuk, Orhan ([2002] 2004). *Snow*, trans. Maureen Freely. London: Faber.

Parker, Walter (1984). 'Globalizing the Social Studies Curriculum', *Educational Leadership*, 42/2: 92.

Parrinder, Patrick (1987). *The Failure of Theory: Essays in Criticism and Contemporary Fiction*. Brighton: Harvester.

Pax, Salam (2003). *The Baghdad Blog*. London: Atlantic.

Payne, Michael, and John Schad (eds) (2003). *Life after Theory*. London: Continuum.

Peet, Richard, with assistants (2003). *Unholy Trinity: The IMF, World Bank and WTO*. London: Zed Books; Kuala Lumpur: SIRD; Johannesburg: Wits University Press.

Pennycook, Alastair (1994). *The Cultural Politics of English as an International Language*. London: Longman.

Pennycook, Alastair (1998). *English and the Discourses of Colonialism*. London: Routledge.

PMLA (2001). *Special Topic: Globalizing Literary Studies*, 116/1, coordinated by Giles Gunn.

Pope, Rob ([1998] 2002). *The English Studies Book*. 2nd edn, London: Routledge.

Powers, Richard (2000). *Plowing the Dark*. London: Heinemann.

Raban, Jonathan (1974). *Soft City*. London: Hamish Hamilton.

Rajan, Rajeshwari Sunder (ed.) (1992). *The Lie of the Land*. Delhi: Oxford University Press.

Rajan, Rajeshwari Sunder (1997). 'The Third World Academic in Other Places, or The Postcolonial Intellectual Revisited', *Critical Inquiry*, 23: 596–616.

Riverbend (2005). *Baghdad Burning: A Young Woman's Diary from a War Zone*. Delhi: Women Unlimited.

Robertson, Roland (1992). *Globalization: Social Theory and Global Culture*. London: Sage.

Rowling, J. K. (1998). *Harry Potter and the Chamber of Secrets*. London: Bloomsbury.

Rushdie, Salman (1981). *Midnight's Children*. London: Jonathan Cape.

Rushdie, Salman (1988). *The Satanic Verses*. London: Viking.

Rushdie, Salman (1991). *Imaginary Homelands: Essays and Criticism 1981–1991*. London: Granta with Penguin.

Rushdie, Salman ([1983] 2001). 'An Interview with Salman Rushdie' – Interview with Rani Dharkar, in Rushdie, *Interviews: A Sourcebook of his Ideas*, ed. Pradyumna S. Chauhan. Westport, CT: Greenwood Press, pp. 47–51.

Rushdie, Salman, and Elizabeth West (eds) (1997). *The Vintage Book of Indian Writing, 1947–1997*. London: Vintage.

Ryman, Geoff (1998). *253*. London: Flamingo.

Said, Edward (1978). *Orientalism*. Harmondsworth: Penguin.

Said, Edward (1983). *The World, the Text, and the Critic*. London: Vintage.

Said, Edward (2001). 'Globalizing Literary Study', Special Topic: Globalizing Literary Studies, *PMLA*, 116/1: 64–8.

Sanga, Jaina C. (2001). *Salman Rushdie's Postcolonial Metaphors: Migration, Translation, Hybridity, Blasphemy and Globalization*. Westport, CT: Greenwood Press.

Sassen, Saskia (1991). *The Global City: New York, London, Tokyo*. Princeton, NJ: Princeton University Press.

Sassen, Saskia (2000). *Cities in a World Economy*. 2nd edn, Thousand Oaks, CA: Pine Forge.

Schiffrin, André (2000). *The Business of Books: How International Conglomerates Took Over Publishing and Changed the Way We Read*. London: Verso.

Scholes, Robert (1985). *Textual Power: Literary Theory and the Teaching of English*. New Haven, CT: Yale University Press.

Scholes, Robert (1998). *The Rise and Fall of English: Reconstructing English as a Discipline*. New Haven, CT: Yale University Press.

Sherry, Simon (1996). *Gender in Translation: Cultural Identity and the Politics of Transmission*. London: Routledge.

Spencer, John (1965). 'A Note on the "Steady Monologuy of the Interiors"', *Review of English Literature*, 6/2.

Spivak, Gayatri Chakravorty (1993). *Outside in the Teaching Machine*. New York: Routledge.

Spivak, Gayatri Chakravorty (1999). *A Critique of Postcolonial Reason: Toward a History of the Vanishing Present*. Cambridge, MA: Harvard University Press.

Spivak, Gayatri Chakravorty (2003). *Death of a Discipline*. New York: Columbia University Press.

Stiglitz, Joseph (2003). *Globalization and its Discontents*. New York: Norton.

Strauch, Eduard (2001). *Beyond Literary Theory*. Lanham, MD: University Press of America.

Tagore, Rabindranath (2001). *Selected Writings on Literature and Language*, ed. Sisir Kumar Das and Sukanta Chaudhuri. New Delhi: Oxford University Press.

Tajfel, Henri (1978). *The Social Psychology of Minorities*. London: Minority Rights Group.

Tajfel, Henri (1981). *Human Groups and Social Categories: Studies in Social Psychology*. Cambridge: Cambridge University Press.

Tanselle, Thomas (1989). *A Rationale of Textual Criticism*. Philadelphia: University of Pennsylvania Press.

Tanselle, Thomas (1990). *Textual Criticism and Scholarly Editing*. Charlottesville: University Press of Virginia.

Theall, Donald F. (2004). 'Transformations of the Book in Joyce's Dream Vision of Digiculture', in Louis Armand (ed.), *Joycemedia: James Joyce, Hypermedia and Textual Genetics*. Prague: Litteraria Pragensia, pp. 28–43.

Theory and Society (1996). 'Symposium on Class', *Theory and Society*, 25: 5.

Thompson, John B. (2005). *Books in the Digital Age: The Transformation of Academic and Higher Education Publishing in Britain and the United States*. Cambridge: Polity.

Toulmin, Stephen (1990). *Cosmopolis: The Hidden Agenda of Modernity*. New York: Free Press.

Touraine, Alain (1981). *The Voice and the Eye: An Analysis of Social Movements*, trans. Alan Duff. Cambridge: Cambridge University Press.

Trivedi, Harish (1993). *Colonial Transactions*. Calcutta: Papyrus.

Tymoczko, Maria (1999). *Translation in a Postcolonial Context*. Manchester: St Jerome.

Tymoczko, Maria, and Edwin Gentzler (eds) (2002). *Translation and Power*. Amherst: University of Massachusetts Press.

Valente, Joseph (2004). 'Joyce's Politics: Race, Nation, and Transnationalism', in Jean-Michel Rabaté (ed.), *Palgrave Advances in James Joyce Studies*. Basingstoke: Palgrave, pp. 73–96.

Venuti, Lawrence (1995). *The Translator's Invisibility: A History of Translation*. London: Routledge.

Venuti, Lawrence (1998). *The Scandals of Translation: Towards an Ethics of Difference*. London: Routledge.

Vertovec, Steven, and Robin Cohen (eds) (2002). *Conceiving Cosmpolitanism: Theory, Context and Practice*. Oxford: Oxford University Press.

Vico, Giambattista ([1725] 2002). *The First New Science* [*Principi di una scienza nuova*], ed. and trans. Leon Pompa. Cambridge: Cambridge University Press.

Vidal, John (2003). 'They Stood up to be Counted – and Found Nobody Could Agree on Totals', *The Guardian*, 17 February.

Vishwanathan, Gauri (1989). *Masks of Conquest: Literary Study and British Rule in India*. London: Faber & Faber.

Wallerstein, Immanuel (1974). 'The Rise and Future Demise of the World Capitalist System: Concepts for Comparative Analysis', *Comparative Studies in Society and History*, 16.

Wallerstein, Immanuel (1991). 'The National and the Universal: Can There be Such a Thing as World Culture?', in Anthony King (ed.), *Culture, Globalization and the World System*. Basingstoke: Macmillan, pp. 91–105.

Wellek, René (1959). 'The Crisis of Comparative Literature', in Werner P. Friedrich (ed.), *Comparative Literature 2: Proceedings of the Second Congress of the International Comparative Literature Association*. Chapel Hill: University of North Carolina Press, pp. 149–59.

Wellek, René (1970). 'The Name and Nature of Comparative Literature', in *Discriminations: Further Concepts in Criticism*. New Haven, CT: Yale University Press, pp. 1–36.

Whited, Lana A. (ed.) (2002). *The Ivory Tower and Harry Potter: Perspectives on a Literary Phenomenon*. Columbia: University of Missouri Press.

Whitehead, Colson (2003). *The Colossus in New York: A City in Thirteen Parts*. London: Fourth Estate.

Williams, Jeffrey J. (ed.) (2002). *The Institution of Literature*. Albany: State University of New York Press.

Wittgenstein, Ludwig (1953). *Philosophical Investigations*, trans. G. E. M. Anscombe. Oxford: Blackwell.

Wolfe, Tom (1987). *The Bonfire of the Vanities*. London: Jonathan Cape.

Wolff, Janet (1991). 'The Global and the Specific: Reconciling Conflicting Theories of Culture', in Anthony King (ed.), *Culture, Globalization and the World System*. Basingstoke: Macmillan, pp. 161–73.

Woodring, Carl (1990). *Literature: An Embattled Profession*. New York: Columbia University Press.

Wright, Richard (1940). *Native Son*. New York: Harper.

Young, Robert (2001). *Postcolonialism: An Historical Introduction*. Oxford: Blackwell.

Zepetnek, Steven Tötösy de (ed.) (2003a). *Comparative Literature and Comparative Cultural Studies*. West Lafayette, IN: Purdue University Press.

Zepetnek, Steven Tötösy de (2003b). 'From Comparative Literature Today Toward Comparative Cultural Studies', in Zepetnek (ed.), *Comparative Literature and Comparative Cultural Studies*. West Lafayette, IN: Purdue University Press, pp. 235–67.

Zipes, Jack (2000). *Sticks and Stones: The Troublesome Success of Children's Literature from Slovenly Peter to Harry Potter*. New York: Routledge.

Zolo, Danilo (1997). *Cosmopolis: Prospects for World Government*. Cambridge: Polity.

Index

Achebe, Chinua, 125–6
Adair, Gilbert, 167–8
  Love and Death on Long Island, 152–3, 155–6, 159
Adamson, Bob, *China's English*, 133
Ahmad, Aijaz, 117–18
  In Theory, 117–18, 119
Albrow, Martin, 4, 5
Aldridge, A. Owen, *Reemergence of World Literature*, 139, 141
Alexander, Jeffrey, *Meanings of Social Life*, 89
Alive (1993 film), 38
Althusser, Louis, 90, 108
Amin, Samir, 119
Amis, Martin, 46
Annesley, James, *Fictions of Globalization* 66, 69–71
ANSWER International (Act Now to Stop War and End Racism), 25
Anti-Capitalist Manifesto, An (Callinicos), 19
anti-war protests 2003, 24–30
Appadurai, Arjun, 8, 88, 91, 94, 101, 119
  Modernity at Large, 88–9, 107
Appiah, Kwame Anthony, 49
Archibugi, Daniele, *Cosmopolitan Democracy* (with Held) 49
Armstrong, Paul, 76
Arnold, Matthew, 128
Ashcroft, Bill, 120–1
Auerbach, Erich, 141
Augé, Marc, 37

Baker, Nicholson, *Checkpoint*, 25, 27–31

Baldick, Chris, 129
  Social Mission of English Criticism, 128
Barthes, Roland, 75, 151
Bassnett, Susan, *Translation Studies*, 147
Baudrillard, Jean, 98, 99, 100, 101, 119
Bauman, Zygmunt, 5, 106, 117
Beauvoir, Simone de, 108
Beck, Ulrich, 8, 49, 118, 119
Belsey, Catherine, 91
Benetton advertisements, 38
Benhabib, Seyla, 48
Benjamin, Walter, 85
Bernheimer, Charles, 139, 140
Bettig, Ronald, *Copyrighting Culture*, 169
Bhabha, Homi, 112, 113, 115, 116, 119
Bhagat, Chetan, 163
Bhopal gas tragedy, 38
blogs, 57–61
Bloom, Harold, 93
Bolter, Jay David, 78, 80
Bonfire of the Vanities, The (Wolfe), 46
Booker Prize, 167–8
Books in the Digital Age (Thompson), 170
Bourdieu, Pierre, 117, 119
Bové, Paul, 93
Brandt, Willy, 7
Brandt Commission report (*North–South*), 7
Brecht, Bertolt, 48
Brennan, Timothy, 50
  Salman Rushdie and the Third World, 103, 104

Brooker, Joseph, 72
Brouillette, Sarah, 165
Brown, Dan, 164
Bryant, John, 81–2, 84, 165–6
Budgen, Frank, 75
Burgess, Anthony, *A Clockwork Orange*
    42
Burke, Sean, 75, 151
Bush, George W., 24, 27, 28
Business of Books, The (Schiffrin),
    160–61

Callinicos, Alex, *An Anti-Capitalist
    Manifesto*, 19
Campanella, Tommaso, *Civitas solis*, 44
Casanova, Pascale, *World Republic of
    Letters*, 142, 144
Castells, Manuel, *Internet Galaxy*, 77
Chakrabarty, Dipesh, 121–2
Chaudhuri, Amit, *Picador Book of
    Modern Indian Literature*, 118
Checkpoint (Baker), 25, 27–31
China's English (Adamson), 133
Chow, Rey, 10, 140
Civitas solis (Campanella), 44
Clement, Robert, 137–8
Clockwork Orange, A (Burgess), 42
CND (Campaign for Nuclear
    Disarmament), 27
Coca-Cola advertisements, 38
Cohen, Robin, 48
Cold War, 7, 44, 67
Colossus in New York, The
    (Whitehead), 41
Communist Manifesto, The, 15, 19
*Comparative Literature and Comparative
    Cultural Studies* (Zepetnek), 140
Comparative Poetics (Miner), 138
Cooper, Dennis, *Userlands*, 58
Copyrighting Culture (Bettig), 169
Corngold, Stanley, 146–7
Cosmopolis (DeLillo), 14–18, 19, 23,
    25, 39, 46, 48, 50
Cosmopolis (Toulmin), 49–50, 51
Cosmopolis (Zolo), 50, 51
Coupland, Douglas, *Generation X*,
    37–8
Crawford, Robert, 129
    Devolving English Literature, 128

Critique of Postcolonial Reason, A
    (Spivak), 118
Cronin, Michael, *Translation and
    Globalization*, 148, 149–50
Crystal, David, 124, 132, 133

Damrosch, David, 144
    What is World Literature? 143–4
Dasgupta, R. K., 141
Death in Venice (Mann), 153, 155–6
Death of a Discipline (Spivak), 141–2,
    147
Debray, Regis, 117
DeLillo, Don, 46
    Cosmopolis, 14–18, 19, 23, 25, 39,
    46, 48, 50
    Mao II, 50, 51, 152, 153, 155–6,
    159
Derrida, Jacques, 79, 90, 101, 108
    Habermas on 94–5
Devolving English Literature (Crawford),
    128
diaries, 59
Dirlik, Arif, 121–2
Dixon, John, *Schooling in 'English'*, 128
Donoghue, Denis, 93
Dow Jones Industrial Average, 38
Doyle, Brian, 129
    English and Englishness, 127, 128

Eagleton, Terry, 91, 93, 118
Easthope, Anthony, 91
Eco, Umberto, 79
Economy of Prestige, The (English),
    168
Elias, Norbert, 94
Eliot, T. S., 48, 97, 102, 128
    The Wasteland, 102
Ellis, Brett Easton, 46
End of a Primitive, The (Himes), 40
End of History and the Last Man, The
    (Fukuyama), 66–8
Engler, Balz, *European English Studies*
    (with Haas) 132–3
English, James, 168
    Economy of Prestige, 168
English and Englishness (Doyle), 127,
    128
English in America (Ohmann), 128–9

English Studies Book, The (Pope), 130–2, 135, 136
Ensler, Eve, *Vagina Monologues*, 31–6
Erikson, Erik, 94
European English Studies (Engler and Haas), 132–3

Fairclough, Norman, 9–10
Falk, Richard, 8, 49
Feather, John, 156, 159–60, 161–2
Featherstone, Mike, 8, 119
  Global Culture, 86, 87, 88
  Undoing Culture, 107
Fictions of Globalization (Annesley), 66, 69–71
Finnegans Wake (Joyce), 55, 79, 84
Fish, Stanley, 93, 166
  Is There a Text in this Class?, 76
Foucault, Michel, 90, 108
Fountain at the Centre of the World, The (Newman), 17–18, 19–23, 25
Francis, Rob, 163
Fukuyama, Francis, *The End of History and the Last Man*, 66–8

G8 (Group of Eight), 8, 18
Gabler, Hans Walter, 83, 84
Gaggi, Silvio, 78
García-Berrio, Antonio, 73
General Dynamics Corporation, 38
Generation X (Coupland), 37–8
Ghosh, Amitav, 162
Ghost Town (McGrath), 40–1
Giddens, Anthony, 3–4, 119
Gikandi, Simon, 121
Gilbert, Stuart, 75
Glass, Loren, 158
Global Culture (Featherstone), 86, 87, 88
Globalization/Anti-Globalization (Held and McGrew), 19
Globalizing Literary Studies (Gunn), 10–11
Godzich, Wlad, 139
Goethe, Johann Wolfgang von, 74, 141
Goffman, Erving, 94
Gorman, Herbert, 75
Gouldner, Alvin, 117

Grabovsky, Ernest, 145
Graeber, David, 8
Graff, Gerald, *Professing Literature*, 129
Greenblatt, Stephen, 10
Groden, Michael, 83, 84
Guillory, John, 93
Gumperz, John J., 94
Gunn, Giles, *Globalizing Literary Studies*, 10–11
Guy, Josephine, *Politics and Value in English Studies* (with Small), 129

Haas, Renate, *European English Studies* (with Engler), 132–3
Habermas, Jürgen, 8, 49, 97, 98, 106, 115, 118
  on Derrida, 94–5
Hall, Stuart, 86, 94, 115
Hannerz, Ulf, 86
Hardt, Michael, 8
Harry Potter and the Chamber of Secrets (Rowling), 158–9, 167
Harvey, David, 98, 100, 101, 119, 120
Hassan, Ihab, 104
Hegel, G. W. F., 66–7, 97
  Phenomenology of Spirit, 67
  Philosophy of History, 67
Hegemony and Socialist Strategy (Laclau and Mouffe), 115
Held, David, 4, 119
  Globalization/Anti-Globalization (with McGrew), 19
  Cosmopolitan Democracy (with Archibugi), 49
Himes, Chester, *End of a Primitive*, 40
Hindess, Barry, *Pre-Capitalist Modes of Production* (with Hirst), 115
Hirst, Paul, *Pre-Capitalist Modes of Production* (with Hindess), 115
Hitchcock, Peter, 124–5, 126
Hobsbawm, Eric, 7
Huggan, Graham, 122
  Postcolonial Exotic, 119–20
Hulme, T. E., 97
Hussein, Saddam, 24, 25, 30–1
Hutcheon, Linda, 98, 101, 105
hypertext, 53–61, 77–85

IMF (International Monetary Fund), 7, 18, 92
In Theory (Ahmad), 117–18, 119
intellectual property, 168–9
Internet Galaxy (Castells), 77
Iraq invasion 2003, 23–4, 27–8, 49, 60
Is There a Text in this Class? (Fish), 76
Iser, Wolfgang, 75–6, 166

Jameson, Fredric, 108, 117–18
  Postmodernism, 99–100, 101
Jay, Gregory S., 93
Jay, Paul, 10
Johnson, B. S., *Unfortunates*, 55
Johnson, David, *Shakespeare and South Africa*, 128
Jordan, Tim, 8
Joyce, James, 25, 48, 103, 104
  Finnegans Wake 55, 79, 84
  Ulysses, 66, 71–2, 73–6, 79–80, 83–5, 102

Kachru, Braj, 123, 125, 132
Kaldor, Mary, 49
Khullar Management, 163
Kidd, John, 83
Kilminster, Richard, 6
King, Anthony, 46, 86
Klein, Naomi, 8
Kojevé, Alexander, 67
Krishnaswamy, Revathi, 121, 122
Kymlicka, Will, 49

La Ville radieuse (Le Corbusier), 44
Lacan, Jacques, 108
Laclau, Ernesto, *Hegemony and Socialist Strategy* (with Mouffe), 115
Lash, Scott, 8
  Sociology of Postmodernism, 106–7
Lauter, Paul, 93
Le Corbusier, *La Ville radieuse*, 44
Leavis, F. R., and Leavis, Q. D., 128, 157
Lefebvre, Henri, 119
  Production of Space, 101
Levefere, André, *Translating Literature*, 147
Levinas, Emmanuel, 108
Linati, Carlo, 75

literary prizes, 167–8
London novels, 41–3, 46
Londonstani (Malkani), 42, 46–8
Love and Death on Long Island (Adair), 152–3, 155–6, 159
Lu Xun, 48
Lukács, Georg, 90
Lyotard, Jean-François, 98, 99, 100–1, 104

McEwan, Ian, 46
  Saturday, 25–7, 28, 30–1
McGann, Jerome, 76, 78–9, 82–3
McGrath, Patrick, *Ghost Town*, 40–1
McGrew, Anthony, *Globalization/Anti-Globalization* (with Held), 19
McHale, Brian, 104–5
McLuhan, Marshall, 6
Malkani, Gautam, *Londonstani*, 42, 46–8
Man, Paul de, 90
Mandel, Ernest, 7
Mann, Thomas, *Death in Venice* 153, 155
Mao II (DeLillo), 50, 51, 152, 153, 155–6, 159
Masks of Conquest (Vishwanathan), 128
Mathur, Anurag, 163
Mead, George Herbert, 94
Meanings of Social Life, The (Alexander), 89
Midnight's Children (Rushdie), 66, 71–2, 80–1, 102–5, 111–12, 115–16
Miller, J. Hillis, 53, 77–8
Miller, Karl, 151
Miner, Earl, *Comparative Poetics*, 138
Modernity at Large (Appadurai), 88–9, 107
Moretti, Franco, 142, 143, 144
Moses, Michael Valdez, *The Novel and the Globalization of Culture*, 66–9, 70, 71
Mouffe, Chantal, *Hegemony and Socialist Strategy* (with Laclau), 115
Muslim Association of Britain (MAB), 26–7

NAFTA (North American Free Trade Agreement), 18

Native Son (Wright), 40
Negri, Antonio, 8
Nehru, Jawaharlal, 111
new social movements, 7
New York novels, 39–41, 46
Newman, Robert, *The Fountain at the Centre of the World*, 17–18, 19–23, 25
Ngũgĩ wa Thiong'o, 125–6
9/11 (terrorist attacks in USA), 23, 40
North–South (Brandt Commission report), 7
Not in Our Name project, 25
Novel and the Globalization of Culture, The (Moses), 66–9, 70, 71
Nussbaum, Martha, 49

Obel, Karen, 32
O'Brien, Susie, 62–4, 65
Ohmann, Richard, 129
English in America, 128–9
Orientalism (Said), 108–9
Our World Our Say, 25

Pakulski, Jan, 115
Palmer, D. J., 129
The Rise of English Studies, 126–7
Pamuk, Orhan, *Snow*, 153–6, 159
Pennycook, Alastair, 126–7
Phenomenology of Spirit, The (Hegel), 67
Philosophical Investigations (Wittgenstein), 101
Philosophy of History, The (Hegel), 67
Picador Book of Modern Indian Literature, The (Chaudhuri), 118
Plowing the Dark (Powers), 1–3, 50, 51, 52
Politics and Value in English Studies (Guy and Small), 129
Pope, Rob, *English Studies Book*, 130–2, 135, 136
Postcolonial Exotic, The (Huggan), 119–20
Postmodernism (Jameson), 99–100
Pound, Ezra, 83, 97
Powers, Richard, *Plowing the Dark*, 1–3, 50, 51, 52
Pre-Capitalist Modes of Production (Hindess and Hirst), 115

Principi di una scienza nuova (Vico), 97
Production of Space, The (Lefebvre), 101
Professing Literature (Graff), 129
publishing industry, 159–66, 169–70

Raban, Jonathan, *Soft City*, 43–4, 45
Reemergence of World Literature, The (Aldridge), 139, 141
Richards, I. A., 128
Rise and Fall of English, The (Scholes), 129
Rise of English Studies, The (Palmer), 126–7
Riverbend, 60
Robertson, Roland, 4, 5, 6, 86
Roth, Philip, 83
Rowling, J. K., 157–9, 164
Harry Potter and the Chamber of Secrets, 158–9, 167
Roy, Arundhati, 162
Rushdie, Salman, 126, 162
Midnight's Children, 66, 71–2, 80–1, 102–5, 111–12, 115–16
The Satanic Verses, 72, 118
The Vintage Book of Indian Writing (with West), 118
Ryman, Geoff, 46
253, 42–3, 54–7, 60, 61, 73, 77

Said, Edward, 10, 90, 110–11, 119
Orientalism, 108–9
Salam Pax, 60
Salman Rushdie and the Third World (Brennan), 103, 104
Sanga, Jaina C., 72
Sartre, Jean-Paul, 48
Sassen, Saskia, 8, 44–6, 47
Satanic Verses, The (Rushdie), 72
Saturday (McEwan), 25–7, 28, 30–1
Schiffrin, André, *Business of Books*, 160–1
Scholes, Robert, *The Rise and Fall of English*, 129
Schooling in 'English', A (Dixon), 128
Seattle anti-WTO protests 1999, 8, 18, 20–3
Senn, Fritz, 84
Seth, Vikram, 162

Shakespeare and South Africa (Johnson), 128
Small, Ian, *Politics and Value in English Studies* (with Guy), 129
Snow (Pamuk), 153–6, 159
Social Mission of English Criticism, The (Baldick), 128
Sociology of Postmodernism (Lash), 106–7
Soft City (Raban), 43–4, 45
Spencer, John, 74
Spivak, Gayatri, 112, 113–14, 119
   Critique of Postcolonial Reason, 118
   Death of a Discipline, 141–2, 147
Stiglitz, Joseph, 8
Stone, Oliver, *Wall Street*, 46
STWC (Stop the War Coalition), 24–5, 27
Szeman, Imre, 62–4, 65

Tagore, Rabindranath, 141
Tajfel, Henri, 94
Theall, Donald F., 80
Theory (literary)
   Appadurai on, 88–9
   institutionalization of, 89–96, 129, 139–40, 147
Thompson, John B., *Books in the Digital Age*, 170
Toscani, Oliviero, 38
Toulmin, Stephen, *Cosmopolis*, 49–50, 51
Touraine, Alain, 115
Translating Literature (Levefere), 147
Translation and Globalization (Cronin), 148, 149–50
Translation in a Postcolonial Context (Tymoczko), 149–50
Translation Studies (Bassnett), 147
253 (Ryman), 42–3, 54–7, 60, 61, 73, 77
Tymoczko, Maria, *Translation in a Postcolonial Context*, 149–50

Ulysses (Joyce), 66, 71–2, 73–6, 79–80, 83–5, 102
Undoing Culture (Featherstone), 107
Unfortunates, The (Johnson), 55
Union Carbide Corporation, 38

United for Peace and Justice, 25
United Nations (UN), 23
Userlands, The (Cooper), 58

Vagina Monologues, The (Ensler), 31–6
Valente, Joseph, 72
Venuti, Lawrence, 146, 148, 162
Vertovec, Steven, 48
Vico, Giambattista, *Principi di una scienza nuova*, 97
Vintage Book of Indian Writing, The (Rushdie and West), 118
Vishwanathan, Gauri, 129
   Masks of Conquest, 128

Wall Street (1987 film, dir. Stone), 46
Wallerstein, Immanuel, 7, 86, 87
Wasteland, The (Eliot), 102
Weber, Max, 17
Wellek, René, 137, 138, 141
West, Elizabeth, *The Vintage Book of Indian Writing* (with Rushdie), 118
What is World Literature? (Damrosch), 143–4
White, Hayden, 108
Whitehead, Colson, 46
   Colossus in New York, 41
Williams, Raymond, 90
Wittgenstein, Ludwig, *Philosophical Investigations*, 101
Wolfe, Tom, *The Bonfire of the Vanities*, 46
Wolff, Janet, 87
Woolf, Virginia, 25
World Bank, 7, 18, 92
World Republic of Letters, The (Casanova), 142
Wright, Richard, *Native Son*, 40
WTO (World Trade Organization), 8, 18, 20, 22, 168

Young, Robert, 110

Zepetnek, Steven Tötösy de, *Comparative Literature and Comparative Cultural Studies*, 140
Zolo, Danilo, *Cosmopolis*, 50, 51